To Chris,
Love, xo

Carrie Stevens

www.EliteRewards.biz

P.S. Spin you wheels with us ♡

Revelations *of a* Rock 'n' Roll Centerfold

A MEMOIR

CARRIE STEVENS

Front cover hair and makeup by *Kimberley Ex-Hill*. Book cover by *Carrie Stevens* and *Don Taylor Atkinson*. Book design by *Don Taylor Atkinson*, Benchmark/MIG Los Angeles.

PHOTO CREDITS: Front cover image and Dedication page photo by *Dean Capture*. Chapter 1 lead photo by *Alberto Figarone*. Lead photos on Chapters 2-6, 8, 11-12 and back cover image by *James Creighton*. Preface page image and Chapter 9 lead photo by *Jon Abeyta*. Chapter 7 lead photo by *Marcel Indick*. Chapter 10 lead photo by *Sarah Orbanic*.

Published by Plethora & Privy, Inc.

ISBN: 978-1-7353644-3-8

PRINTED IN THE UNITED STATES OF AMERICA

Author's Disclaimer:

THIS BOOK was entirely written from my bed and bathtub, on airplanes and trains, and in waiting rooms, pubs and parking lots. Every last word was written by me, Carrie Stevens. This is my life story told from my perspective and based on my memories alone.

This is a work of non-fiction. Some names and identifying details have been changed.

ALISON REYNOLDS PHOTO

Acknowledgements

You might be surprised at how many people it takes to write one's own life story. I didn't get where I am in life by going it alone, and this memoir was no different.

Thank you to:

The Caravello family. Loretta Caravello, Eric Carr's sister, for giving me her constant love and support. Also, Sara-Jean Bartky, Eric's niece, for keeping in close contact with me. I feel his presence when we speak.

Bruce Kulick, Gary and Lenora Corbett, Jack Sawyers, Todd Trent. In our love of Eric, we are forever united.

Chris Jericho, Joey Cassata, Eddie Trunk, Todd Billetts, Monsters of Rock, Shout It Out Loud Cast, The KISS Army and the KISS fans all over the world for keeping Eric Carr's memory alive. A special thank you to Eric Singer.

Jessie Henry, for letting me mentor you. Your loss made my story more meaningful. Our friendship gives me purpose.

Hugh Hefner, for inspiring me to thank him while he was still alive. He gave me endless gifts I am grateful for every day. I will always love him.

My iconic Playmate sisters, for their camaraderie. What a wild ride it's been!

Gene Simmons. This book was his idea. In 2002, Gene not only put me on the cover of *Tongue*, but personally interviewed me for the magazine. Later, when I ran into him at the Playboy Mansion, he suggested I write a book about being on the road with KISS. While I could have written an entire book on the subject, I had secrets that were even wilder and crazier than life on the road with rock stars. There would be a time to tell all. That time is now.

David Lee Roth, who, for better or worse, has influenced me since 1984 like no other. Without Van Halen, I'd be boring. But it's not all about sex, drugs & rock 'n' roll. It was Dave's recent advice to me that inspired me to call my anti-aging and weight loss company **StayYoungandSkinny.com**.

My loving grandparents, who saved every card and letter I ever sent them. Josephine Stevens, Francis E. Stevens, Katherine Pittz and Eugene A. Pittz.

Mr. Mike Richard, my favorite teacher at Quabbin Regional High School, for having us journal at the start of each class. Ever since, journaling has been part of my life. Without the letters and my journals for reference, I couldn't possibly have remembered so much so vividly.

My ex-boyfriend box. Every time I broke up with someone, I'd get on a ladder and climb up to the highest shelf in my closet and drop all their love letters and photos into a black shoebox. Sort of like a coffin. It is hard to write about a love affair, when you can't remember what you saw in the guy in the first place. The ex-boyfriend box served me well.

Allison Burnett, for persistently telling me to write this book. And since he insisted that it would be a success, I had no qualms about asking him for help when I had writer's block. He gave me assignments. I did them but didn't understand his reasoning. Then he put them together like a song. I thanked him, and he humbly replied, "I actually didn't do anything. You did it." The truth is, Allison is not only a brilliant writer and director, but a wonderful friend.

Malcolm Nicholl for helping me get the bones down. For ensuring that I included the tedious, but vital details. And for having the patience of a saint.

Bobby Rock, for all of our deep conversations that contributed to the content. After poring over my first draft with the professionals (Allison, Malcolm, and Bobby), I entrusted it to a few of my closest friends for a read.

And so, I also want to thank:

Nicki Anderson-Jelsma and Christina Scott, for your wisdom and guidance. My faithful friends spent days upon days, and hours upon hours listening to me read chapter after chapter, pestering them for advice. I couldn't have done it without you!

Elena Grace Soto, for saying that reading my book made you love me even more. Bridgette Pratt for telling me that you laughed and cried. Eric Pulier for telling me not to change a thing. Your love and support gave me the courage to publish.

Kent Moyer, for generously supporting all my endeavors, and for introducing me to Don Warrener. Don Warrener, for introducing me to Don Atkinson, who patiently and beautifully designed this book. Thank you all, for believing in me.

I want to thank my oldest and dearest friends, for being a part of my past and for lending me your memories. As I was writing, I would call you for inspiration. You brought me back to my roots. I love you all for keeping me grounded: *Chrissy Purcell-Williams, Tanya Morin, Lori Prentiss, Amy Docherty, Joanne Madsen, John McWilliams, Darren Boudreau, Jan Crutchfield, Susan Reilley-Lehane, Victoria Mariencheck, Donna Wright, Wendy Griffin, Peggy Trentini, Jacob Getz, Anita Pressman, Kathy Henzerling, Nicole Simpson, Eyerly Felder, Antonia Dorian, Bobbie Brown, Shannon McLeod, Gennie Gabriel, Kurt Clements, Donna Anderson, Jaydene O'Connor, Cindy Rakowitz, Randy Castonguay, James and Marie Gonis, Richard Bann, Gary Miller, Adi Greenberg, Rima Kaddo, Ms. Long, Stephen Gustavson, Elena Terrones, Gary Rosenson, Lisa Lascody, Hofit Kaspi, Scott Eirish, Andre Felix, Jessica Denay, James Henry, Doug & Marsha Nelson, Connie Woods, Michael Berk, Rudy Sarzo, Pat Lacey, Pete Merluzzi, Tanya Martin, Tommy Thayer, Tammy Smith, Tony Valente, Cooper Hefner, Ron Litz...and my twinsie, Carrie Peterson.*

My family. Thank you to my beautiful mother for giving me life. My sister, Jill, for encouraging my writing and for always protecting me. My sister-in-law, Elizabeth, for her love and loyalty. My brilliant father, for everything he's done for me. You are my anchor! I can always depend on you and that gives me great peace. My stepparents, Judy and Dave, for being so understanding and kind. My cousin Victor Stevens, for being the family historian.

Shout out to my son, Jaxon, for not being embarrassed by me! Thanks for thinking Mom is cool. I love being your co-pilot.

Julienne Green, (my goddaughter) for texting me: "Carrie, you're a fucking Superwoman. I love you so much. We are always connected, and I feel like I need your guidance always." You got it, babe! Always.

My Irish friends. Especially, Emma and Kiara. The Galway Player. The Galway Street Club. All of the buskers, barkeepers and regulars at Hyde and The Salthouse. Thank ye for showin' me the way home!

Last but not least, a big thank you to all of the insignificant ghosters, who were egotistical enough to ask me if they were going to be in my book. You gave me a good laugh, guys!

For my son, Jaxon...

and our little dog, Jedi.

Contents

PREFACE: *Don't Tweet Before You Think*   1

Chapter 1: *Don't Drop Out of School*   9

Chapter 2: *Don't Have a One-Night Stand*   35

Chapter 3: *Don't Run Off with a Rock Star*   53

Chapter 4: *Don't Drink Straight Whiskey*   87

Chapter 5: *Don't Join a Harem*   107

Chapter 6: *Don't Pose for Playboy*   131

Chapter 7: *Don't Have an Affair with a Married Man*   171

Chapter 8: *Don't Get Knocked Up*   189

Chapter 9: *Don't Fall in Love with a Legend*   219

Chapter 10: *Don't Blow Off Billionaires*   247

Chapter 11: *Don't Believe in Fairytales*   269

Chapter 12: *Don't Think It's Over*   295

Dedication

This book is dedicated to the "readers," a word used in jest, to refer to the rare *Playboy* subscribers who didn't just look at the photos, but read the articles, too. Thank you for the opportunity to take you inside my soul and for not judging a book by its cover.

In loving memory of
ERIC CARR

Preface

Don't Tweet Before You Think

It all started with a tweet. The Harvey Weinstein scandal was dominating the news. You couldn't turn on TV or radio, or visit social media sites, without seeing and hearing another breathless revelation of misconduct. I read a tweet from the *Hollywood Reporter* that I simply couldn't believe. Oscar-winning film director Oliver Stone had expressed sympathy for Weinstein.

Impulsively, I tweeted: *"When I heard about Harvey, I recalled Oliver walking past me and grabbing my boob as he walked out the front door of a party. Two of a kind!"*

I didn't think anyone paid much attention to me and my tweets, but all hell broke loose. Within two hours, my son called out, "Mom! You're trending! You're in Japan! You're in the U.K.!" My phone started to ring, and emails came pouring in. Reporters from all over the world wanted to interview me. I spoke first to the *New York Daily News*. That same evening, they carried the story on their website under the headline: "Former Playboy Playmate Carrie Stevens accuses Oliver Stone of sexual assault after director defends Harvey Weinstein."

I called my friend Christina. "I never said he sexually assaulted me!"

She set me straight. "Carrie, grabbing someone's boob *is* sexual assault."

1

I'd been having my boobs grabbed and my ass groped since puberty. It was obnoxious and rude, for sure, but I didn't know it was a crime. Media outlets across the globe were running with the story. I was accidentally at the forefront of the #METOO movement, along with Rose McGowan, Ashley Judd and every other actress speaking out against Weinstein and Hollywood sexual misconduct. I wasted a week of my life talking to reporters. Most of them didn't do much more than repeat the same quotes. They loved that I had said Oliver Stone grabbed my boob and honked it like a horn. They didn't bother to report something else I told them: that the two-second incident was among the least significant two seconds of my life.

I said to myself, "Wow, people think Oliver Stone grabbing my boob is interesting? If they only knew the rest of it! Maybe I should write a book."

I'd been thinking about writing a memoir for a long time. Lots of people had encouraged me, even though what they knew of my colorful life barely scratched the surface. Still, it didn't take long for me to convince myself out of it. Writing a memoir was not just grueling work, but it would require me to be utterly honest not just about myself, but about others as well, many of them powerful men with a great deal invested in keeping their secrets secret. No sooner had I made up my mind not to tell all, when two more tweets put me front and center of a major scandal: the firestorm over Donald Trump's secret ten-month affair with *Playboy* Playmate Karen McDougal.

I got accused of being the reason the affair was exposed!

In a March 2018 legal filing against American Media Inc., publisher of the *National Enquirer,* Karen claimed that I was the first to reveal the extramarital relationship, which had taken place years earlier during Melania Trump's pregnancy. Karen blamed a series of tweets I'd posted almost two years before, just four days after Trump became the presumptive Republican nominee for president. I remembered the tweets. My close friend, Miss December 1992, Barbara Moore and I were being silly, talking about the women we knew whom Trump had slept with, one of the unlucky chosen was Barbara herself. Her six-month affair with Trump had started in 1993. At the time, Barbara had no idea that Trump's fiancée Marla Maples was pregnant.

My first tweet read: *"@realDonaldTrump from what I've heard... you're the easy one #donaldlovesplaymates @karenmcdougal98."*

The second read: *"I usually don't get involved in politics but why Bill Clinton can't get an extramarital BJ but @realDonaldTrump can. Right?"*

I tagged Barbara. We giggled.

I also tagged Karen because we thought she would think it was funny, too. I thought, and still think, that the whole thing was pretty hilarious. I stand by my *#donaldlovesplaymates* hashtag because it's true. As soon as I woke up the next morning, however, I deleted the tweets. I had realized that I didn't want to get involved in the issue at all.

7.   For several years, Ms. McDougal led a "Hollywood" life, attending events and parties as both honored guest and hostess. During that time, Ms. McDougal had a 10-month relationship with Mr. Trump.

8.   Ms. McDougal moved on from this period of her life and lived in relative privacy for the next decade.

9.   But on May 7, 2016, four days after Mr. Trump became the presumptive Republican presidential nominee, former *Playboy* playmate Carrie Stevens revealed the past relationship between Ms. McDougal and Mr. Trump on Twitter. In a series of tweets regarding Mr. Trump's extramarital relationships, Ms. Stevens said.

10.   Ms. McDougal did not seek hush money from Mr. Trump. But she also didn't sit back and wait to become tabloid fodder. If the story was going to become national news, she wanted to be the one to tell it to ensure that the account was accurate and not lurid grist for the tabloid mill. She hired entertainment lawyer Keith Davidson, who assured her that the rights to publish her story were worth millions. Unknown to Ms. McDougal, Mr. Davidson was working closely with representatives for Mr. Trump while pretending to advocate on her behalf.

11.   Mr. Davidson introduced Ms. McDougal to AMI, a leading magazine and tabloid publisher. He told her that AMI had deposited $500,000 in an escrow account toward a seven-figure

Karen McDougal was using them as her excuse for selling her story to the *National Enquirer* for $150,000. She claimed she wanted control of her own story since a former friend (referring to me) was talking about it on social media. But she contradicted her claim entirely when then she signed a catch-and-kill deal, giving up all control to her story. So, while I'll graciously take credit for outing the affair, I really don't deserve it.

The frenzy of media phone calls and emails began all over again. I knew all about Karen's affair with Trump. We were good friends at the time it was going on, and she had confided in me. I refused to talk to any of the news people. I was afraid that whatever details I offered might be twisted and used inadvertently to hurt the victims of sexual harassment and the #METOO movement. There would be a time after the dust had settled when it would be safe to tell my side of the story, but not yet.

The Oliver Stone and Donald Trump experiences, minor episodes in my eventful life, made me appreciate that I did have a bigger story to tell. Still, I was worried about what people might think. A "nice girl" wouldn't write a tell-all. I worried about the men I would hurt. Then it hit me: I was silencing myself to protect people who, if I died, wouldn't even come to my funeral. I was entitled to tell my story, simply because it was mine, the only one I would ever have. The #METOO movement was emboldening me to speak out about *everything*. Ironically, it also gave me the time to write a book, for the simple reason that my speaking out had already brought my acting career to a screeching halt.

I stopped getting calls for auditions. A friendly producer told me, "We can't risk getting sued just because someone brushes up against you."

What the fuck? I had never sued anyone. All I did was impulsively tweet a couple of times. It was beyond depressing and triggered in me a kind of mid-life crisis, during which I questioned everything I had done with my life. Could things have turned out differently? I'd always dreamed of appearing in publications like *Vanity Fair* with my name alongside that of Angelina Jolie. Now I was headline news but reduced to being described as a "forty-eight-year-old former Playmate." Ugh. It didn't matter that the Oliver Stone thing had happened six or seven years before I became a Playmate and that there had been so much more to my life. This was my identity now, how I was defined... as if I had been born with a staple in my navel.

I wondered, 'How did I get here? Is this what my life has amounted to? What had I contributed to the world?' As the #METOO movement grew to become a worldwide phenomenon, the clear message was: Tell your story. Speak up. It's the only way to create change. As Oprah said in her inspiring speech at the Golden Globes: *"Speaking your truth is the most powerful tool we all have."* Hmm. I wondered if Oprah would sympathize with the experiences of a *Playboy* Playmate. Most people didn't. Most feminists don't like us, and men just want us to shut up and spread our legs. That's just the way it is. Sad but true.

Regardless, it was time to tell my truth.

My decision was confirmed when I got a Facebook message from a woman, a stranger, saying, "When are you sex objects going to realize you are not people?" This is the actual thinking of a lot of small-minded, hateful souls. Just because a woman is sexy, they think she doesn't have feelings. A woman plays a bimbo on TV, and people believe she's dumb in real life. And yet they don't think a man who plays an astronaut on TV is really an astronaut, or even necessarily smart.

Maybe this book will help clear up some misconceptions. Or maybe it will just entertain you for a while. My chapters all begin with the word "Don't," because I did the opposite of everything nice girls are taught to do. I'm not sure who made the rules, but I broke them. It's been a wild ride. I'd like to say that I don't believe in regrets, but considering some of the dumb shit I did, I can't. At the same time, if humans didn't make mistakes, then how would we learn? I forgive myself for my errors and applaud myself for having the courage to talk about them. I have a unique perspective, and I don't expect everyone to relate to me. Either way, by sharing my experiences I feel I'm giving back. This book is about the people I have loved and the lessons I have learned.

Chapter 1

Don't Drop Out of School

I have to wonder what I could have achieved in life if only I had been as ambitious academically as I was in aspiring to fuck David Lee Roth. Not that I'm blaming Van Halen for my moral decline (that's what parents and teachers are for), but something happened to me the first time I saw David Lee Roth strut on stage, his blonde mane wildly blowing, his Spandex-skinned crotch seeming to call out "I love you, Carrie." With his ankles behind his ears, raw rock was in the air at the Worcester Centrum in Massachusetts. His scissor kicks and mile-high splits represented freedom to fly. Fly the coop, that is.

I was coming into my own. It was 1984, and I was a freshman in high school. A boy at school named Shane gave me concert tickets. I think his Dad had a connection. I'd never even heard of Van Halen. I was a virgin. But after laying eyes on Diamond Dave, I didn't want to be one anymore! I plastered David Lee Roth's posters all over my walls and learned all the lyrics to all of Van Halen's songs. I began working out on Nautilus machines in leopard-print leotards. Every thrust and rep, in my mind, was one step

FACING PAGE: A recreation of David Lee Roth's iconic dressing room image from Van Halen on tour, circa 1982.

9

closer to hooking up with Dave. I'd listen to Van Halen's *"I'll Wait,"* and imagine I was the model he was singing to:

> *Are you for real? It's so hard to tell, from just*
>   *a magazine.*
>
> *Yeah, you just smile and the picture sells, look what*
>   *that does to me.*
>
> *I'll wait 'til your love comes down.*

I was only sixteen. I'd do the math in my head over and over again, calculating our age difference and working out the exact date I'd be old enough to make Dave mine. Maybe when I turned twenty, we could get married. He would be thirty-four and ready to settle down. My inspiration was the dozens of Van Halen posters plastered all over my bedroom walls, although I also had some of KISS, one of Billy Idol, and one of Sylvester Stallone as Rambo.

I could never have imagined that by the time I was twenty-one, I would be asked out by every one of these men. How does a small-town girl, growing up on a dead-end dirt road, in a town with more cows than people, create bedroom walls that in five years flat come to life, like an X-rated Disney movie? It's a crazy story. Welcome to my weird existence. It hasn't exactly turned out to be a fairytale.

*****

I was born in 1969 in Buffalo, New York. My parents decided to call me Carrie, not in honor of my grandmother or a famous movie star or anything traditional. My dad, a research scientist, named me after a piece of laboratory equipment, the Cary spectrophotometer. It's an apparatus that measures the intensity of light. I was born to be a shining star.

We moved to Massachusetts when I was a toddler. Soon after, my parents divorced. I am not sure whether it was my father's idealism or his Catholic upbringing that made him think he had to marry every woman he ever dated, but he's been married five times. My mother has only three marriages under her belt. They certainly searched hard for love in all the wrong places, but at least I got some awesome sisters out of the deal.

The earliest memory I have of my father is when I was four years old, and he lost me at the Barnum & Bailey Circus. Mesmerized by the clowns with their exaggerated makeup and crazy costumes, I followed them backstage. Panic-stricken, Dad eventually found me, the happy center of attention, surrounded by clowns performing just for me. Or maybe I was entertaining them, who knows. I do know that this adventure foreshadowed my future, except the breed of clowns I hung out with backstage was much sexier.

Since my parents were divorced by the time I was two years old, I don't remember them ever being together. My mother had custody of me and my older sister, Jill. Mom was a rebellious flower child, a feminist who marched for civil rights and women's rights. After the divorce, there was a lot of moving around. For a while, home was a dirt-floor yurt in a commune of skinny-dipping hippies. We even lived in

Portugal for a few months. When I was six years old, my mother met and married Allen, an eccentric artist with a big ego and an even bigger drinking problem. We settled in West Hardwick, Massachusetts.

My mother was also an artist. Her paintings and sculptures, mostly female nudes, were displayed all over the house. Only one nude male was displayed: Allen immortalized on canvas, with his dick dangling between his legs, every pube presented in vivid detail. In his hand, he held a bottle of Heineken, true to life. As I was just a little girl, it was extremely embarrassing, especially when my best friend, Chrissy, came over after school. Her family seemed so normal, and here I was living among a life-sized penis portrait, sculptures of breasts, and paintings of orchids that resembled flowering vaginas.

I often wondered why my mother didn't like me much. I knew as much because when I was ten years old, I was sitting on her lap and innocently asked, "Mommy, do you like me?" She looked at me long and hard before she replied, "I love you, but I don't like you." Presumably she loved me because I was her daughter, but she didn't like me? Why? We've always had a tumultuous on-and-off relationship. After each incident that caused a parting of the ways, I suffered over what I might have done wrong, but then I always returned to those words: *I love you, but I don't like you.* That's the bottom line. An awful feeling of rejection. I'm not sure if I was a rotten kid or not, but more likely she just resented motherhood. Back then, abortion was illegal. Over the years, she'd tell me that if she hadn't had kids, she could have been a doctor or a lawyer or President of the United States. Also, I don't think it's a coincidence that she declared she didn't like me as soon as I began to develop into a woman. Maybe I was not only a threat, but also a reminder of what she could have been had she not gotten knocked up. Either way, it hurt. My mother also preferred my sister, probably because Jill was more nurturing. She actually mothered my mother. I had an independent streak. Being rejected will do that to you. As I grew older, my friends became my family, and heavy metal music was my therapy.

West Hardwick, Massachusetts was so small that it didn't even have its own zip code. In addition to Chrissy, my best friends were my horse Star, my goat Billy Buck, and my dog Niko, a pure white Samoyed. I'd braid pink ribbons through Star's mane and tail, ignoring the fact he was a boy, and, on hot summer days, bikini-clad and barefoot, I'd ride him bareback all over the neighborhood with Niko trailing along. Poor Niko was always getting sprayed by skunks and quilled by porcupines. The only way to get the smell off of him was to bathe him in tomato juice, so sometimes he was an orange Samoyed. The Quabbin Reservoir was our playground. It was huge, thirty-nine square miles, and had been created in the 1930s by flooding the Swift River Valley, destroying five towns just to supply water to Boston. Star would get excited at the sight of the water and canter right into it, with Niko not far behind. It was illegal to cross the gates of the Quabbin, but there was no one to bust us.

Our home was not large, but it sat on five acres. We had pigs, goats, sheep, chickens, rabbits, geese. My sister and I had lots of chores, starting each morning when we collected eggs from the chicken coop. I hated it. It stank and the chickens pecked my hands as I snatched their eggs. It was rural America with a capital "R." No blacks. No Asians. No Jews. Just a lot of white men in flannel shirts with scruffy beards, chewing tobacco, and driving pickup trucks. One day, Chrissy and I and some other local kids were put in the back seat of one. We thought we were being taken somewhere fun, but the trip was just to a neighbor's house to watch pigs get castrated.

Allen and his drinking buddies had all sorts of twisted ideas about ways to entertain themselves, like getting drunk and cutting the heads off chickens. Then they'd piss themselves laughing as the headless chickens lurched and flapped around our yard. I'd run to my room and cry. One day they roasted Billy Buck for dinner. *My* Billy Buck. It's the cruel side of rural life almost no one talks about.

Sometimes, to my young mind, it seemed as if my mother and Allen materialized out of thin air. I thought maybe she was a witch, and he was a warlock, and that they could magically disappear and reappear. The truth is that I was the one who was invisible. At least that is how I felt. I was a lonely kid. I was only six when they met and ten when they got divorced, so luckily, he wasn't in my life long.

Every other Sunday, I was thrilled when my father would drive two hours from Albany, New York, to see us. He would arrive with my grandparents in tow, and I'd run out all excited, shouting, "Daddy, Daddy, Daddy!" But then I'd get this sickening feeling in the pit of my stomach. Oh, I'm not supposed to act happy to see my dad. If I did, I'd face the wrath of Allen. But I couldn't help myself. I loved him. My sister and I got to spend an hour with them at a local diner. The visits were too short, but at least I felt loved.

My grandparents provided stability in my life. They always told me how much my father loved me. I'm sure they wanted to fix the damage caused by my parents' vicious custody battles, and I'm glad they did. Their nurturing helped a lot. Whenever I wanted to escape, I'd call them up, and they'd drive all the way from Albany to get me. Grandma would have Irish stew waiting on the stove. I'd wake up at their house at three in the morning, and she'd indulge me with a tea and marshmallow party. We'd have middle of the night conversations, mostly about my great-grandparents who immigrated from Ireland, and about her love for my grandfather. She said never marry for money. She said if she had nothing but an orange crate to sit on, she'd be happy as long as she had my grandfather. She instilled good old-fashioned values in me. These are the times I cherish most.

*****

When I was only ten years old, I sat on the toilet and blood came gushing out. I screamed and called for my mother. "This better be good," she said. I had interrupted her while she was painting. I hadn't learned about menstruation yet, as most girls don't get their periods until their teens. Soon after that, my chest began to swell. That's when the sexual harassment started. In 5th grade, the boys snapped my bra strap and slapped their dicks on my desk when the teacher wasn't looking. They teased me mercilessly, calling me "Dolly Parton," and "Little Tits." When the other girls began to develop, I became "Big Tits," and, ironically, "Barbi Benton." Ironic, because she was the long-time girlfriend of Hugh Hefner. Of course, as adults we know that boys are mean to girls as a way to get their attention, but, as a kid, I felt only shame. To try and hide my boobs, I wore a blue satin baseball jacket zippered all the way up to my neck. I was just a wounded, impressionable little girl with hormones and feelings, if anyone had bothered to look past the big blue eyes and the giant boobs.

Being perceived as pretty came with punishment. In fact, the lesson I learned at this age was that it was a mortal sin to be conceited. I was never told I was beautiful. I was just told not to be full of myself. In fact, they took shots at me for my looks. They called me "airhead" and "space cadet," because at that point I was so wounded by mockery that I barely ever spoke. Young girls believe the narrative that is told to them about themselves. It led to a lifetime of a confused sense of self-worth. While other kids were learning reading, writing and arithmetic in elementary school, I was getting a premature lesson in physical and verbal harassment.

*****

In junior high school, I was voted most popular and best dressed. I excelled in creative writing and note passing. Math and science were more challenging. One day I raised my hand in biology class because our teacher, Mrs. Marshall, taught us there was no such thing as a dumb question. Clearly, she didn't mean it.

"Are we supposed to be taking notes?" I asked.

Mrs. Marshall replied, "Pretty face, but nothing in the head."

The class burst out laughing. That was a defining moment for me. The typecasting that Mrs. Marshall bestowed on me that day would replay throughout my life. While the other kids learned about chromosomes, I was being told, "You are to be seen and not heard." I never raised my hand in any class again.

Not all teachers were like Mrs. Marshall. Mr. Richard was different, a wonderful man who taught the journalism and mass media class. He inspired me through the teaching of the history of music and television. He made school bearable. We learned about Chuck Berry, James Brown, Elvis Presley, The Beatles, and even what he called "glam rock," which included KISS. My kind of classroom! I was the entertainment editor of the school newspaper. My friend Tanya worked with me. Both big U2 fans, we were over the moon when we learned that they were going to be playing at the Worcester Centrum as part of their *Unforgettable Fire* tour. We set out to get an interview, writing letters to the band's management. We also reached out to the Centrum, requesting press passes. Our vice-principal and class advisor vouched for us, but there was no reply from the powers that be.

Regardless, Tanya and I got tickets to the show. We were on the side of the stage, close enough to catch the eye of one of the band's crew. He smiled at me. I smiled back. A coy, demure smile. The lights went down. As the lights came back up and Bono darted on stage, I felt a hand slap a backstage pass on my thigh. It was the guy I'd smiled at. I said, "Oh my God! Thank you. Can my friend have one too?" He slapped a pass on Tanya's thigh. I never saw that guy again, but I got my interview. I talked to Bono, The Edge, and Adam Clayton. More significantly, I got a life lesson. I learned the power of feminine wiles. Right then and there, it clicked. *My worth was based on my sexual attractiveness.* It made sense, I mean the odds always seems stacked against me unless I was all dolled up and batting my eyes. When I went with the flow, I didn't fail.

Someone I admired who had all the feminine wiles in the world was Madonna. I used to turn up the volume of my boom box and lip-sync to her song *Borderline*. I was also more than a little jealous of Madonna because I imagined she was singing about David Lee Roth who, in my mixed-up mind, just had to be dating her. In boom-box fantasyland, Madonna was good enough for Dave. I wasn't. He was out of my league. I was determined to change that.

Clutching my hall pass, I'd walk around the school auditorium. Alone in that big room, I felt important and confident I would be famous one day. I fantasized about coming back to that small town in a stretch limo and all those empty seats were full of adoring fans begging for my autograph. In addition to dreaming of losing my virginity to David Lee Roth, I dreamed of becoming an MTV VJ like Martha Quinn, or anchoring the nightly news like Barbara Walters. I had a knack for writing, but I wanted to be on camera. I basically wanted to be liked. If I became famous, it would mean I was likable, proving my mother wrong.

My mother did work hard, traveling to art fairs doing portraits and various odd jobs to put herself through college and put food on our table. But we never had enough money to make ends meet. I was ashamed of being poor and I hated using lunch stamps at school. You wouldn't know we were on welfare, though, from the way I was dressed. I was styling, always decked out in designer jeans, Jordache, Gloria Vanderbilt or Calvin Klein. My grandparents would buy them for me, or my dad would take me on an occasional shopping spree. That's pretty much the only he had the opportunity to show his love. So, in a way, I learned to equate love with material things. I guess that's why my wise grandmother cautioned me against marrying for money. She saw the writing on the wall.

*****

Davey was my first boyfriend. I was a seventh grader, and he was a senior in high school. He was five years older than I was. Davey's father owned the town dump. Davey worked there and I kept him company. The first time I ever had oral sex, Davey went down on me in a tractor, the one he drove to push the garbage into the landfill. I had never even imagined such a thing was possible. He said, "There's something I want to do to you," and stuck his head up my skirt. All I remember is the stench of decaying trash overpowering any other sensory experience I might have had.

One night while my mother was in the living room, sprawled on the couch watching T.V., Davey and I were hanging out in my bedroom, which was right next to it. Just the two of us. A fourteen-year-old girl and a nineteen-year old boy. With the door closed. I was wearing my pink pajamas, the onesie Zoot suit pajamas with their own feet and a zipper all the way to the top. Not the sexiest of nightwear, but that didn't deter Davey, who whispered seductively, "I just love you so much I want to share everything with you." And then we did it. I fell for that corny line. Years later, I questioned my mother why she'd allowed Davey to hang out with me alone in my bedroom. She said he'd promised her he wouldn't do *that* with me. I have no clue why she believed him. She wasn't naive. I mean, nineteen-year-old boys are notoriously horny. What else do they want to do but fuck? So, there went my virginity.

Davey loved to smoke pot, but I didn't. In fact, I was vehemently against it. Whenever I caught him with weed, I'd break up with him. Or at least I tried. He wouldn't let me. He'd hysterically cry and bash his head on the nearest hard surface until it bled, and he wouldn't stop until I agreed to take him back. After high school, he joined the army and proposed to me by mail. He even included a diamond ring with the letter. His parents were livid because of the age difference and they were paranoid, with good reason, that he might get me pregnant. His older sister confronted me in the hallway at school and demanded the ring back. I should have punched her in the face. Instead I handed it over. I didn't really have any interest in marrying Davey, anyway. I was only still a kid, for God's sake.

My mother didn't want me to grow up a small-minded redneck, so in order to broaden my horizons she sent me every other summer to stay with friends in San Diego. When I discovered surfer dudes, I forgot all about Davey. My friend Buffy and I paraded along the boardwalk in our bikinis, drinking gin out of soda cans. We told the boys we were sixteen, when we were fourteen, and eighteen when we were sixteen. We had bonfire parties on the beach, and guys would drive us home. We got drunk and puked in the backs of their trucks but, amazingly, nothing bad ever happened to us. Crazy but fun times. I came home with spiked hair, wearing shark tooth earrings. I subscribed to *Surfer* magazine and was California dreamin'.

*****

Four days a week, my mother was away at art shows, so I was alone a lot. I lived mostly on macaroni and cheese and frozen pizza. Free of parental oversight, I rarely bothered with homework. I had Billy Thibeault, the boy whose locker was next to mine, do it for me. My mom's absence also gave me the chance to throw crazy parties. It was always a blast until either my sister Jill came home, or the police showed up. We'd outsmart the police by quickly hiding the booze in the oven. We drank whatever we could get our hands on in those days, mostly cheap wines like Boone's Farm Tickle Pink and Strawberry Hill. The good thing about Boone's Farm is that, unlike beer, it has no telltale odor. The cops didn't have a clue.

I regularly held parties on Thursday nights while Jill presided over Students Against Drunk Driving meetings. Jill and I were complete opposites. While she was a do-gooder, I turned the house into party central. When the headlights of Jill's car swept up the driveway, everyone ran for their cars, knowing she'd be in a rage. They were more afraid of her than of the police. Ironically, this meant they usually drove home drunk.

When there wasn't a parentless house to party in, we moved into the fields and the woods. We built bonfires, blasted rock music, like Tom Petty, Led Zeppelin and Lynyrd Skynyrd, and drank beer like there was no tomorrow. We were resourceful enough to collect all the empty bottles and cans and cash them in for a nickel apiece. That's how we got money to buy concert tickets. One time, during my sophomore year, my friend Sharon and I wound up in a nightclub after an Aerosmith concert shaking hands with Steven Tyler. I only met him for two seconds. It was all very innocent except for a roadie who did blow off of Sharon's boobs. I have no idea how we ended up in that club. It's all a blur. But, looking back, it's the only time I got to meet the legendary Steven Tyler, so it was pretty fucking cool.

When I was fifteen and visiting my grandparents in Albany, they let me go to a Billy Idol concert with my nineteen-year-old stepsister Tammy and my friend Lori. As he blasted out, "With a rebel yell, she cried, *More, more, more!*" I rushed down to the front row, leaped onto a speaker, jumped onstage, and kissed him. He smiled and actually kissed me back. I was holding onto him so tightly that security had to grab me by my ankles to pull me away, but not before I managed to hand him an antique Elvis Presley pin I'd taken from my mother's collection. I had read that Elvis was his idol and wanted to give him something so maybe he'd remember me. I later saw magazine pictures of him wearing the pin, so it was worth getting in trouble for stealing it, not to mention the embarrassment of giving it to him. Looking back, I would classify my behavior as crazy. But according to the diary I kept back then, I was in love with Billy Idol, and it was the best night of my life. I was over him by the time I met him just a few years later at a valet stand outside an L.A. club called X-Poseur, and he asked me out. That was the same night he wrecked his bike and almost died.

When I was sixteen, I saw KISS in concert for the first time. It was March 23, 1985 in Springfield, Massachusetts, during their *Animalize* tour. Chrissy and I got her mother to drive us to the show. We were sitting on top of some random guy's shoulders. Back in the good old days, that's what we did. We had general admission floor seats and would tap the tallest guy we could find on the shoulder. They'd crouch down and let us climb on top to watch the show. Money can't buy seats like that. I was wearing jeans and a white Flashdance-style, off the shoulder sweatshirt with white fishnet overlay. Paul Stanley kept motioning for me to pull my top up. "Show me your tits," was a thing in the 80s hair band world. It worked with a lot of the other girls in the audience. But I had small town, nice girl values. Paul kept egging me on to show him my tits, but I kept shaking my head no. Eventually, I teased him. I pulled up the fishnet layer, but that left the white sweatshirt covering my tits. I laughed and smiled, and what he did next was as surreal as it was exhilarating. He stopped singing, shined a huge spotlight on me and said, "You! I am going to marry you." In that moment, Paul Stanley made me feel more important than at any other time in my young life. I got a taste of the attention I was craving. But the moment was fleeting. After the show, I made Chrissy go chasing the tour bus down the street with me. The band was probably looking out the window laughing at us. In reality, I was just another high school sophomore, not Paul Stanley's fiancée.

That same year, after a friend of my mom's said I was a classic beauty who should be modeling, my mother sent me to the John Robert Powers Modeling and Finishing School, an hour away in Worcester, Massachusetts. There I learned how to apply makeup and file my nails. We were taught how to sit properly in an "S" position with our ankles crossed. We learned how to walk straight, balancing a textbook on our heads, and how to make introductions, start conversations at parties, and smile pretty for cameras. I loved it. Although there weren't many modeling opportunities in Massachusetts, I did do a few fashion shows and car shows. I figured the experience would eventually land me in magazines where David Lee Roth would see me and fall in love. I'd be the girl he sang to in *"I'll Wait."*

*****

Hunting was a big thing in my small town. Although I despised it and still do, one of the neighbor girls and I once stole two of her brother's rifles and snuck off into the woods, wearing his camouflage and his faux urine that was supposed to attract deer. We had no idea what we were doing. We could have accidentally shot each other or someone else. We didn't and, thankfully, didn't shoot any deer either. That's how I met Darryl. He was the brother whose guns we'd stolen. He was twenty-two and looked just like Rambo in the poster on my bedroom wall. He'd just broken up with the girl he was living with and moved back home, to the house at the end of our dead-end dirt road. I got out of Darryl's pants and invited him into mine. We were crazy about each other. I was only seventeen, but I had a fake I.D. so we hung out in bars. A lot. Our main hangout, a dive called The Q, was kind of like the bar in the movie *Road House* with Patrick Swayze, only smaller and without country music. They played the pop dance songs of the 80s from artists like Prince and Whitney Houston.

Darryl loved to make me mad by flirting with other girls. One night he danced up a storm with a tall, ravishing redhead whom I'd never seen before. I was so jealous I pushed her off of him and punched her in the face. What did she expect? I mean, where I grew up it was the all-white version of *The Jerry Springer Show*. I knew they would kick me out. I didn't care. I had to fight for my man. Eventually I grew some class, and behaved like a lady, but in high school, if anyone messed with me or my friends, I punched them. It earned me the nickname "Rocky."

After the bouncer at The Q kicked me out of the bar, I walked over to Darryl's older brother Harold's house. He lived nearby and I needed to vent and have another drink. I left my burgundy Chevy Impala, a present from my grandparents, in the parking lot. In the middle of the night, my mother got a call from the police department, saying my car had been found totaled in a field. She immediately thought the worst; that I was dead. Well, I *was* dead; dead to the world, fast asleep on Harold's couch. Someone had taken my car for a joyride and crashed it.

My mother figured out where I was and came over and got me. She drove me to friends a few hours away so I couldn't be questioned by the police or, I suspect, have a blood alcohol test. Thirty years later, Darryl confessed to me that the car thief was a twelve-year-old relative of his. He'd been sitting in my car to keep warm, got bored, and decided to teach himself how to drive. He flipped my car in a field, escaped unscathed through the driver's side window, and snuck home through the woods.

Assuming Darryl was the culprit, my mother had had enough. For the first time in my life she decided to lay down the law. "You're in my house. You'll live by my rules," she fumed. She forbade me from ever seeing Darryl again. I thought I was real clever hiding my fake I.D. in the ceiling of my room, but she found it and destroyed it. She had once been a teenager too. What the hell was going on? I was nearly eighteen, virtually an adult, and she was suddenly trying to be strict with me? After all these years of no supervision, she decides to be a parent?

"If you can't live with my rules, get out," she said. So, the next day when she wasn't home, I packed my things and flew the coop. Luckily, my dear, sympathetic grandparents had coughed up $3,000 for another car. Not because they were rich or I was spoiled, but because they truly supported my dreams, and I couldn't get very far without transportation. In return for letting her use my car while I was at school, my friend Lori's mom let me stay at their house. I might have been rebellious, but I was nobody's fool.

*****

My sassy little ass got the last word with Mrs. Marshall, the biology teacher who'd made the humiliating remark about my empty-headedness. She'd been promoted to principal, and I was often called to her office for one infraction or another. This time it was because my friends and I thought it would be a good prank to plant condoms in the cafeteria's big white tub of Thousand Island dressing. We giggled as Mr. Betscha, the English teacher, freaked out when he saw a condom hanging off his ladle. It hadn't been used, so what was the harm? Mrs. Marshall didn't see it that way. She threatened to suspend me from school until I turned the tables on her.

"Do you remember what you said to me when you were my teacher?" I asked her.

I'd learned how to be a good manipulator, or, in nicer terms, negotiator, from watching my CBS soap operas, *As the World Turns* and *The Guiding Light*. When she said she didn't remember, I laid it all out. How her scathing remark had emotionally wounded me so much that it was the reason I had deteriorated academically and behaviorally. If I told the school board or the school superintendent about it maybe that would jog her memory. Mrs. Marshall was very responsive. She apologized. What did I want?

"I want out of school and into the world," I said.

No doubt happy to get me out of her hair, she agreed to let me spend my senior year at the community college in Worcester and still graduate with my class. The following year I would transfer to a four-year university and major in broadcast journalism.

The plan, however, was quickly derailed. I was sitting in my guidance counselor's office going over the college paperwork when we heard police sirens. I looked out the window and saw a police car drive up the school's circular driveway, followed by my mother's car. She flexed her legal strong arm, winning the battle. Since I was under eighteen, I couldn't legally own the car I'd bought with my grandparents' money without her permission. The police returned my car to the dealer. I was taken out of school and sent to a shrink. I think it was more for my mother than for me. It relieved any guilt she might have over kicking me out. I was to be sent to live with my father, who was now working for a pharmaceutical company in Memphis, Tennessee.

We stopped off at the house to pack my things, which gave me the chance to raid my mother's medicine cabinet. After the drama that went down, I truly felt like it was the end of the world. Not only was I being torn away from my boyfriend, I wouldn't be going to college a year early and wouldn't be able to graduate with my friends. My life in Massachusetts was over. My future plans were destroyed. I was done. I decided to end my life. If she didn't want me around, then I really wasn't going to be around. I got hold of her bottle of Motrin, big orange pills (which were prescription meds at the time) and swallowed the whole bottle. I grabbed bottles of aspirin and Tylenol and whatever else was stashed in there. I swallowed them all.

At the psychologist's office she tried to get me to speak but I refused to utter a word. The only thing that came out of my mouth was orange projectile vomit. My suicide attempt was undetected by the incompetent shrink. Neither my mother nor the shrink knew what I had done. I was beaten down to the point that I was willing to take my own life, and they never figured it out.

I realize my mother thought she was protecting me from my reckless self, but I had my shit together. I was going to college a year early. Had she been around more, maybe she would have known me better. Had she not kicked me out, I might have been Barbara Walters or Martha Quinn. I'll never know.

Ripped out of my life in Massachusetts, I went from being the most popular girl in school to an outsider, teased and called "Yankee" by many of the kids at Germantown High in Memphis, the largest high school in Tennessee. It was like being in a foreign country. I was sad, lonely, and homesick. I wrote poetry about it and cried a lot. Since I had nothing to do but study, I was getting A's and B's. Nobody at school spoke to me until I met Susan Reilley. Van Halen had broken up and David Lee Roth was touring with his new band. I was in the front row at the Mid-South Coliseum for his *Crazy from the Heat* concert. I turned around, and there she was, right behind me in the second row. We've been friends ever since. Without even meeting him, David Lee Roth had cured my lonely heart.

In the middle of the school year, a guidance counselor informed me that my records had come in from Massachusetts. I didn't have enough credits to be a senior in Tennessee. I would have to stay back and repeat eleventh grade. No way. I was not willing to go through that misery for another year. So, I dropped out. I would no longer be class of '87. I was no shining star, as my namesake suggested. I was a high school dropout.

But now that I had Susan, life in Tennessee started to get fun. She introduced me to her friends, who were metalheads and party animals. While I worked as a hostess at a Houston's Restaurant, I went to the Memphis John Robert Powers Modeling and Finishing School and booked a few minor modeling jobs. But I wanted more out of life than fun. All of the kids who worked with me attended Memphis State University. Standing there at a podium, handing out menus and robotically repeating "enjoy your meal" wasn't enough for me. If I was ever to become a broadcast journalist, I needed to go to college.

I didn't tell my father or my stepmother, Lynn, of my plan. I took the GED, the high school equivalency diploma test, and passed without even studying. Then I registered for ACT, the college entrance exam. I didn't tell them about that either. I was too nervous to talk about it. I got accepted to Memphis State and started college the same time as my classmates who'd graduated high school in their caps and gowns. My parents were not in the least encouraging. The first day of college my stepmother chased me out to the car with a pen and paper telling me to write down every book I bought and every class I failed, because I'd have to pay her back. My father said, "What makes you think you are going to graduate? You've never finished anything in your life." I was only eighteen, a little young to be judged so harshly. Maybe he was trying to show me tough love, but I would have preferred a vote of confidence.

Nevertheless, my independent streak won the day. I was having a blast. I studied hard and partied even harder. I fell in love with Memphis's eclectic music scene. From touring Elvis's Graceland and Sun Studios, to listening to the blues on Beale Street and head-banging in in the heavy metal bars, this outrageous new city offered me opportunities that changed the course of my life forever.

Chapter 2

Don't Have a One-Night Stand

November 17, 1987. It began in the lobby bar of The Peabody Hotel, the South's grand hotel in downtown Memphis. It's famous for the parade of ducks that waddle to and from the lobby fountain at 11:00 a.m. and 5:00 p.m. every day. My friend Mary and I weren't there to see the ducks. We were there to see Rolling Stones' guitarist Ron Wood and an exhibition of his art.

Mary and I made a striking pair. Mary was half-Japanese and always dressed like she'd just stepped off the set of the music-dance TV show *Soul Train*. She was wearing a zebra-print miniskirt, a red crop top, and high-heeled pointy shoes. I, a curvy, all-American girl with fair skin and auburn hair, wore a low-cut acid-washed denim dress and white leather fringe jacket. Mary had long black hair down to her ass; my hair was shoulder-length with bangs teased really high, thanks to my generous application of Aqua Net hair spray. We were hard to miss.

After the exhibit, Mary and I headed to our stomping ground, the lobby bar, of course. Sitting at the table next to us were three rockers. One of them, from the back of his head, looked just like KISS front man Paul Stanley. But according to their tour schedule, they should have left town the night before. It couldn't be Paul. And it wasn't. It was Eric Carr, the drummer, who I'd always thought was the cutest guy in the band. With him was Steve, the tour manager, and one of the road crew guys. I overheard them talking about getting a cab to a bar we frequented, The Midway Café, to see one of our favorite local bands, The Willys. I seized the opportunity, boldly interrupting, "I've got a car. I'll take you!"

That's how I met Eric.

Outside, we all piled into my brand new, white Toyota Celica. Eric took the front passenger seat. We had instant chemistry. Sparks were flying. He didn't stop cracking jokes. When he wasn't laughing, he was asking me about myself in his sexy, soft-spoken voice. He had an appealing way of nervously moving his lips when he spoke to me. He told me that two of KISS's concerts had been canceled, so the rest of the band flew back home for a few days, but he and the road crew were biding their time in Memphis. Up until then, I'd only see him from afar. But now he was looking right into my eyes, fixated on me, and it felt so natural, as if I had known him my whole life. He was not at all intimidating. I was comfortable with him.

Then it hit me: *rock star Eric Carr was sitting right next to me in my car.*

I'd always been a KISS fan. When I was nine years old, in 1979, my girlfriends and I dressed up as KISS for Halloween. I was Peter Criss, the original drummer. We put tinfoil on our arms and wore black leotards and tights. Ace got grounded, so we were a three-man band. We wore some crap makeup that came in a KISS kit that we bought in the Halloween section of Kmart, and we all broke out in rashes the next day. Nevertheless, I joined their fan club. I was a member of The KISS Army.

The first time I saw KISS in concert was that time in Springfield, Mass., during their *Animalize* tour when after I'd teased Paul Stanley, pretending I was going to show him my tits, he'd stopped the show, shone the big spotlight on me, and announced he was going to marry me.

Now, two years later and living in Memphis, whenever KISS blew into the south my girlfriends and I were on their trail. Four nights earlier, we'd made the 400-mile round-trip to Jackson, Mississippi to see their *Crazy Nights* concert. Two nights earlier, we'd seen them perform at the Mid-South Coliseum in Memphis.

I was there with Mary and two other friends, Kathy and Donna. Kathy was a seasoned rocker chick. I mean she went to Woodstock, which is badass. But that was the year I was born. She was thirty-five, and I was just eighteen. She was a petite blonde with a southern drawl and a shit-ton of makeup. Donna was a cute, bubbly blonde, and a hard-core metal chick. Before the concert we were at The Peabody where the band was staying. Kathy knew all the rock stars, so of course she'd met Eric in the past. When the elevator doors opened, and he appeared, she broke away to say hello and snag us some backstage passes. Then Eric rushed down the hotel corridor to leave for the venue.

Eric didn't seem to notice me, even though I was wearing a hot pink leather mini skirt and metallic silver halter top. But Gene Simmons certainly did, slyly slipping a folded-up piece of hotel notepaper into my hand as he nonchalantly walked towards the exit. Scrawled on the paper was his room number. I was flattered. But Gene had a reputation. I was probably one of a dozen girls that night to be invited to his room. God knows how many girls would be knocking on his door. I had no intention of being one of them, so I crumpled the paper into a ball and threw it away. Besides, Gene scared me. He was larger than life, and that made me nervous. Anyway, I had a date for the show, a nineteen-year-old named

Mark. He was a handsome long-haired guitar player from Little Rock, Arkansas whom I had met at the Mall of Memphis where I worked in a record store. After hanging out at The Peabody, the girls and I met up with Mark at the KISS concert. We all had a blast. But that night Eric didn't know I existed.

Tonight, I had his full attention as I navigated our way to the Midway Cafe. And it wasn't long before we had a real connection. I remember leaning against an antique jukebox with him, where we had gone to steal some private time away from the others and the loud music. One moment, I was captivated by the deep, serious gaze in his eyes; the next, I was laughing at some quick-witted remark. He was kind, fun, and very sexy. As we listened to The Willys, we held hands, kissed, and downed Long Island Iced Teas. Too many Long Island Iced Teas, a potent concoction of vodka, tequila, rum, triple sec and gin. Oh, and don't let the bartender forget the splash of Coke, or you'll choke.

At closing time, they kicked us out and we stumbled into my car. On the way back to the hotel, all five of us had an urgent need to pee. None of us could wait the ten minutes it would take to get to The Peabody. I stopped the car on Poplar Avenue, and we all relieved ourselves in the middle of the street. Yes, we were that wasted. Eric suddenly decided that I was too drunk to drive and insisted on getting behind the wheel. But he wasn't exactly capable, either. When we got back to The Peabody, he plowed straight through a thick chain blocking the parking lot entrance. The chain whiplashed, spiraling through the air, over the car, and smashing my taillights. We were all so drunk we didn't care. The other two guys went their separate ways, and Mary and I followed Eric to his room. It's not what you're thinking. The thought of a threesome absolutely wouldn't have crossed my mind back then, although it might have crossed Eric's. I mean he was a guy, wasn't he?

I called my dad and told him I was going to sleep over at Mary's house. I assured him that I would go straight to class at Memphis State University in the morning. I hung up and went to the bathroom. When I came out, Mary, in her drunken stupor, had Eric pinned on the bed, straddling him. At least she still had her clothes on.

I was livid. I was the one Eric had been kissing all night. We'd connected. She knew it. And yet she was moving in on him! Drunk girls aren't just easy. They are emotional. They either scream or cry. I screamed.

"What the fuck are you doing, you slimy slut?!"

Mary started to cry hysterically. Eric tried to calm things down.

"Why don't you take her home and come back?" he suggested.

That made sense to me and Mary didn't argue. I can't believe it, but I did just that. Even though it was 3:00 am, I drove Mary to her home in Frasier, about thirty minutes away, and drove back to The Peabody. I think the adrenaline from the fight must have sobered me up, because I somehow made it back alive. I knocked on Eric's door, and he opened it. Naked. And happy to see me. We had hot, sweaty sex until we fell asleep exhausted. He was by far the most experienced guy I'd ever been with and by far the most endowed. I skipped school in favor of sex education from Eric. We paused to share stories about our lives. He admitted he got lonely on the road. I'd taken care of his loneliness, at least for a day. Much to my horror, he admitted that he'd once shared his bed with five girls at the same time. I'm not sure what that was a cure for. I was just glad I didn't catch anything.

I knew I was just a one-night stand for him. I mean, what thirty-seven-year-old rock star would take seriously an eighteen-year old who'd slept with him the night they met? And yet, as absurd as it sounds, he stole a little piece of my heart that night.

*****

KISS continued their *Crazy Nights* tour, and I went back to being a college girl rocker chick. I told myself that Eric and I had had our wild, crazy night (and day) and logically that's all it would ever be. But all the while, deep inside of me, I had a feeling there would be more to our story. Seven months later, I was proved right. I'd gone to New Paltz, New York to visit my sister, Jill, who attended college there. I was honest with her and told her I'd fucked Eric. She was much more conservative than I, and protective of me, so when she told her classmate, Tina LaRue, about my encounter with Eric, she made it sound more like a relationship than a one-night stand.

It so happened that Tina had a friend she grew up with in New Paltz, named Danny, who was a KISS fanatic. He collected all kinds of KISS memorabilia. He even had a KISS pinball machine. We called him "green teeth." You can guess why. The two of them surprised me with tickets for a KISS concert on the Fourth of July, a couple hours' drive away in Swanzey, New Hampshire. Danny drove, while Tina and I fought over who got to take the back seat. Neither of us wanted to sit up front because Danny's feet smelled so bad. Don't get me wrong. He was a cool guy. We really liked him. We just didn't like the stench. Tina and I shared the burden and swapped seats whenever we made a stop to buy beer or use the restroom.

As we were parking at the Cheshire Fairgrounds where the show was being held, Tina turned to me with a big smile on her face, and asked assertively, "Well, since Jill told us you're dating the drummer, you can get us backstage, right?" Oh, shit. They'd got the tickets. It was my job to get us backstage. And it shouldn't be a problem should it since I knew Eric so well? Yikes.

I had to confess what had really happened. Nevertheless, Tina convinced me there was no harm in asking, right? As humiliated as I was, I felt obligated to put in the effort for Tina and Danny. Apprehensively, I handed a note for Eric to a security guard at the backstage entrance which basically said, "Hello, it's Carrie from Memphis, and I'm here."

A few minutes later the guard returned. Eric had told him he didn't know any Carrie from Memphis. Mortified,

I walked away. While we waited for the show to start, we walked around the fairground, wallowing in the conflicting aromas of the sugary-sweet smell of the cotton candy and the rank odor of fried onions lathered on greasy hot dogs. It was a blistering hot day, so I was wearing cut off shorts and a turquoise triangle bikini top. It got me a lot of attention, but I was in no mood for it. I felt defeated.

At the show, a roadie named Romeo, who told me he was Gene's bass tech, came on to me. A few minutes later I saw him on stage with Gene pointing at me. He returned and invited me backstage. I was deathly afraid to meet Gene. He was such a huge presence, an icon, and there was that *tongue*.

"I'm not going to be with Gene Simmons," I said.

"No, no, you are coming to hang out with me... don't worry," said Romeo.

Oh sure. No need to worry? He had no idea how paranoid I was that he'd discover I'd not only spent a night with Eric but had just sent him a note and been rejected. I went anyway. Romeo led me by the hand through the crowd. The band was on stage. The show was about to begin. With a great display of chivalry, Romeo brought out a high wooden bar stool for me. There I was, the only person watching the show from the side of the stage, perched on this stool like a princess.

It was hard to enjoy the performance, though. I was so tense. I sat there, eyes fixed firmly on Bruce Kulick, the guitar player, and Gene and Paul. Anywhere but the massive drum kit, and the man sitting behind it. The jerk who'd blown me off. The jerk who surely remembered me, but obviously didn't like me enough to ever want to see me again or even have enough courtesy to acknowledge my existence! The last thing I needed was for him to spot me on stage and tell the guys he fucked me in Memphis.

After the show, it was still daylight, and there was a tent set up with a barbeque for the band and crew. Invited to stay, I got Romeo to allow Tina and Danny backstage. They were impressed. I'd pulled it off, after all. We sat at a round picnic table, my back to the entrance. Tina, sitting across from me, excitedly blurted, "Oh, my God. Here he comes, here he comes. Your drummer friend. He's here." Eric walked right past us, heading for the buffet. My heart was pounding as I watched his every move. He got a huge plate of food and came to our table. Oh, my God. I looked down, I wanted to crawl into a hole. Tina and Danny seized the initiative and introduced themselves. Just as Eric was about to take a bite of one of the three hot dogs on his plate, Tina said, "Oh, and you already know our friend Carrie from Memphis." When I looked up at Eric his jaw dropped, causing the hot dog to fall out of his mouth.

"Wow. I don't remember you being so beautiful," he said.

Regardless of the butterflies dancing wildly in my stomach, I wasn't about to lose my cool.

"Well, if you had," I quipped, "Maybe you wouldn't have said you didn't know me."

Eric must have been starving, judging from the pile of food on his plate, but after speaking to me for a few minutes he seemed to lose his appetite. I made him nervous. I thought it was cute. We picked up the conversation where we'd left it seven months ago, like no time had passed. He seemed more like the down-to-earth guy I'd met in Memphis than the rock star who just a few minutes earlier had been on stage in front of thousands of adoring fans. Eric was sitting at the other side of the table next to Tina, who was dominating the conversation. He kept looking at me, kind of transfixed, sort of like a love-sick puppy. Was this for real? What was going on?

Paul Stanley sauntered in like the cat who ate the canary. He swung one leg over the bench I was sitting on, commanding my attention. My mind was blown. What if Gene and Romeo came backstage? They'd been nice enough to bring me up on stage. Would they be pissed off? Paul was seriously hitting on me. What if it all came out and I was thought of as nothing more than a groupie who'd had a one-night stand with Eric? Paul zoomed close in on me, nose to nose, with relentless intensity. He had one mission, and one mission only, and that was to get me back to his hotel room. He was trying to persuade me to leave with them in the band's limo. Right then. Can you imagine? Me riding in the limo with Gene and Paul and Eric? It might sound like every KISS fan's dream come true. I was so stressed that I was shaking.

I asked Paul if he remembered shining that spotlight on me in Springfield when I was sixteen, and, of course, he said sure, he remembered. But I knew he was just floating my boat. It was part of the show. He probably picked a girl out of the audience to propose to every night. But this was Paul Stanley.

How could I not be flattered and charmed? Eric was trying to act cool, chatting with Tina, while eyeing what was happening between Paul and me. What was happening now was that Paul was whispering seductively in my ear, "Come back with me now, baby." He was really pushy and I have to admit I had a little fun knowing that Eric was squirming in his seat, worried he might lose me to Paul. I didn't have the balls to turn down a huge rock star. I just couldn't find the word, "No." So, I told Paul I couldn't leave without my friends, but would follow him to the hotel in their car.

"Be there," he encouraged. "Room 224. Be there."

Of course, I had no intention of going. And I'm sure he got over being stood up as soon as his head hit the pillow that night. I wasn't tempted in the least. Why? Because I'd already traded phone numbers with Eric and made a date for the next night. He was staying with his parents in upstate New York, only thirty minutes from my sister's home. I smiled victoriously. I wasn't a one-night stand anymore. I had a real date.

*****

For our first date, Eric met me at a restaurant in New Paltz. Jill and Tina had given me a ride there and tried not to be obvious about lingering around long enough for photo ops. There was no way he didn't notice their scheme. A less gracious celebrity might have found it obnoxious, but Eric was a good sport. I sat on his lap so we could all squeeze into the frame of the camera. Today I cherish those photos.

After dinner, we got a room at the Holiday Inn, because of course we wanted to have sex and the hotel bed was definitely a better option than the backseat of his silver Porsche. To say it was wild, crazy sex would be putting it lightly. It was even better than the first night and day we'd spent together in that Memphis hotel room. I had never felt a physical connection like that. I had actually never had an orgasm with anyone besides myself before I met Eric, so he now had a spell over me. I was addicted. It's scientific knowledge that when people have orgasms, the body releases a hormone called oxytocin which makes a woman feel like she is in love, and a man feel territorial. Because we shared crazy chemistry, we couldn't resist each other. We had as many dates as we could fit in during the time we were in the same area.

A few days later, when Eric turned thirty-eight on July 12th, 1988, I bought him a card with a little bird on the cover and inserted this poem I wrote as a birthday gift:

For Every Berry There is A Bird

You wake me by the rise of light
As your strength searches for my warmth
Waiting, I feel you behind me
The curling waves of your back are the rhythm
of my breath.

I am the berry, the sweetness... half your age
You take me like a vacation

To return from where we came
You're painting me hot crimson and gold
With our moisture... over and over.

Then a waterfall; an electrifying crash
You rest your face between my breasts,
Your sweat drips like teardrops then evaporates,
Simultaneously with the morning dew.

Helpless, I cry inside!
You are the blackbird who must fly away.

We had to go our separate ways: Eric had to prepare for a twenty-city European tour, and I had to return to school in Memphis. This time it was different, though. This time we vowed to keep in touch. Even though he was thirty-eight and I was now nineteen, I didn't think about the age difference. He was a rock star; he seemed ageless. And even though there was a physical distance between us, we spoke on the phone all the time. We grew close. I was his "ear." His confidante. I'd listen to all his problems and give him advice. Even about his other girlfriends. His most recent had been Charisse, of the all-female metal band, Hari Kari, but I knew he was seeing others. He was a big stud on the road. But he was honest about it. He was also a very generous and helpful person. He gave Tina LaRue, today a successful entertainment attorney, her first job in the music industry managing Hari Kari while she was still in college. That was wonderful of him, but a little awkward for me. Especially when Tina booked their tour and had them stay at my house in Memphis and play at the nightclub I went to every weekend, The Stage Stop. I was expecting Charisse to try to kill me, but thankfully she didn't. Maybe she didn't know I was having sex with her ex-boyfriend.

I was doing well as a journalism major at Memphis State. I had all A's and B's, but I was restless. My father wouldn't let me live at the dorm. So that I could focus on school, he wanted me to live at home and didn't want me to get a job. So, what did my rebellious ass do? I got two jobs: one at a record store and one working the front desk at a Ramada Inn. With the money I made, I decided to take a vacation and met my old friend Marie from Massachusetts, in Los Angeles over Christmas break, so we could ring in the New Year together.

Los Angeles in the 80s was a rocker chick's paradise. On any given night, hundreds of gorgeous long-haired guys from different bands swarmed Sunset Boulevard passing out flyers for their upcoming gigs. Hard rock and heavy metal bands played up and down the strip at clubs such as Gazzarri's, The Whisky-A-Go-Go, The Roxy, and The Coconut Teaszer. We went to see Faster Pussycat at Madame Wong's on New Year's Eve. Every night we'd go to a show and end up afterwards at the Rainbow Bar and Grill at 1:00 a.m. for last call. It was always packed with scantily clad girls and skinny guys in snakeskin pants. We could barely get through the sea of leather and lace to walk down the aisles.

When I returned to Memphis State, I couldn't focus anymore. All I could do in class was daydream about moving to L.A. I had a phone conversation with Eric about it, and he wasn't exactly supportive. He was concerned, knowing most nice, small-town girls get corrupted when they get caught up in the Hollywood scene. But he also mentioned he was going to be there recording KISS's new album, *Hot in The Shade*. That sealed the deal. I was determined to relocate to L.A., so that I could be close to him. I called my friend Jan, who had also been talking about moving there. Did she still want to go? "Hell, yeah." I packed my suitcases and hid them behind my bed. In case my parents tried to stop me, I was going to leave without saying goodbye. But my stepmother found my bags. My dad was furious when I told him my plans. He told me not to expect any financial help from him.

"You'll be back in two weeks," he predicted.

For the record, it's been thirty years and counting.

Before I left for L.A. on Valentine's Day, 1989, I made a recording of *"Love Song"* by Tesla to help Eric get over his breakup with Charisse. I sent the cassette to him, labeled "Valentine's Day 1989."

> *So, you think that it's over,*
> *That your love has finally reached the end.*
> *Any time you call, night or day,*
> *I'll be right there for you if you need a friend.*

I was so in love with him, as only young love can be. The song goes, "You'll find love again, I know." That would be me. I knew I was his true love. That was the subliminal message I was trying to convey. I just had to get him to realize it!

Chapter 3

Don't Run Off with a Rock Star

L.A. was rock and roll heaven. I shared an apartment with three other girls on Orange Drive in Hollywood. Between us, we had every band that played on the Sunset Strip come through that apartment, a revolving door of rock stars. I was nineteen; one of the other girls was only seventeen, and wild. She was with so many guys that she got three STDs in the first six months. None of us had any money. We'd buy a cheap jug of Carlo Rossi wine and drink it in the apartment before we went out. Sometimes at the Rainbow, where we hung out five nights a week, we'd order one Long Island Iced Tea (the strongest drink available) and split it among the four of us. That way we could all get buzzed on a budget. We would go to Happy Hour at a Mexican place called La Villa Taxco, where the food was free if you bought a drink. We'd buy a diet soda and all of us have dinner. My friend Amy from high school had also moved to L.A. and landed a job at a department store. We would shop there and then return the clothes after we'd worn them. We didn't suffer. We had fun figuring out how to survive.

I worked the front desk at the Ramada in West Hollywood, usually the graveyard shift. Sometimes as many as ten gay men would book one room to presumably have an orgy. Something I'd not seen back in Massachusetts, or Memphis, for that matter. I remember one night a nice young married couple from the Midwest checked in. Later, the husband came down and blew the bellman in the closet. The bellman was proud of it, but I was in shock. Some nights, I was the one who got lucky. Eric would come visit me, and, on my next break, we'd go into one of the rooms and make love.

During these early days in L.A., I also got modeling jobs. I was 5'5" and too short for fashion modeling, so I did what's called "commercial print" or "product print." In one ad for a Toyota truck, I was cast alongside a rail thin, flat-chested blonde beauty and a cute surfer dude. We posed in the back of the truck, pretending to be laughing, enjoying a sunny day. I was kicking back in a large, black inner tube while the other two models stood next to me.

Suddenly, the photographer scowled. He stopped taking photos and called a meeting. The crew huddled together but were too far away for me to hear their animated conversation. I hadn't a clue what was going on until the wardrobe stylist asked me to follow her into the trailer. Wasting no time, she pulled down the top half of my one-piece bathing suit and announced that the photographer thought my breasts were saggy and unattractive. They needed some help. Then, expertly wielding a roll of silver duct tape, she proceeded to tape my breasts. First from underneath, lifting them up, and then back across to smash them down. Humiliated, I walked back onto the set all taped up like a mummy, knowing everyone was staring at my now-acceptable chest. As if that wasn't painful enough! It was nothing compared to the moment when the tape was ripped off.

Around the same time, my friend Wendy, who I'd met shooting a music video for the band Lizzy Borden, arranged for me to test shoot with a well-known poster photographer. His problem wasn't my boobs; it was my weight. He insinuated I had a weight problem. Seriously? I weighed about 110 pounds. This asshole must have weighed three hundred pounds, and *I* was too heavy? Admittedly, I had a slight bulge on the outside of my thigh. We used to call them saddle bags, but now, thanks to the Kardashians and J. Lo, they're coveted curves, in style. The fat photographer told me I needed liposuction. Looking back, I think he was trying to do a psychological number on me, trying to tear me down so he could play hero, build me back up, and hit on me.

Finally, I got "discovered." I was at my dentist's office in Burbank when a woman approached me and asked, "Union or non-union?" What? Like a coal miner's union? I had no idea what she was talking about. All I knew was that I wasn't in any union. So, I replied, "Non." Her next question: "Would you like to go on a cruise to Mexico for a week?" Hell, yeah. The union she was referring to was SAG, The Screen Actors Guild. I guess everyone assumed everyone was waiting for their big break while waiting for the dentist. Maybe people did get discovered every day of the week in everyday situations. I went for it. The project was an *NBC Movie of the Week*, a teen comedy called *Class Cruise*. The audition consisted of me walking into the producer's office in a bikini and letting them eyeball me. I got the job, along with three *Playboy* Playmates.

All we had to do was parade around in our bikinis for a week. Basically, we were glorified extras, more set decoration than actresses, but it paid $100 a day, good money at the time. Strange as it may seem, I didn't consider myself beautiful like the Playmates were. I didn't think I compared to them. I also didn't win any points with those girls. I found them worldly-wise and intimidating. They didn't like me because I was an innocent little flower who asked stupid questions. Probably the worst: "What do your parents think of you being a Playmate?" The experience of being on the set for a week, however, was invaluable. It gave me the opportunity to see acting as a real profession. Now I knew for sure what I wanted to do with my life.

*****

The following year I got another break, while working as a cocktail waitress at The Laugh Factory on Sunset Boulevard. A tall man with salt and pepper hair handed me a business card that read "Spotlight Enterprises." I assumed he was just hitting on me and was about to throw the card in the trash when the club's owner, Jamie Masada, stopped me.

"That's Bob," he said. "He's really powerful. He can help you. He represents Jerry Seinfeld and Jay Leno."

I went to Bob's office for a meeting. He sat me down and said something flattering yet crazy: "You've got the *'it factor.'* There's something about you. You remind me of Madonna." That's the part that sounded crazy. I didn't think I was anything like Madonna. He went on, "When you're ready to come into my office and say, 'I am going to be an actress and nobody is going to stop me,' I will sign you."

Bob motivated me to work on my acting career. I took out a $3,000 student loan, enrolled in acting classes, and got some headshots done. The first day at orientation, the teacher asked, "How many of you think you'll get work as actors?" The entire class of thirty raised their hands. Then he dropped the bomb, proclaiming that only one or two of us would ever work. He pointed at me and said, *"You* will get work just because of the way you look." The rest of you better work hard and hope for good luck. I'd been singled out yet again because of my looks. It was not the negative message that Mrs. Marshall sent in biology class. It was meant to be a compliment, but the message was the same. It told me that my worth was based on my beauty.

After three months of training, I had the confidence to stride into Bob's office and repeat the words he needed me to say: 'I am going to be an actress, and nobody is going to stop me.' True to his word, he signed me. Soon afterwards, I booked a national TV commercial for Lexus, which not only earned me my SAG card, but also $50,000 in residuals. The commercial called for me to wear a wedding gown. I tried on a succession of beautiful gowns, joking it would probably be my only chance to wear one. I must have jinxed myself. Thirty years later, I'm still not married.

Eric was always supportive of my acting. When he was on tour, I'd fax my scenes to his hotel, and he'd help me learn my lines over the phone. He was so proud when I got the Lexus commercial that he had the KISS office staff find out from the ad agency every time it would air so he could tell everyone to watch. When he was on the road, the guys all had dressing tables with mirrors that unfolded. Eric's mirror had my black and white headshots all over it, you could hardly see the mirror. And he was a vain guy, so that was a sacrifice.

Unfortunately, Bob had a huge gambling problem and the agency went bankrupt. Just my luck. I had to pound the pavement, trying to find new representation. It wasn't easy. I got tons of rejections. Most agents said I was too "green," inexperienced. One told me I was beautiful, but I would be more beautiful if I had better teeth. Okay, I could get those fixed. Another agent turned me down, saying I'd never get a part in a soap opera because my jaw was too big; I looked like Maria Shriver. What a bitch. What did she expect me to do, have my jaw reconstructed? Anyway, I always thought Maria Shriver was beautiful. I like her big, square jaw. Within a year, I proved the agent wrong when I secured a recurring role on *Days of our Lives*. I was tempted to write the bitch and rub it in her face, but I didn't.

*****

While KISS was recording *Hot in The Shade,* I often stayed with Eric in his apartment on Larrabee Street in West Hollywood. I was so lovesick that I'd even wait for him to come home while he was out having dinner with another girl. I would write "I love you" in the dust on his coffee table, waiting for his return. I was such a pathetic doormat. But I knew what I wanted — a permanent, exclusive relationship. He didn't want to be my boyfriend; I had to *make him* be my boyfriend. Even when we were together twenty-four hours a day, he'd still maintain we weren't an item. It wasn't that he was a douchebag, he just couldn't envision a serious long-term relationship with a girl half his age. I'd insist, "Whether you like it or not, you're my boyfriend." Eric said he wanted a normal girlfriend. So, I got a normal job as a secretary. He was delighted and sent me flowers to my office with a card that read, "I am in love." I was elated, until he told me the flower company had made a mistake. He didn't actually say that. Devastated, I quit the stupid job. I got immersed in acting again and started seeing Marq Torien, the singer for the Bullet Boys, whom I'd met in Memphis and ran into again in L.A.

After a night partying with Marq at his place in Manhattan Beach, I came rolling home about 5:00 a.m. only to find Eric parked outside my apartment. Eric couldn't bust me, because I wasn't cheating on him. You can't cheat on someone unless you are committed. Without a commitment, I was free to date other guys. I had never been interested in anyone else until Eric said the florist wrote "I am in love" by mistake. I had no intention of being his doormat anymore. Eric called and asked me out and I said no. Five minutes later, he called again and said, "Please" and I said, "I can't, no." Another few minutes went by, and he called a third time, begging me. So, I went over. Like most men, Eric didn't know what he had until it was gone. Marq was just the wakeup call he needed. That night Eric decided he was madly in love with me and wanted an exclusive relationship.

Eventually, Eric thought of me as an extension of himself and treated me like we were a team. I was indispensable! Finally, I overheard him on the phone tell someone, "Well, my girlfriend and I..." I said triumphantly, "See? I *am* your girlfriend." I was always paranoid that he was going to cheat on me. He openly admitted he'd cheated on every girlfriend he'd ever had. He maintained I was the exception. I professed to believe him and that meant a lot to him, but I'm not sure I truly ever did. I thought, "Well, if he cheated on everybody else, why wouldn't he cheat on me?" I never caught him, not once, although there were always girls sending him cards and phone numbers. He was a rock star, what did I expect?

Now that Eric and I were both in L.A., we were able to spend a lot of time together. The day I walked into The Fortress recording studio and met Gene for the first time, he looked me up and down appreciatively, then looked at Eric, and said, "You should marry her. Look at her. I mean it. Marry her." I doubt he meant it literally. It was his way of saying I was beautiful, a charming compliment. But I didn't know how to handle it. I was a small-town teenager and these were middle-aged men, hugely famous, larger than life. I bashfully clung to Eric's arm, stared at the ground, and mumbled, "Thank you." Whatever his intent, the statement was quite a big deal, as Gene was known for being anti-marriage. Then Eric and I went off together, into the tiny bathroom at the studio, locked the door behind us and did what we liked to do best.

The first time Eric took me on a trip with him was when he had to do a radio show with Paul in Portland, Oregon. He traded in his first-class ticket and got us two coach seats. Paul was not happy about it at all when Eric told him I was coming. He berated Eric, "This is not a trip for you and your girlfriend." But when we got to the The Four Seasons, we saw Paul in the lobby. He was in a great mood. He was all smiles and generously told us to get massages at the spa and charge them to the room. I had never stayed at such a fancy hotel. It was the first time I had ever seen a mini bar. I was so excited I started tearing through all the snacks. Eric said, "You know those aren't free. Right?" We laughed. I had no idea.

Dating a rock star is kind of a nightmare. In the beginning, it's thrilling. But then when they're on the road, it's brutal. Sure, it's fun when you join them in yet another city, but then it's miserable when you eventually part. You miss them so much. And then there are the "complications" of life on tour. Once I decided to surprise him, and it totally backfired on me. Eric's birthday was July twelfth (he was born Paul Charles Caravello, July 12, 1950; Eric Carr was his stage name). It was two days apart from the birthday of KISS's offstage keyboardist and Eric's best friend, Gary Corbett. Gary's wife Lenora thought it would be a great idea to show up in Virginia and surprise them. I eagerly agreed. I knew that at the same point during every song Eric's drum tech, J.W., always handed him a glass of water. I came up with the scheme that when Eric turned to grab his water I would be there instead with his glass of water and a big smile, "Happy Birthday, babe!"

How did it backfire? I somehow got wind that the band had hired a stripper to prance onstage with a cake, singing Happy Birthday, and they abruptly canceled her when I unexpectedly showed up. It wasn't Eric's fault. He knew nothing about it. But I was so mad. I tried not to show it at the party we had for him in our hotel room. Gary and Lenora were there as well as Bruce Kulick and Gene Simmons. Gene cut the cake and took a whole piece in his mouth and spit it out, then took another piece and did the same thing. Maybe he was rehearsing for the blood he spits out on stage at night. I really had no idea, and it didn't matter. I was preoccupied with the idea that had I not shown up, a stripper would have been at this party with Eric instead of me. There is video footage from that night. Recently, Eric's sister Loretta (whom I consider my eternal sister-in-law) played it for me. In the video, Eric sweetly introduces me as his future wife, but added, "You know when people are smiling, but they're really not happy?" He was right. I wasn't happy. Later, I started a fight over the stripper. We argued the rest of the night, and he slept on the floor. Now I'm at an age where I'd say, "Who cares? It's harmless." But I was so immature back then, and I felt threatened. I would give anything if I could go back in time and make it right.

Unlike most of the rock bands, KISS wasn't a party band. Apart from Eric, the guys didn't even really drink. None of them did recreational drugs. Eric made it clear to me that if I ever did, he would dump me. He only ever got high once, by accident, and that was in Amsterdam when someone gave him a cookie laced with marijuana. One time in Concord, California, Gene said the wrong city when he was onstage, and the crowd booed. He made a quick recovery… "Oh man, I'm so fucked up tonight!" The crowd went wild cheering. They loved it! I was laughing because I knew it was all an act. Gene was brilliant.

Eric and I were high on life. One time, we wrecked a hotel ballroom in Maine. You might call us partners in love and crime. We had idle time on our hands. Everything had been set up for a banquet, and we trashed it. We just went on a rampage, dragging tablecloths off tables, throwing silverware and plates all over the place. He went down on me under the podium while I gave an Oscar acceptance speech, and I blew him in the elevator. We pressed every button to every floor, ready to be caught in the act. Another time we were backstage before a show in the guys' locker room when we realized Paul was in a bathroom stall, getting head from a groupie. We saw four feet under the stall and heard Paul's groans. Eric and

I tossed all the coins we could find, pennies, dimes, whatever, over the top of the stall trying to hit them and interrupt their rhythm. I never did get a look at the groupie. Eric and I ran away as fast as we could, laughing like children, so we wouldn't get in trouble with Paul.

Eric and I were a little crazy and a lot crazy in love. But not as crazy as the weird lady who followed us on that tour, convinced she was Eric's wife and that he was cheating on her. She even made up an I.D. for herself with his last name on it. She threatened to kill me, and she had a knife. It got so bad that the security guys had to escort Eric and me separately onto the tour bus.

Oftentimes, Eric would fly me out to be with him when he had a few days off from touring and didn't want to stay at the same hotel as the band. He liked to use his free time on romantic getaways and to get a break from the same faces he worked with day in and day out. Once we coupled up with Gary and Lenora and stayed at a cabin in the Catskills. He presented me with a box from Victoria's Secret, and I did a private fashion show for him. Another time, we checked into a couples-only hotel in Chicago called Sybaris. Our suite had a heated swimming pool, an indoor waterfall, Jacuzzi, waterbed, and a hook hanging from the ceiling. What the hell is that for, we both wondered. Then we opened up the closet. There we found a swing with a hole in the bottom that you could attach to the hook. We quickly figured out what to do with it.

It was a great achievement for Eric that the *Hot in The Shade* album would include a song written and sung by him called *"Little Caesar."* Every musician wants their work featured for the royalties it generates, but for Eric it was much more than that. It was also an acknowledgment of his creativity. Eric was a master of his craft. He was the first heavy metal drummer to incorporate electronic drums into his live solo. He was technically advanced, regarded in the industry as a "drummer's drummer." For the longest time, he'd wanted to do more, but was creatively frustrated because Gene and Paul made all the decisions and had all the control. In effect, they owned the Eric Carr persona. It was emotional torture for Eric. Especially when they took his drum solo away. KISS was really Gene and Paul's band, while Eric and lead guitarist Bruce Kulick were the hired guns working for a salary. That's probably one reason Eric and Bruce were such good friends; they could relate. The three of us and Bruce's then wife, Christina, went out a lot together.

For my twenty-first birthday on May 1st, Eric took me for a romantic dinner at Wolfgang Puck's original Spago Restaurant on the Sunset Strip. I was in love and already knew I wanted to marry him. Over dinner, I blurted out that I wanted a ring. He said, "This time next year, if things are going as good as they are now, you'll get a ring." Sadly, things would change dramatically before I reached my twenty-second birthday.

It was a special evening. Eric also sent me a giant arrangement of flowers along with a card that read, "You are only twenty-one once, make the day as special as you are. There is nothing you can't accomplish. Dare to conquer your dreams. I believe in you." It was a typical motivational message from this good man, the one person who always gave me the courage to become a model and an actress. He was the one who supported me every step of the way, soothing my insecurities and boosting my self-confidence. I remember exactly where I was sitting at Teru Sushi in Studio City when he asked, "What exactly do you want to do with your life?" I found the courage to admit I wanted to be an actress. Most people would say, "You're crazy," or "You'd better have a back-up plan." Eric simply asked, "What can I do to help you?" And he paid the expensive fees for SAG and AFTRA (the unions you had to join in order to work in film and TV.)

Once we were lying on his bed at his Manhattan apartment. There were mirrors on the walls, mirrors on the ceiling. We could look at each other, every which way. As we lay there naked, after another of our mammoth lovemaking sessions, he eyed the images of me in the mirrors and said, "You know, you've got one of those bodies like those girls in the magazines."

"What magazines?" I asked.

"You know, *Playboy*."

"Really?" I said. I'd never thought of myself that way.

"You should do it. I'd be really proud of you," he said. He suggested I talk to Shannon Tweed, Gene's Playmate girlfriend. But I was more afraid of Shannon than I was of Gene. They were both intimidating, but at least Gene was friendly. Shannon was the queen. I didn't exist. She never even said hello when we were in the same room. It was a long time before I had the self-confidence to try out for *Playboy*. If you even dared to mention such an aspiration in the sticks where I grew up, you'd be laughed out of town.

Eric reveled in my body. He couldn't get enough of it and wanted reminders of me when he was on the road. He loved to take pictures of me. And video. We had lots of 'naughty' pictures. He was a bit careless with them, giving film to some random tour assistant to go and get developed. I said, "Jesus, Eric. Don't be giving those photos to strangers, I'm naked in some of them." I'm grateful no one ever stole them and published them. It's good that they didn't. That would have ruined my chances of being a centerfold. *Playboy* didn't accept girls who had posed nude before.

Eric was so supportive that he even came with me for my first TV audition. It was on the Sony lot a Fox sitcom. I didn't get the part and openly wondered, "Maybe I'm just not pretty enough." Eric replied, "You could never not be pretty enough." It's something I've carried with me through years of casting calls. I look around the room at the competition and say to myself, "You could never not be pretty enough."

When Eric was staying with me, and I had to go to work, he'd do my laundry, make me a packed lunch, and send me on my way. He loved my low-rent North Hollywood studio apartment, preferring it to his fancy Manhattan condo. He was such a super sweet guy. Especially to his fans. He didn't have a rock star attitude. He was just really a normal person with his own insecurities. He had a great sense of humor and was always thoughtful. He used to send me a postcard from every city, (I still have them all) and he'd come home with little gifts he'd bought at truck stops. He was such a sweet guy, he even endured Tiffany, my fluffy black and white cat who hated him. Every time he came by, she pissed in his shoes or on his clothes, but it didn't stop him from coming over!

The *Hot in the Shade* Tour was a coast-to-coast epic of one hundred twenty-three concerts that officially launched in Lubbock, Texas on May 4th and finished in New York's Madison Square Garden on November 9th. Around this time, Eric's behavior towards me became erratic. We'd loved and fought, fought and loved. At first, I didn't think much of it. Someone wise once said, "If you are not psycho, you're not in love." But Eric's behavior was getting worse.

Once I flew three thousand miles to join him on the East Coast. I got there. We had sex. He jumped in the shower. When he came out, toweling his massive head of hair, he calmly announced, "I think I want to break up." I'd just arrived. There'd been no fighting. We'd had great sex. What happened in the shower that could have possibly made him want to break up with me? I was flabbergasted.

"We're not breaking up, and I'm not going anywhere," I said. "I'm here to stay!"

It was an awful week. In public, we pretended that everything was fine, but behind closed doors we barely spoke.

I was so hurt. He was distancing me. He would even put a pillow between our heads at night. It had always been a tempestuous relationship, yes, but this was something else.

I remember lying in bed, hidden beneath the covers, tears spilling down my cheeks, knowing that in a few hours I would be catching a plane back to L.A. After the way he'd treated me, I assumed it was all over between us. Suddenly, Eric got up, walked to my side of the bed, fell to his knees, and gently pulled back the covers. He whispered: "I'm sorry. I'm sorry. I don't know what's wrong with me. Please don't leave. I don't want you to be gone. I love you." And then he asked, "Do you want to come with me to my parents this weekend?" He swayed from one extreme to the other.

Eric's physical health had seemed fine to me. He certainly had no problems in bed. But guys on the tour later said he'd shown signs of being unwell; he'd had weird leg cramps and looked drained at the end of a show. The last week of the tour, he did it to me again. In front of everyone else, he acted like everything was perfect, his arm always affectionately wrapped around me, but then at night, back in our room, he wouldn't talk to me. He wasn't speaking to Paul and Gene much either, due to creative differences. I was surprised to learn he'd also shut Bruce out. Bruce didn't deserve that. Bruce was a hired gun, just like Eric. And he wouldn't hurt a fly. We were both confused by Eric's behavior, and Bruce apologized for Eric more than once. He found me crying in elevators and hallways and consoled me more times than I can count.

Something was tormenting Eric, and I was tired of bearing the brunt of it. I'd spent years chasing him and kissing his ass. I was done. I'd finally had enough. I flew back to L.A. and changed my phone number. He sent cards. I sent them back, unopened, marked "Return to Sender." He'd broken up with me once too often, and I just wasn't taking it anymore. The tables had turned. Naturally, he went crazy, as most guys do when they want something they can't have.

I got on with my life. I went to auditions. Hung out with friends. Kept active. Did everything I could to erase thoughts of Eric. He didn't make it easy. He started calling my family, my mother, my sister, my father, desperate to get back in touch with me. My mom phoned me one day and said, "You should talk to him. He's really sick."

"What's wrong with him?"

"He has the flu or something."

My attitude was, so what? It's the flu. He'll get over it. And then I found out it wasn't the flu. It was a tumor. Eric needed open heart surgery to get rid of the tumor that had buried itself in his left ventricle. We started talking, day and night. But he refused to let me fly out to be with him for the surgery. "I don't want you to see me like this."

In April 1991, Eric went in for the surgery and recuperated very quickly. Three weeks later, he came to L.A. He was proud of his scar, a four-inch-long, raised, red line down the middle of his chest; he was always showing it off. We'd be in a convenience store, and he'd happily lift up his shirt so the cashier could get a look. All of our fights were forgotten. It was a fresh start. Then, as we were beginning to find ourselves again, our world turned upside down. We got the dreadful news that a biopsy of the tumor showed it was malignant. He had a rare cancer of the heart. So rare only about fifty cases have ever been noted. Even the Mayo Clinic only sees one a year. Worse still, the cancer had spread into his lungs. He needed chemotherapy. The harsh medical verdict: he had just two to five years to live. He was only forty-one. It was impossible for me to grasp. Eric went back to New York for more doctor's appointments and I stayed with my friend Wendy. I remember sitting on the floor of her Beverly Hills apartment, talking to him on the phone, stifling my sobs so he wouldn't hear. But nothing could have prepared me for what lay ahead.

I dropped everything and went to be with him in New York. I gave up my budding career and my North Hollywood apartment, and gave everything in it to my roommate. Possessions just didn't seem important. In between chemo-therapy appointments, Eric and I spent the summer doing fun things and enjoying each other. We were so goofy. We'd walk the streets of Manhattan singing in the rain, jumping in puddles, ducking into cafes for Mexican coffee, and then back into the rain to sing and jump some more. We went to all the museums and the zoo. We went horseback riding. We did all the fun things people don't usually take the time to do. He wasn't moping around, thinking, "I'm going to die." His mindset was, "We don't have chemo today. Let's go have an adventure.'" We spent memorable time with his parents and my grandparents. We visited my hometown of Hardwick, Massachusetts. I'd always dreamed about taking my future husband to see where I grew up, so I'm glad we shared that. And we continued to have an active sex life. Even when he was bald and bloated from the side effects of the chemo, I would be trying to jump his bones.

"Why would you want me, looking like this?" he'd ask.

I'd tell him, "I'm attracted to you, not your looks. I love you for who you are and not what you look like."

It was true. We were closer than ever, and I could not get enough of him.

Some of the most tender moments between us were during those days. I'd go with him to Sloan Kettering for the chemo treatments. Often, we lay in his hospital bed together. Sometimes the doctors would walk in and not know which one of us was the patient. It wasn't grim and terrible, and Eric never felt sorry for himself. He dealt with it a lot better than I did. Eric was a courageous guy. He'd shown that in 1974 when a deadly blaze swept through a nightclub where he was playing, Gulliver's, on the New York-Connecticut border. Twenty-four people died but Eric saved the life of one of the band's singers. Now he was fighting for his own life just as bravely.

We played pool and ping pong. We watched movies. Sometimes we went up to the arts and crafts ward and made jewelry for each other, necklaces and keychains, with melted stones. Ceramics, too. We'd take the elevator up to that room and say, "We got off on the wrong floor." What we really meant, was the wrong floor in life. Like, 'we're not supposed to be here, in the arts and crafts room of the cancer ward. You're this rock star; I'm a budding starlet.' It was unreal. Eric impressed me when he didn't freak out after his hair fell out, a victim of the chemo. Yes, his trademark long hair that he was so proud of, that he teased and made as big as possible with liberal applications of Aqua Net. I salvaged the remaining strands into a braid and braided mine to match. We wore matching bandanas. I didn't want him to feel different; I did everything I could to make him feel normal.

He took a lot of naps, during which I was often a nervous wreck, checking to make sure he was still breathing. We did a lot of spiritual work. We read Louise Hay books, repeated affirmations, and focused on relaxation. We learned that the point of power is in the present moment. We never had a conversation about death. But Eric must have thought about it. How could he not? He told me he had two regrets: not having had children and not finishing the animated cartoon series he created, *The Rockheads*. He was taking this time to work on it and named a character, "Cariel," after me and the character from one of our favorite movies, *The Little Mermaid*.

Before chemo started, the doctor at Sloan Kettering had warned Eric that the treatment could make him sterile. We decided to freeze his sperm so that we could have children someday. Because he was confined to the hospital, he had to produce a sample right there into a container. I couldn't bring myself to help him out; strangely, I was embarrassed. My job was to transport the precious sample to the sperm bank. Holding the container under my shirt, pressed against my stomach, trying to keep it warm and alive, I took a cab across town on a mission I'd never imagined. I remember thinking, "Wow, I could be carrying our baby." But it was too late. When they tested the sample, there were no sperm swimming around. The cancer had already made him sterile. How would I break the news? I walked through Central Park formulating in my head the words I would use, trying to ignore the throngs of people enjoying the simple acts of life. Hoping to soften the blow, I went into a store and bought him some little gifts and a card, and his favorite tuna sandwich, while rehearsing my words over and over in my mind. It wasn't necessary. As soon as I walked into his hospital room, he took one look at my face and knew.

"It's too late isn't it," he said, more as a statement than a question.

I silently nodded. My eyes stung from holding back the tears. We held each other for a long time. I felt him trembling.

That wasn't the only setback. KISS was in L.A. recording *"God Gave Rock 'n' Roll to You II,"* without him. Drummer Eric Singer was filling in for my Eric. It was obvious he was being groomed as Eric's successor, and it ate away at Eric. He was increasingly frantic about it. They'd already taken his solo away from him, after twelve years. And now this. I was focused on Eric's health, but I was aware business and financial discussions were going on. Paul often called Eric's home late at night, waking us up and pressuring him to resign. They didn't want KISS to look bad for firing a sick dude. Jesse Hilsen (Paul's former shrink who ran the band's business office) called making threats about taking away Eric's insurance if he refused to cooperate. This was evil, but as I have matured over the years, I choose to believe that everyone was doing the best they could with the knowledge they had at the time. Nobody knew Eric was going to die. If Eric had lived, both he and the band would have come out looking better to the public if Eric had resigned rather than been fired. But Eric was no quitter. He refused. He really believed he was going to get well, so why should he resign?

Gene and Paul weren't so optimistic. Their priority was their brand, and their brand was the band. The show must go on. They didn't want to risk being on tour and having to cancel shows if Eric suddenly became ill, losing them millions. I'd like to think they were concerned about Eric's health because they cared about him as a friend and not just an employee, but who knows? Honestly, I was just twenty-two years old. I didn't know all the ins and outs of what was going on with Gene and Paul. My relationship was with Eric, not them.

Gene could be charming and engaging. I think he genuinely cared about Eric but didn't understand him. He was confused, just as I was, when Eric suddenly became anti-social on the *Hot in The Shade* tour. I remember arriving on tour once, and when Gene saw me standing with Eric, he asked him, "Is this what's been wrong?" Obviously, Gene wondered if Eric was so quiet and sad because he missed me when I wasn't there. I never got to know Paul much. He seemed uncomfortable in his own skin around me. He was never as friendly again as he was the day that we met at the New Hampshire show. I guess you can't blame him. I stood the guy up. He was always polite to me, just standoffish. But the roadies had another impression. They thought he had acted like a woman with PMS and behind his back they called him "Phyllis." Obviously, Eric wasn't the only one with mood swings.

At the end of the day, KISS is a money machine. Gene always said, "Time is money; money is time." And because Eric was so sick, they decided his time was up. But I believed in miracles. And I saw one with my own eyes: one day Eric and I went to his doctor for a check-up, and they took X-Rays. They were completely clear! In the beginning of this nightmare the X-Rays had been cloudy, with spots everywhere, and now they were clean as a whistle. The chemotherapy had worked. Eric was in remission. It was amazing! When we got the news, we were hysterically happy, both of us crying tears of joy.

Eric and I went back to L.A. and got right back into the groove. Even though he hadn't played drums with KISS in the studio on *"God Gave Rock 'n' Roll to You,"* Eric had sung the *a cappella* line "...to everyone, he gave his song to be sung." He insisted on appearing in the video. The band was apprehensive about letting him play. I was furious at them for not being as positive as I was. Sure, Eric was pale and puffy and had to wear a wig, but, aside from his appearance, you would have never known he was sick. He beat those drums louder than thunder and faster than a fox for fifteen straight hours that day. I was on the set cheering him on. Now that the worst was over, I wanted Eric to feel alive and inspired. I wanted him to continue to be part of the band. Being the drummer for KISS meant everything to him.

One night, around this time, Eric and I went with Bruce and Christina to see Van Halen on their *F.U.C.K.'N Live* tour. This was after David Lee Roth's departure, when Sammy Hagar was fronting the band. Word about Eric's cancer had gotten around. Backstage, after the show, Eddie Van Halen put his hands on Eric's shoulders and kept saying, "Oh, man. I'm so sorry. I'm so sorry." As he continued gushing over Eric, in true rock-raunch style, Eddie whispered in my ear, "Nice tits." In the limo afterwards, I told everyone what had happened, and since it was rock god Eddie Van Halen, Eric wasn't mad at all. Bruce said to Christina, "How come *you* didn't wear something low-cut tonight?" Only Eddie Van Halen deserves that kind of respect.

*****

Eric got me an apartment in Studio City and generously paid the first six months' rent up front and put all the utility bills in his name. At IKEA, he bought me furniture, silverware, plants, everything I needed because I'd given everything away. We sat outside the store in my car, stuffed with all these trappings of domesticity. I don't know where it came from, but I said, "I'm sorry." And he looked me straight in the eye and said, "I know. Me, too." Neither of us said what we were sorry for. There was no need. Everything that had happened before we faced his mortality as a team was petty. Nothing else mattered but this moment.

I told him, "You really don't have to do all this for me."

And he said, "I want to. I want to give back to you because you've given me my life back." He wanted me to resume my career and achieve my dreams.

I thought, "This guy deserves a party after all the suffering he's been through." So, I threw him a surprise bash at Club Black and Blue in L.A. The next day he flew back to New York and called me. The first words out of his mouth: "Will you marry me?"

I started laughing.

"Why are you laughing at me?" he wanted to know.

"Because you're not serious."

"How do you know I'm not serious?"

"Because you know us," I replied. "We'd get to the end of the aisle, look at each other and go, 'Nah!'"

We both laughed.

A couple of hours later, I got a call from Bruce. Had I heard about Eric?

"No what?" I said, "I just talked to him."

He's home alone. He gets a blinding, mind-numbing headache, the kind of pain that makes you feel your head is going to explode. He takes aspirin... there's an open bottle on the counter. A 911 call. Paramedics rush into his apartment... he's collapsed on the floor, phone off the hook. At Bellevue Hospital, they realize he's had a brain hemorrhage. Then a series of seizures wrack his body. He slips into a coma.

I got to New York as fast as I could. I walked into the hospital room. It was silent other than the beeping of the blood pressure and heart monitors. Eric lay in the hospital bed, almost unrecognizable. His skull was stitched up, and he was covered in bandages, wires and tubes. He was alert and aware, I could tell by the look in his eyes, but he couldn't speak. The hemorrhage had severely damaged his brain, leaving the entire left side of his body paralyzed. Only Eric's closest friends and family were allowed in intensive care. I saw the look of despair on the faces of Eric's parents. I felt so helpless. I couldn't fathom how difficult it was for them to see their son lying there suffering. I was seeing the same unimaginable suffering, but denial is a powerful thing.

I never thought he wouldn't get well. Eric was a fighter. Within a few weeks, he began to improve enough for them to move him back and forth from the bed to a wheelchair. He wasn't able to hold his head up straight anymore, so it hung to the right. All he would do was the only thing he was capable of. He kicked. He angrily kicked and kicked his left leg, the only leg he could move. Sometimes he would try to say "Fuck!" He could only make the sound of the letter "F," but I knew what he meant because his eyes flashed with fury. There are almost no words to describe the torture he endured, trapped inside his own body, struggling to communicate. I gave him a pad and a pen, but he couldn't write legibly. Even though Eric played guitar and drums right-handed, he was left-handed.

9-16-91 5:32 PM

Dear Eric –
I think your undergoing surgery right now. I am a mess. You shocked me this time. You've got to stop this! I feel, I feel, I feel so much. Mostly I'm scared. I'm fucking horrified to be blunt. I feel so helpless and far away. I can't help but ponder what happened. All my thoughts hurt. Even to breathe brings me tears. I'm trying not to bark with God – If he was listening I would have given the world away for you. I love you. You are the most wonderful person I know and I want you to always be in my life, somehow. I don't know what's going to happen. I'm scared.

9-19-91 6:59
Eric!!! When are you going to wake up? I miss you so much! I'm used to ta[lking] to you everyday. I'm so [caught] as cold. You kn[ow] [how] run down I get when

Dear Eric..... (morning) Sept 22, 1[9..]
I had a dream last night, or maybe it was real. You tapped into my brain while I was asleep. You communicated with me through our sleep. It was so real. Your voice was so clear. It was a very happy conversation, but I don't remember what was said. It is possible that it was real. The sub-conscious is a very mysterious thing – all we know is that it's much more powerful than the conscious (I can't spell that word). And right now it's the only state you're in! But after last night I have a feeling that you're going to wake up real soon. If not before I get here, then right when I'm there.

I just wanted to feel 11:41 PM
close to you, so I'm!

but wonder how you feel. I hope soon you'll tell me. I love you always and forever and through bad and good – sickness and in health.

— Sept. 23, 1991 1:56 PM

Hi Sweetie – I guess I don't have much to say. I'm just getting ready to come to New York. Just doing errands and tying up loose ends. Your caesar salad is still in the fridge – it's looking pretty gross. I'll clean it out before I leave. The weather is beautiful. I think today is the first day of fall. Well I'm going to do some laundry now. Last time you did it thank you for that. I love you.

I stayed there twenty-one hours a day. I read to him, adjusted the headphones playing his favorite music, brushed his teeth, massaged his feet. As bad as things were, it never occurred to me that he might die. I knew he would never be normal again, but so what if I had to spend the rest of my life dressing him and buttoning his shirts? I never imagined I might be without him. I held back the tears as I watched over this virile, energetic rock star, who'd once twirled his drumsticks and hammered the shit out of his massive drum kit night after night in city after city in front of thousands of adoring fans. Now the man that I loved more than life itself was disintegrating before my eyes. I lay awake at night, praying to God to give me his pain. I'd sleep on a little wooden bench in the waiting room and Eric's sister, Loretta, would see me there every time she visited.

"Are you still here?" she'd ask.

Finally, his doctors, family and friends, all told me, "Carrie, you can't keep this up. You're young. You've got your whole life ahead of you. Take a break and go back to L.A. for a while." I reluctantly agreed. I think they were concerned for my sanity. I really didn't know where Eric ended and I began.

After I went back to L.A., they moved Eric to a rehabilitation hospital. It was going to be a long haul. He had another hemorrhage, and then he improved again. The doctors were really pleased with his progress. I was told he was doing great and would probably be able to talk on the phone soon. I wrote him letters every day, and Lenora

Corbett, who lived in Brooklyn, visited him every day and read them to him.

Meanwhile, I found a job as a cocktail waitress at a five-star hotel on the Sunset Strip. On my break one night, I went to the pay phone to pick up my voicemail messages and heard Lenora telling me to call her. She said it was important. Over a pay phone, I got the news that Eric had passed away. It was November 24, 1991. I fell to my knees. The phone hit the marble floor. I wailed so loud I think all of West Hollywood heard. Security came and took me to their office. I was sobbing so hysterically that I couldn't speak. I could barely see through my tears, but I managed to scribble Bruce Kulick's phone number on a piece of hotel paper, and the security guard called him and his wife and I spent the night on their couch. It was hard to breathe, knowing that Eric wasn't. The doctors had given him two to five years; he'd survived for only eight months. As I was packing to go to New York for the funeral, it came on the evening news that Eric had died. I stood there, watching the T.V. saying to myself, "Eric would never have imagined he'd make the nightly news." He was so humble.

Ironically, Freddie Mercury was in the headlines, too. He'd died the same day.

The hardest thing I've ever done was walk into that funeral home. My legs buckled as I made my way towards the open casket. It was a traditional Catholic wake, closed to the public. I sat in the front row, in disbelief, watching his friends and family pay their respects. I'd been looking at his embalmed body for two days, yet the finality of death felt sudden and shocking when it was time to say goodbye. I felt guilty leaving him there. I stared at his beautiful face for the last time and slipped a photo of the two of us into the casket.

The next day, fans were gathered outside St. Joseph's church in Middletown, N.Y. Some dressed appropriately, some in KISS T-shirts and ripped jeans. Just before the service, an older gentleman announced to them, "Against the better judgement of Mrs. Caravello, she has decided to let you people come in. Eric's sister said that this is what Eric would want. Please, do not make her regret her decision." They were escorted past the stained-glass windows and seated a few pews away from the band. Under that vaulted ceiling, we were all equal in God's eyes.

I rode to the burial in the limousine with Eric's family, trailed by a two-mile-long procession of mourners, including Gene and Paul, in a blue Lincoln Town Car. Eric died being exactly who he wanted to be, still the official drummer for KISS.

When I got back to L.A, I held a West Coast Memorial for those who couldn't attend Eric's funeral in N.Y. I wrote my own eulogy to honor this wonderful man:

There are people who are special. Lights do turn green just for them. Everybody likes them the instant they meet.

Eric was one of those people. He had a heart of gold. He was generous beyond his means. He always cared about his friends and made time for his fans.

*Words cannot express how thankful I am
for the time we shared together. In that time,
he helped shape who I am today. For that he will
always be in my presence.*

*I believe there are really only two things
in life we are supposed to do: to love and to learn.
But love is stronger than death or heaven.*

I love you, Eric Carr.

Eric Carr, 41; drummer for group Kiss

Associated Press

NEW YORK — Drummer Eric Carr, a member of the face-painted rock group Kiss, has died at a Manhattan hospital of complications from cancer, his publicist said Monday. He was 41.

Carr, who joined the band in 1980, died Sunday at Bellevue Hospital, said his spokeswoman, Carol Kaye of Kayos Productions in Manhattan. She said he had been hospitalized since September after suffering a cerebral hemorrhage.

Though initially conscious, Carr suffered a second hemorrhage shortly after entering the hospital and never regained consciousness, Kaye said.

Carr had been diagnosed as having a malignant heart tumor in April. was removed but doctors discovered cancerous growths in his lungs. underwent chemotherapy treatments at Memorial Sloan Kettering cer Institute in June.

Everything looked all right after the treatments," said Kaye. "He in remission. He went to the MTV awards in September — that up being his last public appearance. Two days later he had the rhage."

who lived in Manhattan, was single. There was no immediate t from Mercury Records, Kiss's recording company.

oined the group in 1980 after one of its Peter Criss, left. Other origin Paul Stanley and Ac in 1972

ERIC CARR MEMORIAL JAN. 6 1992 7 PM

Through your memories he will live.
Through the music he left behind he will be felt.

CHURCH OF THE BLESSED SACRAMENT
6657 Sunset Blvd.
Hollywood, Ca. Los Angeles

Chapter 4

Don't Drink Straight Whiskey

Back in L.A., I was working as a waitress while looking for acting roles. I was an easy target, young and vulnerable, and I got harassed and hit on a lot. The worst incident happened during my shift at a five-star hotel on the Sunset Strip. Late one night, in the cold dark room that was like a big fridge for liquor, the bar manager tried to rape me. We were alone, closing out. He was a big guy, muscular, and strong. He pressed hard against me, trying to kiss me. When I resisted, he smashed my face sideways, his hand pressed against my mouth to stifle my screams. Terrified, I struggled with all my might. I wasn't strong enough to budge him with a push or a shove, so I kicked him, again and again, with my heels, as hard as I could. He buckled, enough for me to break free and escape.

The next day I reported him, but none of the other employees believed me, or maybe they just didn't care. The female head bartender was a friend, but she just shrugged and smiled, as if to say, *'Oh well. Just another Tuesday. I love you, but I'm staying out of it.'* That's how things were back then. There's probably not a single woman who doesn't have a similar story, which is why #METOO went viral. The bar manager hated me for rejecting him, and he hated me more for reporting him. The tension made it impossible to work with him, so I quit.

Even before that attack, I was having a hard time. I was still reeling from the psychological trauma of watching Eric suffer. I'd come home from work and as soon as I got inside the door, I'd fall to my knees sobbing. I'd manage to hold myself together in public, but once I was in the privacy of my apartment, the emptiness and the grief would wash over me. Crumpled in a heap, I'd lie there sobbing until, totally drained, I'd fall asleep. In the morning, I'd wake up on the floor and drag myself to face another day. Somehow, I scraped myself together and carried on. How did I do it? I don't know. Except that I was sure Eric would want me to get through it.

After quitting my job at the hotel, I got a job as a hostess at a Burbank restaurant, across from Warner Brothers Studios. The owner fired me because I wouldn't date him. Then he called and offered to lend me money. So, I agreed to have dinner with him, but with absolutely no intention of meeting him. I stood the fucker up. I wasn't going to touch his money, no matter how badly I needed it. And I did need it. Eric wasn't sending me grocery money anymore. The harsh reality of adult life was setting in.

Mostly, I tried to keep busy. I threw myself into my career. I went to auditions, but instead of performing the scene, still grief-stricken over Eric's death, I'd bawl my eyes out to random casting directors. My manager had to hold me back for a while, telling casting people that I "wasn't ready." Obviously, I wasn't coping well. I thought I needed anti-depressants, but a wise therapist told me that I was sad, not depressed. She suggested she support me through my grief instead of medicating me through it. I only saw her for a month or so. I just couldn't afford the three-times-a-week treatment plan.

I wasn't raised in any religious faith. I struggled to understand why Eric had suffered. Why had he been taken? Where was he now? Why was I breathing fresh air and he wasn't? The questions plagued me day after day. Both of my parents were brought up in strict Catholic families, and both rebelled against the church. Neither instilled in me a belief in the afterlife. Quite the opposite. As a child, they told me that once I grew up, I could choose my own religion. But when did I have a chance to study theology before I was twenty-two and my boyfriend was dead?

Because I wasn't raised with religion, I never really understood why it was such an important part of many people's lives, until I needed comforting. I was truly a lost soul. My scientist father advised, "He is just a memory now, move on." My artist mother was emotionally overwrought, sobbing over the phone, "I can't believe he's gone." I had to console her when she should have been consoling me.

I tried to socialize, but I'd often end up in the bathroom alone and crying, or worse, crying in public. I had night terrors. I'd bolt up in bed having dreamt about Eric's body decaying in his white-satin-lined, metallic-gray coffin. I'd lie awake, hyperventilating. This wasn't a nightmare. This wasn't my imagination. Eric was now behind the cement wall of a mausoleum. I could not accept it, but I had to. It was best I didn't go out socially. I preferred staying home and, when I had the time, reading spiritual books by candlelight. I read as many as I could get my hands on, desperately trying to figure out what life and death were all about. I read somewhere that death is like slipping out of a tight shoe. I read that love is stronger than death or heaven. I held onto whatever pieces of wisdom made sense to me.

I never found one particular religion that gave me any peace of mind. Shirley MacLaine's books, especially *Out on a Limb*, helped me more than anything else. She made me believe that Eric was vibrating; his energy was real. That resonated with me because I could still feel him. And the concept of reincarnation gave me some hope. Besides, I am the daughter of a scientist. If you think about it, energy never dies. It changes form. So when we die, doesn't it make sense that we change form? These are the things I contemplated as I came to terms with the fact that Eric and I would never splash through puddles in Manhattan streets again, or play practical jokes on members of KISS, or enjoy long nights (and days) of passionate lovemaking, oblivious to the rest of the world.

I wanted to get into another relationship, hoping that it would relieve the pain, but my heart wasn't open. I had put so many walls up. I could never get serious with anyone because I felt like damaged goods, as though I had a giant "X" across my forehead. I was broken. For the longest time, I couldn't look at any sort of musician. I especially couldn't look at a drum set or even go to a restaurant if a live band was playing. Everything reminded me of Eric. I stopped hanging out at the rock 'n' roll clubs and made the transition to hanging out at Bar One, where the glamorous people in the Hollywood movie industry gathered. Coincidently, David Lee Roth seemed to have the same inclination at the same time.

I'd met him many times before. The first encounter was on a hot summer night in 1989. I'd only been living in L.A. for a few months when I walked through the door of Bordello, a West Hollywood club that all the cool rockers went to on Thursdays. I was wearing a white T-shirt and blue jean shorts. Not the way I'd normally dress for a place like that, but I'd spent the day with my girlfriends, drinking Margaritas on the boardwalk at Venice Beach. On the way home, we were driving past *Bordello* and had decided to drop in and say hello to our friend Keith, who was the doorman.

I was barely past the front entrance when I saw Dave standing right there, not four feet away. I couldn't stop staring at him. David Lee Roth...was...close...enough...to touch. My stare must have burned through the back of his head because he turned and looked right at me. He smiled, nodded, and said, "Hi," probably just to confront me for staring so hard. I was totally starstruck. I gasped and turned my head really quick, looking down, embarrassed. All that time in high school I'd spent dreaming about him. All that time my friend Susan and I had followed his *Eat 'em and Smile* tour all over the South with backstage passes, even though he never once came backstage. And now he was just feet away. I planned to return the following Thursday and be more prepared just in case he showed up again.

At the time the glam metal band, Cinderella, had a music video for the song *"Nobody's Fool,"* that featured two not-so-ugly stepsisters wearing black-and-white polka dotted mini-skirts. That was the look I wanted. Eric found great humor in all of this. He even went with me to the Beverly Center Mall where I found a similar outfit. But no matter how much makeup I applied, no matter how high I teased my hair, I couldn't look like a slut. I had that nice girl, innocent thing going on, and the dirty rocker boys loved it. In the 80s, the guys wanted to wear the makeup, and they preferred a girl who didn't need it. Now I was ready to meet David Lee Roth.

I'd made note of the guy he was speaking to at the bar, his bodyguard/manager, Edmund. So, the following Thursday I perched on the barstool next to Edmund. I was chatting to him when Dave arrived. He didn't seem to recognize me from the week before. Why would he? I looked totally different. I saw Dave lean in and asked Edmund to introduce us. My bait worked, and that night we began a flirtation that went on for years.

Eric thought my little obsession with David Lee Roth was cute. Or maybe he thought I was being ridiculous. Or both. Eric was nineteen years older than I was and not into clubbing, especially after he'd been working in the studio for hours. So, I'd get home around 2:00 a.m., wake him up, and say, "Guess who was flirting with me tonight?" He knew the answer. He'd roll his eyes, and, with a deep sigh, reply, "David Lee Roth." And then he'd say. "Okay, just come to bed; let's get some sleep."

I'd often walk into a club, and Dave would be there with a booth full of girls, and he'd have his bodyguard shoo them away to make room for me. He and I would drink Jack Daniels and talk all night. Well, mostly he talked, and I just sat there enamored with him, hanging on his every witty word. When fans came up to meet him, he'd introduce me by saying, "And this is Carrie. I love you, Carrie." One night there was a bikini contest at the club, but he didn't even look at the girls strutting their stuff. He only had eyes for me, whispering in my ear, "What do you look like in a bikini, Carrie?" I basked in his attention until last call when the ugly lights turned on and then I always did my disappearing act and went home to Eric. Then it would happen again. I'd run into Dave at *Bordello* or the *Rainbow* and the flirtation would continue. He never pressured me. Never asked why I always disappeared on him. He was always just happy to see me. I did think it was strange that Dave never actually asked me on a date or asked for my phone number, but since I had a boyfriend, I kept my mouth shut. What would be the point of encouraging a date I couldn't accept?

By the time I ran into Dave again, things had changed drastically. Eric was no longer with us. It was my twenty-third birthday, May 1, 1992, six months after Eric's passing, and my friends forced me to go out. I was dressed to kill. A black sequined strapless bra under a tiny cropped vest with multi-colored sequins which showed off my tiny waist and my naturally full 34Cs. I paired the bra and vest with ripped-up, cut off denim shorts, over black fishnet stockings, you know, the kind with the line up the back. And high heels, too.

I had every reason to live each day like it was my last, and there he was, Diamond Dave, with a giant smile on his face and ten hot girls sitting in his booth. As usual, he got rid of them to make room for me. I was happily by his side. Dave sang in my ear, "Happy birthday to you, sweetheart." Tonight, had to be the night. I mean, my goal in life was to lose my virginity to David Lee Roth. Better late than never. But I was so nervous that I walked up to the bar and ordered three shots of whiskey, hoping it would give me the guts to make my dream come true. The next thing I knew, I woke up on a living room floor. My head was fuzzy. I had no idea where I was. I just lay there for a minute, trying to figure out how I had gotten there. Then suddenly someone put his arm around me. David Lee Roth. Oh. My. God. I was on Dave's living room floor. Naked. I just lay there in shock, stiff as a board, my eyes bulged wide open as he kissed me "Good morning."

Dave gave me one of his white T-shirts to wear home. It had "Ms. Olympia" in black ink printed on it, the female bodybuilders competition. Female bodybuilders were trendy in the 80s, and he used them in some of his music videos and photshoots. Dave drove me home, back to the valley over Laurel Canyon and stopped at Caioti to get us fresh squeezed orange juice while I waited in the car. I was dying. He looked so damn sexy as he walked toward me and climbed back into the driver's seat. He handed me some juice. "This is for you, sweetheart." My heart was pounding. I could barely speak. I had *"Panama"* lyrics running through my head.

Ah, I reach down between my legs...
Ease the seat back...

Riding alone in a car with David Lee Roth driving was exhilarating. I'm sure the sex the night before was just as exhilarating, assuming we'd had sex. Unfortunately, thanks to the straight whiskey, I didn't remember anything. I wondered if he knew he was with an obsessed fan. Then again, *he* was the one always who acted obsessed with me, while I did my best to appear normal. So how could he know? When Dave dropped me off, he got out of the car and opened up the trunk to get a piece of paper and a pen to write my number down.

He never called, but I'd finally conquered David Lee Roth. Sadly, I didn't remember doing it, but I was too much of an emotional train wreck for it to go any further anyway. Still grief-stricken, I wore the pain of Eric's loss on my sleeve. One night, soon after our hook-up, I ran into Dave at Bar One. I couldn't stop talking about Eric. Dave, politely but very directly, put me in my place, "Carrie, no man wants to hear a woman talk about another man." My heart sank. He was right. I realized that I was not mentally capable of being involved with anyone. Not even David Lee Roth. I was grieving and damaged. There was nothing I could do but accept it. I didn't know how to heal. I can't explain the feeling of isolation that goes with not being emotionally available enough to pursue present desires.

Like most of the VIPs at the clubs, Dave kept walking back into the club's mystery kitchen. I assumed it was to do coke because his nose would be running into his mouth while he was talking to me, and he clearly couldn't feel it. How could I tell him? "Uh, Dave, you may not be aware of it, but there's snot dripping into your mouth." Nothing could make me think Dave wasn't the hottest thing alive, except snot. When I found out that bands like Motley Crüe were doing hard core drugs like heroin, I was stunned. I was never around it. Thanks to KISS, I escaped that decadent era unscathed. I am grateful to Eric for never doing drugs and to David Lee Roth for never offering me any.

*****

It was also at Bar One where I connected again with producer Ted Field. I'd met Ted on the music video set when KISS recorded *"God Gave Rock 'n' Roll to You"* for the soundtrack to one of his movies, *Bill & Ted's Bogus Journey*. When I met him at Bar One, he said of course he remembered me. He said when he met me on the set with Eric, he'd asked himself, "How come the rock stars get all the beautiful girls?"

Ted and I became good friends, and he kindly took me out many times, knowing I was still finding it hard to deal with Eric's passing. One night he invited me to his home where he was hosting a party for Oliver Stone. This is where the incident occurred that I tweeted about: As Oliver was leaving the party, he grabbed my boob and honked it like a horn. He hardly paused before walking out the door with a self-satisfied grin on his face, as though he'd got away with something. I was humiliated but didn't want to complain. Stone had behaved like an immature middle-school kid who snaps your bra and thinks it's hilarious. The encounter lasted no more than a couple of seconds. I dismissed it as the juvenile act of a jerk who felt entitled to use the body of any young woman that he encountered in any way he pleased.

*****

How did I get through these years? With a little help from my friends. Jan Crutchfield and Anita Pressman, whom I'd met working at The Laugh Factory, who were always there for me. Nicki Anderson, my first friend in L.A., had me over for dinner every Sunday night. We never talked about Eric, but I knew that she invited me every week to help me heal, and it meant everything to me. I remained in close contact with Bruce and Christina and Gary and Lenora, as well as Eric's family and my own family. My sister Jill was wonderful.

My friend Wendy Griffin was instrumental in my healing. She told me about a woman named Maren Nelson who gave rebirthing sessions. I had no idea what to expect, but since Wendy was raving about it so much, I decided to give it a try. It was a guided meditation paired with connected deep breathing. It was a hundred bucks a session, and I couldn't really afford it, but it gave me so much peace that it was more important to me than eating. It felt like I was in a huddle with my spirit guides and that Eric tapped into this energy. My fingers went numb and levitated, a transcendental experience. My spirit guides told me that Eric was needed somewhere else, to be of service. I got the message that he was helping children and doing other valuable work. He had a greater purpose and that's why he was taken. He was still connected to me, but we were not meant in this human life on Earth to understand it all. I got more healing through this rebirthing process than anything else.

A truly valuable spiritual relationship came when the bonds of friendship deepened between me and drummer Bobby Rock. Less than eighteen months after Eric's death had thrown my life into a tailspin, Bobby's girlfriend Sherri Foreman was stabbed to death at an ATM in Sherman Oaks, a suburb of Los Angeles. She was thirteen weeks pregnant. When I saw it on the news, I contacted Bruce Kulick to ask if he could get Bobby's address for me.

I had met Bobby backstage in NYC while he was playing for the band, Nelson. When Bobby heard that Eric had cancer, he sent him a Juiceman Juicer. It impressed me so much. And now this horrific tragedy had shattered Bobby's life. I felt the need to reach out to him and share with him what I knew about rebirthing and the healing of grief. We were kindred souls and had deep meaningful conversations. For years, we leaned on each other and learned from each other. Not too many people lose someone they love when they are so young and have so much to offer. Bobby and I understood each other like no one else could. He could look at my face and know how I felt without my speaking a word, when it would take hours to explain my feelings about loss to anyone else.

One night, I made another longtime friend. It was at The Roxbury, a trendy club with a crowd similar to Bar One's. All the paparazzi and famous faces were there. I remember I wore a red velvet dress that night, but at the last minute, before leaving my apartment, I'd decided the dress would look better as a shirt. So, I took a pair of scissors and, while I still had it on, chopped the dress off at the waistline, and tucked it into a pair of faded Levi's. I grabbed my black leather *Hot in The Shade* KISS tour jacket, and I was ready to roll.

At The Roxbury, my friend Pamela and I were standing at the bar where I had rested the jacket on a stool. I wasn't paying attention, and it was almost stolen by some random girl, until she was stopped by a cute, aspiring actor by the name of Matt LeBlanc (he soon became famous for his role in *Friends*). We hit it off, and he drove me home on the back of his motorcycle. I realized just how right my instincts were chopping that red dress and wearing jeans instead. Matt was intimidatingly adorable, and we dated on and off for years. I wanted to be in a serious relationship with him, but my heart simply wasn't open. The spirit of Eric always hovered over me. It probably wasn't fair on Matt or to any of the guys I dated, but Eric was omnipresent in my life. Not that it mattered much, because a natural disaster soon came between us.

*****

The most terrifying experience of my life happened at 4:30 a.m. on January 17, 1994. I literally woke up in mid-air, having been tossed out of bed as a massive earthquake rocked the Los Angeles area. Instinctively, I grabbed my pillow to protect my head from flying debris, and rushed into the living room where Nicki, my roommate, had fallen asleep on the couch. Our entertainment center had crashed on top of her and, adrenaline pumping, I lifted it off of her, even as the room continued to quake. It was like being in the middle of a snow globe that was being furiously shaken by an unseen giant. Anything not bolted down was hurled. Glassware and chinaware were smashed to pieces, strewn all over the floor.

Nicki and I ran out of the apartment, knowing we had to get away from the building. We were on the ground floor of a duplex. Congregated in the driveway, dressed in our pajamas, neighbors met each other for the first time, all of us panicked. Massive aftershocks continued to rock and terrify us. We were all well aware that this huge quake, which turned out to be a magnitude 6.9, might very well be followed by an even bigger one.

Power lines were down and sparking. Sirens wailed as the emergency services went into action. Phones weren't working. We didn't know what was going on. We hung out for hours until the aftershocks calmed down, and some of us were brave enough to dash back inside and grab our booze. Then it was a neighborhood block party in our pajamas. We lived on the Sherman Oaks-Van Nuys border, not far from the epicenter of what became known as the Northridge Earthquake, which killed fifty-seven people, injured more than 8,700, and caused billions of dollars of damage in one of the most destructive disasters in American history.

My apartment was condemned. A crack in the middle of my bedroom wall was so big you could stick your finger through it. Across the city, bridges were destroyed, freeways closed, older buildings crumpled. The devastation was so widespread that it was obvious that L.A. was going to be a mess for a long time. It was enough to scare anyone out of living there. Why would I want to live in a disaster zone for who knew how long? I didn't have a family in L.A. or a relationship. Nothing was holding me down. I took it as an opportunity to do something different.

My father arranged a flight to New York where I became roommates with my friend Stacey Lynn, a Penthouse Pet whom I knew from my rocker-chick circle. She was a leggy blonde with a raspy voice and a girly giggle. She told great stories, having dated guys from Warrant, Extreme, Ratt and Bon Jovi. My father was living in New Jersey at the time, so I'd be able to see more of him. Since I wouldn't need a car, I sold the Mazda Miata I'd bought with money Eric left me and used it to pay for acting classes at The Circle in the Square Theatre School and the Actor's Studio.

When I was at Circle in the Square, I took a full-time program that included dance and voice classes. Eric always told me I had the worst voice he'd ever heard, so I was petrified to sing in front of anyone. The teacher, a shriveled-up, gray-haired, old lady who'd been at the prestigious school for thirty years, lectured us on the first day that there was no such thing as tone deafness. Even so. I procrastinated and went last. I sang Elvis Presley's *"Suspicious Minds."* The teacher immediately changed her mind about tone deafness.

"Okay," she said, "You have problems."

"Don't try to sing again," she said. Speak the song as a monologue. I was so embarrassed I never went back to that class and hung out in Central Park instead.

This was perhaps one of the most wonderfully ordinary times of my life. It was the days before the Internet when I was anonymous. No one in my acting class knew of my past. No one knew me as Eric's girlfriend. No one knew I'd been on the road with KISS. I blended in with the other students as if none of that had ever happened. Sometimes I sat on a bench outside Eric's old high rise at 36th Street and First Avenue, just thinking about him and the good times we'd shared; other times, I visited his grave at Cedar Hill Cemetery & Mausoleum in Newburgh and said a few prayers.

I loved Manhattan, although the sudden loud rumbling of the subway sometimes triggered flashbacks to the earthquake. Mostly, I threw myself into work all hours of the day and night and partying the rest of the time. After all, New York is "the city that never sleeps." I landed an overnight job as a cocktail waitress in a club called Le Bar Bat, that went on until six or six-thirty in the morning. During the day I worked at the original Equinox gym, where hot male models worked out; guys like Marcus Schenkenberg and Michael Bergin who were on the Calvin Klein underwear billboards. I was at the front desk drooling every time they came in.

Stacey and I made good roommates, although she was a lot wilder than I was. I managed to keep away from drugs until one night when we were at a club called The Tunnel, and she persuaded me to try Ecstasy. We'd had some problems with our friendship. It would help us bond, she said, giving me the impression that she wanted me to do it because she cared about me. It worked. Suddenly, I loved techno music. The sounds. The lights. The colors. Everything was intensified. It was like taking a happy pill. I loved everyone. And everything. Stacey was right. Whatever our issues, all was forgiven.

I continued to get caught up in the party scene until one day I came to my senses. It was about 11 o'clock and I was sitting in a booth in a dark, seedy basement club in the East Village called Save the Robots. I was talking to drag queens about our acting techniques; which was better, the Meisner Technique or The Method? When you're high you really get into what you're saying, and you think every word that trips out of your mouth is brilliant. I was giving the drag queens the benefit of my educated opinion when I had a sudden epiphany. It was not 11 o'clock at night. It was 11 o'clock in the morning. I was a loser. Here I was bonding with a bunch of people I'd never seen before and would never see again. What the fuck was I doing? I staggered out of the club, blinded by the dreadfully bright sunshine. I could make out Eric's condo in the distance. Guilt washed over me. This isn't what he wanted for me. Every twenty-five-year-old should live in Manhattan once, as long as you know when it's time to leave. And that time had come for me. Saying goodbye to Stacey and the new friends I'd made was bittersweet, but my time in New York City had reached its expiration date.

JACOB GETZ PHOTO

Carrie with Anita Pressman *(top photo)*;
with Nicki Anderson-Jelsma *(above middle)*;
and with Matt LeBlanc *(photo at right)*.

Chapter 5

Don't Join a Harem

As the Singapore Airlines flight descended onto the Island of Borneo, the thought crossed my mind that I might die there. I might be snatched up, sold into white slavery, raped, murdered, never to be seen again. But it didn't bother me. I don't know if it was a death wish or my innate sense of adventure, but instead of being afraid, it was exhilarating. I had nothing to lose. Absolutely nothing.

I was a broke actress in love with a dead guy. I hadn't sincerely smiled in four and a half years. I refer to those years after Eric died as the lost years. I had been making all of $8.00 an hour as a hostess in a trendy Beverly Hills restaurant and nightclub called Sanctuary. It was a cool place to work, but I could barely afford to put food in my stomach and gas in my car. And gas was more important than food. I needed it to get me to work and to my auditions. But I still couldn't pay for an acting class or a headshot.

All the celebrities hung out at Sanctuary, as I stood at the hostess podium unnoticed. Jenny McCarthy and Pamela Anderson were there all the time. Pamela was part owner. The rich and the beautiful walked through its doors. I seated them and on the nights that I was doubling as a coat check girl, took their coats. Most of them ignored me. The only one I recall hitting on me was Robert Downey, Jr. back in his drug addict days. I don't even know what he was on, but I know what he was wearing: lopsided sweatpants, the kind with elastic around the ankles. He had one pant leg pushed up to his knee, and only one shoe. I was leaving for the night, headed to my car, when he and a friend, just as disheveled, startled me. They seemed to jump out of nowhere. Robert asked for my phone number. It was easier to give it to him than refuse and create a scene, but when he called, I didn't answer. I'm a big fan, but in that state, he was scary. I'm glad he's got it together now.

Stevie Nicks came in once. When my sister Jill and I were growing up, while I had posters of David Lee Roth hanging all over my bedroom walls, she had posters of Stevie. I teased her mercilessly about being a lesbian, even though I didn't know for sure if she was gay. Later, when I found out that she was, I felt horrible that I'd been so mean. I took the opportunity to make it up to her by getting Stevie's autograph and framing it for her.

Every night, all these gorgeous actresses I'd see on auditions were at Sanctuary having dinner and dancing while I worked. And then I started to hear rumors from a few of the regulars who always chatted with me. (By the way, two years later these same guys fawned over me after my *Playboy* centerfold came out, starstruck like they'd never seen me before. I wasn't that memorable until seen naked in a magazine. Pretty funny and very telling.) Anyway, these regulars told stories about this little island on the other side of the world, in the far, far East. They talked about girls who'd gone out there as if they were rock stars who'd scored the chance of a lifetime. One told me I'd be crazy not to go. It was an opportunity to mingle with royalty, to party with a real live prince, the younger brother of the Sultan of Brunei, the richest man in the world. This guy said he had connections in the prince's circle and offered to send my photos to them. Sure. Why not? It sounded like an exotic adventure. A perfect escape from reality.

*****

My phone rang at 1:00 a.m. It was a representative of the prince. I was booked on a first-class flight out of LAX at 7:00 a.m. With just a few hours to get my affairs in order, I furiously packed everything I owned, which wasn't much, and left. I didn't tell my family or my agents or my manager. I just disappeared. It was a better option than driving off a cliff or slitting my wrists. Since Eric's death, I'd suffered crippling anxiety attacks. Disturbing visions flooded my head. I'd be driving and imagine my car flying off the edge of a cliff, tumbling over and over again until it burst into flames. I visualized my family in my apartment after my death, sorting through my belongings. I was detached from reality. My heart was on the other side of eternity, with Eric. I'd been chewed up and spit out by fate, and by every casting director in town. I was worn out and alone with no hope. So, no, I didn't care what I had to do, or what became of me in Brunei. I didn't really know what to expect. I just took my chances.

On the plane I was surprised to meet three other girls who were also invited guests of the prince. I don't know why, but it hadn't occurred to me I might not be the only one. We had the front row seats, first class all the way, the most luxurious flight I'd ever experienced. The girls were nice. Two of them were from L.A. — Cindy, 18, and Alexandra, 25. The other, 22-two-year old Jennifer, was a gorgeous American-born Filipino, an exotic Las Vegas dancer. As we sipped champagne, waited on by flight attendants in adorable red hats and uniforms, we traded information.

There were all sorts of different avenues for girls to wind up in Brunei, entertaining a prince who wanted to be surrounded by a roomful of beautiful women every night. In return, there'd be some appreciative gifts at the end of our stay. Possibly *very* appreciative gifts. Some girls, it was said, were able to buy cars and homes. That's appreciative. Jennifer's boyfriend's sister was a Playmate already in Brunei, so that was her hook-up. Alexandra, who looked more like a librarian than a harem girl, was hired as a singer. I'm not sure about Cindy's connection. I was more interested in her story about dating Billy Idol who, she told us, used to pick her up on his motorcycle from Beverly Hills High School.

The four of us had an overnight layover at an upscale hotel in Singapore. In the morning, we boarded a smaller Royal Brunei Airways plane off to Borneo. When we reached Bandar Seri Begawan, our destination airport, I wondered where we were supposed to go. We were flying blind, jet lagged, dazed and confused. I hadn't been to Asia before and everybody seemed so small. Not so small was a giant portrait of the country's ruler, the sultan, in a white military jacket bearing an array of colorful medals. It dominated a wall of the arrivals lounge. Two smaller portraits depicted his two current wives, both impeccably made up and wearing diamond tiaras. We hadn't been given much in the way of direction. But it seemed there was no cause for concern. Four pretty, young American girls stuck out like sore thumbs, and our ride instantly spotted us. He shuffled us outside, the tropical humidity washing over us as we stepped into a van. Off we went, staring out the windows, wide eyed, as we rolled through the unfamiliar jungle like landscape. Suddenly, after getting a phone call, and without any explanation, the driver did a fast U-turn and headed back to the airport. He ignored our questions. Shrugged his shoulders. Maybe he didn't speak English? The four of us looked at each other as if to say, 'what the fuck have we gotten ourselves into?'

Safely transferred to another vehicle with another driver (who was just as uncommunicative), we tried to figure out what had happened. Could the first driver simply have picked up the wrong passengers? But how many pretty young American girls were arriving that day? And where were we going now? A welcoming cocktail party? A tour of the palace? No such luck. We were driven straight to a medical clinic where they took blood and urine samples. Everyone was very courteous but didn't explain a damn thing. They didn't say what they were testing for, but the reality of our invitation to party in Brunei was quickly becoming apparent; we assumed they were checking for drugs and STDs. We were officially in the Twilight Zone. It was all so surreal. It was like I was sleepwalking from one weird experience to the next. Like I was on a conveyor belt taking me from one bizarre adventure to the next.

Finally, we were escorted to the royal palace. My first awestruck impression: pools, monkeys, and lots of gold. More gold than Trump Tower. I later read that the palace had 1,788 rooms, 257 bathrooms, five swimming pools, its own mosque, a banquet hall for 5,000 people and a 110-car garage. It was the biggest residence in the world, home of the sultan. Our ultimate destination was more of a mini palace, the Assurur Palace, that belonged to the sultan's brother, our host Prince Jefri. It was going to be my home and was way bigger than any home this small town girl had ever seen.

The four of us were taken to a round room, a kind of office, also adorned with gold fixtures, where we were asked to surrender our passports. I wasn't happy doing that, but just went with the flow. We had to sit there for a while. I think it was so that the prince could check us out via hidden camera. All very mysterious and alarming. The longer we sat there, silently waiting to discover what would happen next, the full impact of what I'd done dawned on me. I was on the other side of the world. My family and friends didn't know where I was. How could I have gotten myself in a situation like this?

But it was too late now to back out. My fate would become apparent soon enough.

The only interaction was with Alex, the prince's stiffly formal right-hand man, and Mr. Bal, a chubby little guy dressed in khaki pants and a polo shirt. Both were Malaysian and could speak English, but they didn't bother with small talk; they only issued instructions. There was no orientation, no tour, no front desk, no guidance. We were taken to our living quarters, one of six identical houses spread along a huge driveway that encircled the compound. Each house was at least five thousand square feet with four bedrooms. Six girls lived in each house and were assigned roommates. It was obvious we'd have to rely on girls that were already there to show us the ropes. Initially, they were slow to explain to us newcomers how everything worked, and my first roommate, Liat, was such a raving bitch that I ended up switching rooms.

Most of the girls were lovely, American, and from all walks of life. Some were models and others were known socialites from the L.A. club scene. One was an MTV video vixen. There were Playmates, wholesome college girls, a preppy actress, a cute Laker's cheerleader, a *Penthouse* Pet and one of Vince Neil's four ex-wives. There were also Asian girls, but we saw them only at the parties, as the six houses in our compound were filled only with Americans. I don't know where the Asian girls were housed, but probably somewhere more fabulous, considering that one of the Thai girls was Prince Jefri's favorite. The Filipino women were mostly professional singers and in charge of karaoke at the nightly parties. The girls varied in age, between eighteen and the cut-off age of twenty-six, with one exception. Vince Neil's ex was thirty and had managed to squeeze her way in as part of a package deal with her younger, hotter sister. The youngest of the Americans was only sixteen. She was placed in the harem of the prince's son and was there with her parents' consent, although I'm not sure that makes it any better. She belonged in high school not a harem, for God's sake.

I didn't know how to explain the situation I'd got myself in, so I told my grandparents I was doing fashion shows for the royal family. They said, "Stay and make the money." I never heard any of the girls say their families objected to their strange trip to a far Eastern country and accommodation in a royal palace. I don't know what they told them except that it was an exotic and potentially rewarding adventure. Even the most conservative of people understood the value of a good opportunity.

Our only official duty was to attend a party every night from 10:00 p.m. to 4:00 a.m. A mirrored ball above the dance floor flashed lights as pop disco music blared. Some of the girls sang karaoke to entertain Prince Jefri, who sat on the steps outside with wife number four and their toddler. In the whole time that I was there, he never once joined the party. You'd think he'd be sitting on a throne, wearing royal robes, but instead, he was outside on the steps, wearing a track suit. An intensely attractive man with dark swept back hair, a goatee, and copper complexion, he looked young, about forty and physically fit. Usually he had five or six of his friends in attendance, paired up with Asian girls. The American girls were off limits to them, so they barely spoke to us.

There were some strange rules and customs in Brunei. Five times a day, we heard the Muslim call to prayer, which only reminded us that we were a long way from home. For some reason, women at the palace weren't allowed to eat papaya or yogurt. We were also warned not to show the bottoms of our shoes, as it was considered deeply insulting to someone of the Muslim faith.

On the fourth night, I got a call after the party, around 4:30 a.m. It was Mr. Bal. "Are you okay?" he asked. I didn't realize the question was code. He was checking to make sure I was not on my period. I hadn't been there long enough to know that. None of the girls had clued me in. I replied simply, "Yes, I'm okay." Because, well, I was okay. Then he said I would have to be ready at 8:00 a.m. And added, "No makeup." I wasn't told anything else. But my imagination ran riot. This was the moment of truth. I'd joined a harem! And harem girls didn't just sit around looking pretty, eating bon bons all day. We were expected to do more than perform karaoke. By reputation, the prince had a healthy sexual appetite. My time had come. Was I going to be the main dish on the menu?

It pained me to sacrifice my lip gloss, but on the stroke of eight, conservatively dressed in a subdued skirt and jacket, and low heels, I stepped into a black chauffeur-driven Mercedes. As we headed off, destination unknown, I settled comfortably into the plush leather seats and stared out the tinted windows at scenes I'd never seen before. We drove past houses on stilts with laundry hanging over balconies, alongside a dirty river crammed with slim boats, a shanty town of structures that seemed on the verge of collapse, the worst kind of slums imaginable. A shocking contrast to the posh palace compound with its manicured grounds.

We pulled up to a high-rise building which seemed to be a regular office block. Without any explanation, the driver opened the car door. Another person, already standing there waiting for me, motioned for me to follow. As he ushered me through the doors, yet another man, wearing a uniform and red hat, followed inches behind me vacuuming every step I took. I later discovered the prince would not walk on the same ground as I until it had been cleansed!

I was escorted into a large, opulent room, much nicer than the building's bland exterior, decorated in the same lavish style as the palace; everything trimmed with gold and the floor covered with lush patterned carpets.

"Wait here," I was instructed. "Sit."

The chair was placed in the middle of the room. I did as I was told. What else was I going to do? I looked around, absorbing everything. Family photographs in beautiful ornate frames looked back at me from a large mahogany desk, beautiful women in stylish gowns and smiling children. An uncomfortable, eerie feeling crept over me. I looked up. Dead center above my head was a black dome camera. I was being watched. Presumably by the prince, who was sizing me up. I shuddered at the thought, a peeping prince.

I waited for what seemed like hours, anxiously wondering what was going to happen next. Finally, Prince Jefri, wearing a beautifully tailored business suit, strolled in.

"Hello. I'm Robin."

That's how he introduced himself, but, of course, I knew who he was. He liked to be known by this assumed Western name, which was just as well because when I looked him up later, I discovered his full name was His Royal Highness Pengiran Digadong Sahibul Mal Pengiran Muda Sharif Jefri Bolkiah ibni Al-Marhum Sultan Haji Omar Ali Saifuddien Sa'adul Khairi Waddien.

Robin made the same sort of small talk one would expect in an L.A. bar. Where did I live? What did I do for a living? Where did I grow up? Where did I go to school? How many brothers and sisters did I have? That kind of thing. It went on for about twenty minutes. Then he suddenly said, "Come on," and led me into another room.

What a contrast. Big black bed. Black walls. Drapes and sheets of lustrous black silk. The ceiling and an entire wall were covered in mirrors. This was where the prince had sex with his harem girls. I was sure that he probably videoed all of us. My heart was thumping. I'd never been so scared at the prospect of getting beneath the sheets with someone. Except this wasn't just someone. He was a genuine prince, part of the richest family on the planet, and to him I was a harem girl. Would this be an adventure I'd quickly regret? Lying on the bed kissing me, he asked me to stand up and show him my tits. He liked real breasts and mine were real. Then he motioned for me to join him back on the bed and to my surprise he went down on me. He was attractive, so it was easy to put my nerves aside and enjoy it. But it was surreal. Like I was watching it happen to someone else.

He tried to stick it in the wrong hole, and I stopped him. I'm pretty sure it was an accident, as I learned later that Prince Jefri's thing was oral, not anal. I also learned later that the sultan was different, and that any girl who took it in the ass from him received hundreds of thousands of dollars. Some of them had been there for years and become multi-millionaires. But at this point, I hadn't been schooled on such things. In the small town where I came from, nice girls didn't do that, so my rejection was instinctive. Boy, was I young and dumb. Obviously, Prince Jefri wasn't looking to marry me, so I have no idea why that "nice girl" narrative played in my head. I never met the sultan, so I was never faced with the opportunity to become a backdoor millionaire by, ahem, catering to his desires.

After the prince had his way with me, which only lasted about five minutes, I got dressed, and was led straight into a room filled with eight men. They were obviously dignitaries of some kind, all with unique foreign accents, including one American clergyman wearing a long, white robe. They were discussing what sounded like important world issues that were probably not meant for my "civilian" ears. But they treated me respectfully and made an effort to include me in the conversation. It was truly mind-blowing. One minute my legs were in the air and the next I was daintily sipping tea and eating finger sandwiches in the company of international dignitaries. It ran through my head that the men must have known that the prince just had his way with me, yet everyone acted as if there were nothing out of the ordinary. To me, it was anything but ordinary. It was enthralling. It was 007. Only there was no danger. Thank God.

*****

I was driven back to my house through the large iron gates, guarded by uniformed men wielding machine guns. I tiptoed up the stairs before anyone woke up. It was one in the afternoon but most days the girls slept in. So, it was my secret. I later found out the girls liked to gossip about who did or didn't get "called on" by the prince. That was the one and only time I ever got called on during my entire six-month experience. Some of the girls never got called. I guess Prince Jefri wasn't that into me, but I didn't care so long as I wasn't sent home. Some of the girls were freaked out by the guards having machine guns, but it made me feel safe. Being in the Brunei harem was an escape from my sad reality in L.A., and I wanted to stay.

My theory is that to the prince we were like paintings. Just as art collectors have their precious works of art to study and admire, we were a gallery of sorts. Or, if you want to look at it another way, it was like a wine connoisseur with a cellar full of fine wine. You know it's there and you can open a bottle whenever you want. But you might never take a drink. The prince also had over two hundred luxury cars and the last time I checked you can't drive more than one at a time. What could be a bigger status symbol than a collection of paintings or fine wines or exotic cars? Women. A harem of beautiful young women at your beck and call.

It took a while to adjust to life in the harem. There were two maids assigned to each house, who catered to our every need, tiny Malaysian women dressed in black pants and a white coat, like a chef's, with a name tag. We wrote down what we wanted to eat, and it appeared in our kitchen in tin containers the next day. I was a pescatarian and thankfully they had the most delicious fresh fish. I fell in love with lychee fruit. I'd never had it before or even heard of it.

The only demand on our time were the nightly karaoke parties which I came to regard as "going to work." I'm the world's worst singer, but I often made it fun, tunelessly singing my heart out. Sometimes, we'd go horseback riding on the beach, splashing through the waves of the China Sea or around the muddy racetrack. We went to polo grounds, stylishly suited up in the proper boots, pants, and caps. On Chinese New Year, we were all given traditional Malay dresses to wear and flower leis. The best part: we were also each handed $10,000 in cash. I used some of this money for spa treatments, which we could book at the clinic, but were at our own expense. But most everything else was free. We even brushed our teeth with Evian. We could use the pool or the gym or play badminton, but I rarely did. Something in Brunei's humid air made me have terrible sinus allergies, so most of the time I stayed inside. It was okay because we had a huge catalog of movies and whatever DVDs we ordered were delivered right away. I watched hours of T.V. I read. I slept a lot. I drank champagne every night. Yes, that was life in a harem.

Birthdays were a big deal. On my birthday, I was presented with $10,000 cash and a gorgeous gold Rolex watch with a turquoise face. I loved it. After the nightly karaoke duty, the girls threw a wild after-party for me at house five. We smoked cigarettes and danced, and I recall one silly drunk girl giving a blow job to a banana, before the night ended in a chocolate cream pie fight.

It might sound like we had everything we could want (besides the opposite sex) but being in captivity of any kind gets boring, and, in a way, it was captivity. We were allowed only one phone call a week on a giant prehistoric mobile phone, which we had to pay for ourselves and which was outrageously expensive. At one point, I wrote to my grandparents saying I couldn't call for a while as I'd already blown five grand using the phone. I desperately wanted to call home as I got homesick. My spirit was breaking down. I stopped riding horses or going to the spa. I stayed confined to the palatial compound writing letters to my friends and family and counting the minutes until I would see them again.

One blessing that got me through the days in Brunei was the arrival of Maria, my closest friend in L.A. I had given her photo to Alex and managed to get her invited to join the harem. Maria was tall, blonde, and stunning, an aspiring actress who worked as a waitress at Sanctuary. Six months before I left for Brunei, I was the maid of honor at her wedding. Having the familiarity of Maria there made it even better for me, although I became great friends with some of the other girls. One girl had also lost a loved one to cancer. She and I would get up before everyone else and, over coffee, have deep, healing discussions, bonding over our grief. Another girl had a two-year-old son back home, and we watched movies of him that her parents sent over. Those were some very real moments in an unreal world. And even though I was so far removed from the life I'd had with Eric, he continued to have a presence. I was tormented by a recurring nightmare:

He's alive. He was discovered buried alive, and he'd never had cancer. It was all a mistake. He's at his apartment in New York, but I can't get in touch with him. I'm calling his number and he's not answering. When I finally reach him, he doesn't remember me.

I'd wake up crying, bawling my eyes out. Every time I had this nightmare, I couldn't shake it off. It would ruin my entire day. Occasionally, I still have nightmares like this, but thankfully they're far less frequent.

After almost five months in Brunei, Mr. Bal told us we'd be moving into different houses and to get our things packed. None of us were happy about that. We'd settled into comfortable routines. We were fine with the houses and roommates we already had. Packing up all our belongings was a pain in the ass. Why would they want to disrupt everything? They hadn't made us switch houses so we were nervous at this unexpected development. To our absolute delight, it turned out we weren't moving houses at all. They just wanted us to be ready to leave for London at a moment's notice! We were thrilled to discover that they were flying all the American girls, about twenty of us, on the royal 747 to the U.K. In London they gave us our own floor at the five-star Grosvenor House Hotel in the ritzy Mayfair area. Then, to top it all, they casually handed each of us a black garbage bag full of cash, the equivalent of $100,000 in British pounds.

"Go shopping. Do whatever you want," Alex encouraged us.

The hotel rooms were all paid for, we could order as much room service as we wanted, and we had phones to connect us with the outside world any time we wanted, free of charge. Some of the girls took the opportunity to call their boyfriends or husbands and fly them over. It sounded too good to be true, but it was all real.

Of course, we went crazy. After months of being cooped up, we were on the loose. We went to West End shows. We shopped all over town, Harrods, Oxford Street, Regent Street, Bond Street, the Kings Road. You name it, we were there. My roommate Jennifer and I had so many shopping bags we couldn't see the floor of our room. That's when we invested in another extravagance: boob jobs. We had all these clothes, we needed to fill them out appropriately. The prince had a fondness for Jennifer, but she knew she'd be safe from getting called on because he was at a polo match for two weeks. This was her chance.

She was determined to get her boobs done, so we randomly picked a plastic surgeon from the phone book and booked a consultation. I wasn't looking for a boob job; I was more interested in liposuction as I always thought I was a little overweight. No, said the doctor. You don't need lipo. But my natural 34Cs were sagging a bit and a small implant would lift them up nicely. So, we both signed on the dotted line and plunked down the cash.

It all went well, except that Jennifer was given Vicodin, and all I got was Advil. She got the Vicodin because her procedure was considered more painful. As she started off with a flat chest, her implants were placed under the muscle. In my case, the doctor opted to do over the muscle breast augmentation since I already had a lot of skin and tissue. I should have demanded Vicodin! As we took a traditional black taxi back to the hotel, every time we hit a bump in the road electric shocks pulsed through my new breasts. I was in so much pain, I thought I'd die. Jennifer was blissfully high from the Vicodin, flicking her cigarette ash in her Coke can and then obliviously drinking from it.

One afternoon in London, I went shopping by myself to the upscale department store, Selfridge's. After a successful mission, I stepped out into the craziness of Oxford Street, loaded down with six shopping bags. Nevertheless, as it was such a beautiful, sunny day I decided to take the short walk past Hyde Park back to the hotel. It was a safe area crowded with tourists and locals. Three in the afternoon. I didn't have a care in the world.

Suddenly, out of nowhere, two men attacked me. One came up from behind and pressed a knife hard against my throat. In that split second, as I gasped for air and felt his breath on my neck, I feared the blade was going to slice right through my windpipe. At the same time, the other attacker grabbed hold of my wrist and seized the strap of my watch. He furiously yanked it back and forth, painfully tearing my skin until my precious Rolex broke free. It all happened so fast and was so brutal. Two armed men working in tandem with ruthless efficiency. They didn't say a word, which somehow made it even more terrifying.

"Help! Help!" I screamed at a dozen passengers who'd just gotten off a bus. Every one of them ignored my pleas, pretending they weren't witnessing this savage assault in broad daylight. The blank stares of these cowardly bystanders made me angrier than the attack itself.

Adrenaline transformed me into some kind of super-hero. Instinctively, without thinking of the consequences, I kicked the guy who'd grabbed my watch in the balls and, quickly spinning around, knocked the knife out of the other guy's hand and yanked the baseball cap off his head. All somehow without dropping a shopping bag. As they ran off, I scooped up the knife and the hat and, in my high heels, chased them down the street. I might have kicked the shit out of those fuckers, but they were still getting away with my watch. That watch was five months of my life. I had earned it.

In no time, a police car pulled over. The cops couldn't help wondering what this crazy American girl was doing running down the street, carrying six shopping bags and wielding a knife. I explained the assault, jumped in their car, and we drove around trying to find my attackers, but no luck. I later read in a local newspaper that a crime ring was stalking women who shopped at high-end stores and robbing them of their Rolexes.

Fighting back probably wasn't the smartest thing to do, but it was my gut reaction. My throat could have been slashed, and I could have bled to death on the sidewalk in one of London's fanciest neighborhoods. Luckily, I wasn't badly hurt. Paramedics just had to tape up my wrist. The prince and his entourage were told all about it, or at least that's what I heard through the grapevine, but I never got a call from them. They must have assumed I was fine since I was at the hotel and not in the hospital. It's such a shame that those thugs got away with the $32,000 Rolex. But I learned a lesson that day. I never wanted another expensive watch again. What's the point of having one if you can't wear it?

A few weeks later, I was on my way back home. A year later, I was shocked when newspaper headlines screamed that American girls had been held as "sex slaves" at the royal palace in Brunei. It all stemmed from a lawsuit filed by a former Miss USA, Shannon Marketic, against Prince Jefri, the sultan and an L.A. agency that organized girls for the harem.

Marketic alleged she accepted a $3,000 a day assignment in Brunei for "personal appearances and promotional works," but instead was drugged and sexually manhandled.

She claimed she was held against her will for thirty-two days before she was put on a plane back to the states. The sultan called the accusation "worse than murder." After he and the prince claimed diplomatic immunity, the case was dropped.

Vanity Fair once described Prince Jefri as "Brunei's notorious royal playboy, who has probably gone through more cash than any other human being on earth," and that he and the sultan had "allegedly sent emissaries to comb the globe for the sexiest women they could find in order to create a harem the likes of which the world had never known." That was probably true. But Marketic's accusations were nothing like my experience. Consider the source. A few years later, she was arrested for public intoxication at Dallas/Fort Worth International Airport, and, a few years after that, was charged with stealing almost $90.00 in merchandise from a Target store.

Marketic was in Brunei for just five weeks. I was part of the harem for six months. I got to know dozens of girls during my time there and not one said anything that remotely resembled her allegations. Everyone I know had a positive experience and wished she could go back for another well-rewarded vacation! At the end of my time in the harem, I came away extremely thankful for the prince's generosity with gifts worth about $700,000. He more than lived up to the rumors of rewarding us for our time there.

Brunei was a realization of a different world, a materialistic world where for the prince and the sultan money was no object. Was I destined to have this wild experience? Had my upbringing led me on this path? Eric was gone. I was alone, struggling and failing to make it in Hollywood. Was that why I'd recklessly plunged into the unknown? Another explanation is that I was only twenty-two when Eric died. My brain wasn't even fully developed. I suffered PTSD from the trauma of watching him suffer. Given that it's common for trauma survivors to become risk-takers, perhaps it's not surprising that I landed in a harem without weighing all the consequences.

The financial gifts from my time in Brunei were astronomical, for sure, but I actually think of the time itself as the greatest gift. It gave me the opportunity to work on my mental, physical, and spiritual health, all while living for free. Well, as free as you can live when you're mostly confined within the walls of the palace compound, allowed to make only one phone call a week. I'd also had an extraordinary series of experiences that few people could ever imagine. I'd had time to reflect on my life and recharge my batteries. Plus, there were no distractions. No rejections from casting directors. No laundry to do. No bills to pay. It allowed me to reflect and heal my broken heart.

Brunei was also a turning point in my life in another way. It marked the death of my innocence. I wasn't a small-town girl anymore. I was becoming the hardened, L.A. woman that Eric cautioned me about when I told him I was thinking of moving to the 'City of Angels.' His concern: what happens to "nice girls" like me. He was right. I was unintentionally becoming the sort of girl whom David Lee Roth sang about in Van Halen's *"Girl Gone Bad."* I guess it was inevitable.

PASSPORT
United States of America
BUF NY 142
Mrs. Stevens
Parkhurst Blvd.
40 Sen
BRUNEI DARUSSALAM
$1
BRUNEI DARUSSALAM
Mr. + Mrs. Stevens
959 Parkhurst Blvd
NY 14150

Chapter 6

Don't Pose for Playboy

While writing this book, I examined the external factors of my evolution and realized I wasn't born a sex object. I was bred to be one. I was perceived as pretty and treated like I was stupid from the time I developed breasts at the tender age of ten. Young girls believe the narrative that is told to them about themselves. Growing up I learned that my worth was based on my sexual attractiveness. So, I went with the flow.

Eventually, I decided that if people saw me as a sex object, I would be the best damn sex object. Period. What better way to prove my prowess than to pose for *Playboy*? Ever since hearing Van Halen's *"I'll Wait,"* it was my dream to be in magazines. But now I was an actress. I knew that posing for *Playboy* could be the kiss of death for my acting career, but it might also be a stepping stone. If I was going to take the risk, it was now or never because not many Playmates are published when they're in their late twenties.

Most girls who become centerfolds say they were inspired by finding their father's *Playboy* collection and admiring the beautiful women inside. My inspiration came during a rebirthing session, seemingly through spirit guides when I was in a deep meditative state. My confidence was boosted by having just been in Brunei, in the company of some centerfolds. But the seed had been planted almost a decade earlier when Eric said to me, as we lay in that bed surrounded by mirrors, "You've got one of those bodies like those girls in the magazines." But at the time I was nineteen and didn't have the nerve.

Later, when I found the courage, I realized that I had a connection that might be able to make it happen. My friend Peggy Trentini, whom I had known when she was married to Dana Strum from the band Slaughter, was a member of the Swedish Bikini Team, a group of five models who starred in a TV advertising campaign for Old Milwaukee beer. The girls in the "team" portrayed the stereotypical image of Scandinavian women as blond and busty, and they'd been featured on the cover of *Playboy.*

Peggy agreed that I could make it as a Playmate and excitedly offered to call the editor. She would collect a $1,000 finder's fee if I was selected. It was a long shot, as I heard their L.A. office alone received 5,000 submissions a month for each Playmate of the Month spot. I went all-out. I hired a personal trainer and worked hard, sometimes twice a day, to get into stellar shape. I put myself on a strict diet. Every day for four months, my breakfast was an egg and a piece of toast, lunch was tuna salad, and dinner was fish and vegetables. I was physically ready, but there was one final condition I imposed on myself. I was up for the Pauly Shore Fox sitcom, *Pauly,* as the hot girl with one line, competing against all of the perfect tens in Tinseltown. I said to myself, if I get the part, if I am impressive enough to get this part, then I am good enough to pose for *Playboy*. Sure enough, I got it. Now, I just had to pass the Playmate audition.

Even though the staff was expecting me, thanks to Peggy's referral, I still had to show up for the regular Thursday open call. I sat there nervously and almost decided it wasn't for me. It wasn't too late to back out. The girl who went in ahead of me looked like a streetwalker, while I was smartly dressed like a nice girl in a business suit. I'd read an interview with Jenny McCarthy who said that that's what she wore to her *Playboy* test. If it had worked for Jenny, maybe it would work for me. She was not only Playmate of the Year in 1994, she was hosting a show on MTV and on the cover of *Rolling Stone*. She was the "it" girl in 1997. She was a perfect example of why I decided posing for *Playboy* was worth the risk.

I got past my nerves, strode through the door into the studio, and put on a brave face. Everything else I had to take off. I was auditioning to be a centerfold, after all. I disrobed, and, just as I was taught to do as a teenager at the John Robert Powers Modeling School, I put one foot in front of the other and tilted my hip, the most flattering angle for the camera. I stood there in nothing but that brave face, and my high heels. I also brought my charm school skills into play, as I'd been told it was not only important to look good, but also be pleasant, since you'd be a brand ambassador for the company.

I had no qualms about nudity; it was natural to me, having been raised in a home with nude artwork all over the walls.

Billy White, the photographer who conducted the audition, made it all seem business as usual and put me at ease. He directed me to strike four classic poses. I sucked it in and stuck it out. The whole process took no more than ten minutes. Within a matter of days, I got a call from Marilyn Grabowski, *Playboy's* West Coast Photography Editor. For years, along with Hugh Hefner, of course, she decided which girls made it into the magazine. She had the power to make your career and open doors to clothing lines like Guess and TV shows like *Baywatch*. I was excited to hear from her personally. She'd just got back from a trip, she told me. My photo was on top of her pile. Could I come in for a full test shoot?

In less than a week, I was back at the studio for an entire day's shoot with the team that produces the magazine: photographer Arny Freytag, makeup artist Alexis Vogel, a stylist, an assistant, and Marilyn Grabowski, herself. The "A" team. It went so well Marilyn wouldn't let me leave, and the one-day test turned into an entire month of shooting both stills and videos. Even after a shoot like that, a lot of girls get shelved for a year or more. But *Playboy* put me in the first available issue.

Three months later, I was Miss June 1997. The photos and story ran under the headline "Carrie's New Life: Miss June's Fairy Tale is Anything but Typical." In it I talked about my belief in rebirthing, and they wrote, "More of a style of deep meditation than reincarnation, rebirthing is Carrie's way of expressing her spirituality." The article quoted me as saying, "There is a wholeness to life. I nursed Eric and sort of helped him out of this world, just as he had helped me grow up in the world. Now it's time to take the next step." That sounds lovely, but I wished I hadn't spoken about Eric to *Playboy*'s writer, because he also referred to me as a KISS "groupie," a derogatory slur for what had been a loving, intimate relationship. Reducing me to a groupie was an unfair slap in the face.

The June issue of *Playboy* features the Playmate of the Year and comes out on May 1st. An extra special day for me to make my Playmate debut, as it's my birthday. An added benefit to my being the June Playmate was that they hand out a copy of the issue to everyone attending the annual Playmate of the Year Luncheon. That event was my first time at the Playboy Mansion, one of the most famous residences in the world, a sprawling five-acre property in Holmby Hills, home to Hef's menagerie of flamingos, peacocks, parrots, and monkeys, and to the infamous Grotto, the steamy cave-like pool, reputedly the scene of many romantic and sexual escapades.

The Playmate of the Year Luncheon is an elegant, white-tablecloth event attended by past Playmates, decked out in floral summer dresses. The champagne flows freely and the food is out of this world. I wore a floor length lilac-colored skirt with a halter top, an outfit I'd bought in London. Bare midriff. I hardly had a chance to take it all in. Paparazzi were lined up, cameras flashing, calling my name. As the current Playmate of the Month, I was in demand, and I was determined to make an impact. I later discovered I'd made more of an impact, particularly on Hef, than I could ever have imagined. As I watched stunning Swede, Victoria Silvstedt, be crowned Playmate of the Year, I said to myself: Next year that's going to be me. It's every Playmate's goal.

Even before the June issue hit the newsstands, my life got glamourous. Monique St. Pierre, who was the Playmate of the Year 1979, was now working as a stylist for *Playboy.* She took a liking to me during my video shoot and invited me to a party thrown by billionaire Steve Bing. Every celebrity you'd ever dreamt of meeting was there. Mick Jagger introduced himself to me, although he didn't actually speak, as the man is a legend who needs no introduction. He simply walked over and stopped about six inches from my face. He jutted his neck and head out like a rooster, just as he does when he is performing. He repeated the rooster-move several times as he made direct eye contact with me, then he scanned the rest of me and abruptly walked away. I guess I wasn't his type, but I was excited to "meet" him anyway.

I met Michael Keaton at the foot of the spiral staircase. There was no question I was his type. It didn't take long before we broke away from the crowd and found ourselves smooching in a closet upstairs in one of the bedrooms. We were trapped in there for quite a while because Johnny Depp, Matt Damon and Ben Affleck came into the room. Out of respect for me, Michael didn't open the closet door as he knew the guys would assume the worst. He called me later that night from his home and asked me out. The next day we began dating. I was thrilled with my new life as a Playmate dating a movie star and was soon caught up in a whirlwind of posh, red-carpet events and public appearances, where people lined up to get my autograph. Overnight, it seemed, *Playboy* had made me a celebrity.

One person not so thrilled was my mother. Even though she knew full well that I'd posed for *Playboy*, when the issue came out, she decided not to speak to me, again. She claimed she almost got fired from her teaching job because of her daughter's brazen nakedness. This went on for six months until I wrote her a letter along the lines of, "You raised me to honor the nude body. Your artwork taught me that the nude body is a beautiful thing. My choice to pose for *Playboy* is an extension of you and all that your art influenced me to be." After that, once I'd made it all about her, she started speaking to me again.

Her mother, my Catholic, conservative Grandma Jo, was more tolerant. I'd sent her and my grandfather, my Papa, a signed copy of the magazine with a little note explaining I was afraid to tell them about it, so I thought it would be easier to show them. They called me roaring with laughter. Grandma Jo said, "I need to buy you some underwear. You're not wearing any panties."

Everyone else was supportive even though I was the last person you'd expect to become a Playmate. My friend Allison Burnett, a writer and director I'd worked with (who despite his name happens to be male) said, "You mean I've wanted to see you naked all this time and now all I have to do is pay $6.95 for it?" My friend Frank, an actor, told me I was helping people and didn't know it. I had no idea what he was talking about until he explained he earned extra cash at the sperm bank and my centerfold was in the private room where men came up with their deposits.

Being a Playmate is kind of like being a rock star. I was basically on tour. Besides photoshoots, I traveled the world signing autographs, appearing on TV shows, doing radio interviews, and hosting all kinds of events. I had a guest star role on Beverly Hills 90210, hosted a few shows on E! Entertainment TV, appeared in music videos and commercials, and became the Killian's Red beer girl. The red velvet ropes opened at clubs, men in bars gave me standing ovations. Suddenly, I was famous. I remember walking into the gym, and it dawned on me that everyone now knew how I groomed my pubic hair. Those were moments I hadn't anticipated.

Being a Playmate meant traveling the world getting paid to look smokin' hot, sign autographs, and pose for photos with fans. I made lots of new Playmate sisters, since we were usually traveling in pairs. Two of my favorite promotions were launching *Playboy T.V.* in Brazil with Layla Roberts (Miss October 1997) and hosting a party in Cannes with Jaime Bergman (Miss January 1999) during MIPCOM, which is the TV version of the film festival.

The only time I wasn't comfortable doing a *Playboy* promotion was when I was given away for a charity date in Washington, D.C. I'd gone to a radio station, and they gave me away to whoever called in with the correct answer to their trivia game. I was given a chaperone to make sure I was safe. Gary Rosenson, who is one of my best friends to this day, was assigned the job of babysitting me. A new hire in *Playboy's* marketing department, he was very conservative. I was the first Playmate he'd ever chaperoned and probably his worst nightmare. During dinner, the man who'd won the date told me that he heard voices inside his head telling him to kill his ex-wife. I quickly gave Gary the cue that it was time to bail and vowed never to do another job like that. The next day, as Gary drove me down Pennsylvania Avenue, I told him, "Gary, I'm flashing the White House." I stuck my body out the car window as far as I could and pulled my shirt and bra up, exposing my tits. I could see the security guys on the roof watching me through their binoculars, so they got a good eyeful. Gary's eyeballs got wide and his jaw dropped. I smiled in an effort to calm him down and said, "Oh, come on. I'm only Miss June once! Got to make the most of every moment." This was right before the Monica Lewinsky scandal hit the news. I had never thought of any long-term implications from being a Playmate, but now I was wondering if my breasts might get subpoenaed.

At the time I hoped my Playmate experience would be a stepping-stone to my acting career. I thought that the only people who would see my layout would be readers of the magazine and that over time my notoriety for being a nude model would fade away. This was just before the Internet took over our lives and made me eternally naked for all to see.

Don't get me wrong. I'm not complaining. Far from it. Becoming a Playmate was the springboard to so much more, and it all happened so fast. It was, indeed, a new life, accurately predicted in the title of my Playmate Pictorial, "Carrie's New Life." Celebrities and billionaires called *Playboy's* publicity department wanting to get together with me. Casting directors were requesting my availability for projects. People knew who I was, and they were pursuing me. It felt great. I didn't have time to be sad anymore. I was too busy being Miss June.

*****

Soon after my *Playboy* issue was released, I was having dinner with my friend Dennis, a tour manager, at Casa Vega, a rocker hangout in the Valley. I complained to him about Michael Keaton, whom I'd been dating for about three months. He took me out to dinner only once a week and that wasn't enough of a relationship for me. He didn't seem interested in getting serious. All he talked about was wanting to have a threesome and it got on my nerves.

"Why don't you let me set you up with Enrique Iglesias?" suggested Dennis.

Enrique was already a big star in Latin America, but wasn't well known in the U.S. The name didn't mean anything to me.

"I don't want to go out with some dude that doesn't speak English," I told him.

Dennis's response was to get up from the table and get a T-shirt from his car. On the front was a print of Enrique. That changed everything. I took one look at his handsome face and said, "Okay. I'll meet him."

Enrique was playing at the Honda Center in Orange County, so a girlfriend and I went down to see him and booked a hotel room where the band was staying. We met him briefly backstage before the show. During his performance, I was totally taken aback when the only words he spoke in English were, "This song is dedicated to a beautiful girl I met tonight." And he pointed at me.

I melted.

At the time, Enrique sang only in Spanish, but he said that line in English *for me*. That night we ended up in the hotel's Jacuzzi looking up at the stars and talking. He was raised in Miami and spoke perfect English. He was only twenty-two. And I was twenty-eight. Normally, I wasn't into younger guys, but he became the exception. It was the beginning of a relationship that lasted for three years. Not an exclusive one, but a special friendship with benefits.

Our lifestyles fit. After Orange County, we met the following week in Chicago. He had a show there, and I was shooting a catalog at the *Playboy* headquarters. We often found ourselves in the same cities, especially Miami where he lived, and, of course, L.A. We liked and respected each other. We were passionate. We trusted each other. But I was seeing other guys, and I'm sure he was seeing other girls. It was what it was. It was just fun.

When Enrique recorded *"Bailamos,"* his debut single in the English-language market, I was in the studio giving him feedback. One memorable night, as we lay in his room at the Four Seasons in LA, he put his earbuds in my ears and played the final version. I knew it would be a huge hit and, sure enough, it raced to number one on the Billboard Hot 100. Enrique was following in the footsteps of his famous father, Julio Iglesias, but he never talked much about him. I sensed they weren't close. Enrique was determined to make it on his own two feet, which he did.

One of the things I loved about Enrique, believe it or not, was his taste in music. He liked all the same 80s rock that I did. We used to play name that tune. He'd sing "...every cowboy sings his same sad, sad song," and I'd say "Poison." He'd sing "...like a tramp, like a video vamp," and I'd guess "Def Leppard." I thought it was cute when he told me he'd hung my poster (my centerfold) on his wall before we met. I'm not sure I should have believed him, but I did. I also believed him when he said he'd handle my Mexican gardener since I couldn't speak Spanish and my gardener didn't speak English. Later, I discovered it was Enrique's manager who was making the calls to my gardener. It was a little white lie that he personally called the gardener. In the big picture, he got the job done, and I appreciated it.

It worked between us as long as it did because we were both on the road. Neither of us was looking for a serious relationship. We just had fun when we were together. I'd set my girlfriends up with his buddies Andre and Carlos when they were in town. It was all very casual. We are both stubborn Tauruses, so we would argue but not fight. It was more of a playful banter. We were extremely attracted to each other. We were definitely "in like," but not in love.

It came to an end at a *Playboy* Super Bowl party in Atlanta in 2000. Enrique was there to perform at half time along with Christina Aguilera. We'd talked on the phone and made plans to meet after the party. But when I got to the *Playboy* party, he was there. On my turf. He barely acknowledged me and, as the night went on, flirted outrageously with actress Shannon Elizabeth and some of the other Playmates. I'd found out he'd given his phone number to Playmate Brooke Richards. I was pissed. Sure, we weren't exclusive to each other, but his behavior was disrespectful. I left, and the next day we argued on the phone for two hours. He screamed at me, "This is why I don't want a girlfriend!" That was that. The relationship had run its course.

*****

About six months after my issue came out, I was at Barfly, a trendy spot on Sunset, when Hef's doctor, Mark Saginor, came over to say hello and invited me to join him and Hef at a table in the corner. I was surprised Hef was there. Everyone knew he never went out. We chatted for a while, and he told me that his wife, Kimberly, was going to be furious if she heard we'd been in the same restaurant together. I was speechless. Racing through my head was the thought, "Oh, Jesus. His wife's going to hate me. I'm definitely not going to get Playmate of the Year." I was even more shocked when he said her accusations went back six months.

How could that be? What had I done? I'd only been to the Playboy Mansion twice: once for the Playmate of the Year Luncheon and once for a Sunday dinner at the invitation of Marilyn Grabowski when I'd met Mr. & Mrs. Hefner. I'd been warned to always say hello to Kimberly first if you didn't want to get on her bad side. I'd been really nervous and had gone out of my way to be polite and respectful. Kimberly, who had been Playmate of the Year in 1989, showed no signs of jealousy or animosity. She was lovely.

"Why would she accuse me of anything?" I asked him.

"Well, the problem is, I want the accusations to be true," he said.

My jaw hit the floor. The revelation was overwhelming. I couldn't believe it! Hef went on to say he'd been so taken with me at the Playmate of the Year Luncheon that he couldn't handle it; he'd had to go inside and watch me through his bedroom window on the second story of the Playboy Mansion. I never did find out why Kimberly would accuse him of having an affair with me. Perhaps she caught him staring at me from the window? Maybe he was spending too much time looking at my photos or videos? I don't know. She had no reason to be threatened by me. Hef told me he'd been faithful to her for the entire decade they'd been married.

The next day, however, he called and asked me out.

"I'm sorry," I said. "I can't. You're married."

The last thing I needed was his wife on the warpath and my chances of becoming Playmate of the Year ruined. About a week later, he called and asked me out again. I gave him the same answer.

"Well, we've split up," he revealed. "There will be an official announcement in the press this Friday."

The disclosure destroyed my excuse. I had no idea his marriage was unraveling. I had no choice other than to say yes, but I wasn't going to go alone. I asked if my sister's funny, chubby, and slightly obnoxious friend, Tina LaRue, could join us. She was fresh out of graduate school and staying with me. He graciously agreed, but when his limo picked us up, we brought her cat along, too. The cat, a calico, was entertained by Hef's bodyguards, Kent Moyer and Gary Miller, while we had dinner at Dan Tana's and then went to the House of Blues to hear live music and meet up with some of Hef's friends.

Tina and I went out with Hef often. Sometimes Hef's friend Richard Bann came along, and sometimes it was just the two of us. Hef was humble and full of life. It was easy to forget he was a legend. He seemed especially human when he would have the limo pull over at gas stations to use the restroom. It was easy to overlook the age difference until he told me that he had not driven a car since 1969 (the year I was born) or until he turned on his 1940s music. Big band stuff. I was only twenty-eight, I wasn't interested. But I adored him. He opened up and talked about life and his divorce. I supported him emotionally but made it perfectly clear I didn't want to date him.

I didn't want to be a reflection of Hugh Hefner or anyone else for that matter. I wanted to be my own person, independent and self-sufficient. I'd been the girlfriend of KISS's drummer for four years, and I knew what it was like to be in a celebrity's shadow. I've always been strong-willed, always done things my way, and I wasn't going to have that taken away from me. Hef asked me if our age difference was what was holding me back. I lied, and said no. Hef's personal secretary, Mary O'Connor, told me Hef loved me for my honesty and that there were not many girls who turned him down. I didn't deserve the compliment, but I was unique in my perspective. Sometimes things are better left unsaid. After enduring the pain of losing Eric, it was hard enough to open my heart again, never mind let myself fall in love with someone whom I was almost certainly going to outlive.

A few months later, I was in my paternal grandmother's hospice room in Albany, New York. While she slept, I was watching TV. One of the tabloid shows came on, *Entertainment Tonight* or *Access Hollywood,* I can't remember which, when my photo flashed on the screen. The headline was "Up next, the younger Playmate who stole Hef's heart." Thank God my grandmother was asleep. She'd been a strict Irish Catholic her entire life. She had no idea I had posed nude. She would have pulled the I.V. out of her arm and slapped me upside the head if she'd been coherent. The TV reporter quoted "insiders" who said I'd been seen at the mansion with Hugh Hefner. Bullshit. I'd only been there twice and never alone with him. My beloved grandmother died that day. Hef sent flowers to her funeral, but instead of being addressed to Mrs. Pittz, they were sent to Mrs. Tittz. My grandmother would roll over in her grave if she knew Hugh Hefner sent flowers to her funeral. Never mind the terrible Freudian slip! But it gave us all comic relief on a painful day.

The flowers were a thoughtful gesture, but I was still fuming about the tabloid stories. As soon as I got back to L.A., I called the Playboy offices and told them in no uncertain terms I wouldn't do any more promotions and not to bother inviting me to any parties. I was done. I still had the small-town nice girl mindset. Embarrassed by all the publicity, I felt that everyone was gossiping about me. At that point in time, I still cared what people thought of me. I was mortified. Now my name was all over national TV labeled as Hugh Hefner's homewrecker. I got a call from Mary O'Connor, mother hen to all the Playmates, a strong woman who ran Hef's life with purpose and precision. She gave me a good talking to and said there was a party that night, and I needed to get my ass up there with my head held high. Which I did. I later figured out, when I became wise to the ways of the P.R. machine, that the "Younger Playmate Who Stole Hef's Heart" story had been planted by his people. It wouldn't be good for his image or the Playboy brand to look like he was dumped by his gorgeous young wife. Some girls would have gone along with it on the basis that any publicity is good publicity, but I didn't see things that way. One of my friends on the PR staff, Donna, kept trying to convince me, 'you *should* go out with him, you and I could run the company!' But that wasn't on my agenda.

*****

I was hot favorite to be Playmate of the Year for 1998, until I was the victim of a series of poison pen letters. Someone wrote to *Playboy* threatening that if I got the title, they'd expose the fact that I'd been in the Brunei harem. They also alleged I'd been working as a hooker doing "in call." This set off a huge investigation. Playboy executives showed me the letters. *Do you recognize the handwriting? Do you have any enemies? Who would do this to you?* They bombarded me with questions. I felt like I was a defendant in a court of law. I had to write a twelve-page memo, detailing the daily routine in Brunei.

I didn't know what "in-call" was. Neither did Marilyn, the photo editor. They had to explain it was when a client visits a prostitute's home. So ridiculous. Things got more ridiculous when *Playboy* called to tell me that someone had informed them that I'd hooked on a cruise ship sailing around Eastern Europe. I'd gone on the trip, on the Queen Elizabeth, with my friend Maria in place of her husband when they were splitting up. We were the only two single girls on the ship, besides some of the crew. All of the other passengers were elderly couples. We weren't getting into bed with anyone. Far from it. Our time was spent on cultural group tours walking around churches and museums with a bunch of senior citizens. I had to write another memo, outlining every boring thing we did the whole time we were on the cruise. I got really agitated having to defend myself like this.

Hugh Hefner and I put two and two together and worked out who was behind the sabotage. When I told Hef that a girl (I'll call her "Missy") had called Maria's husband and told him the same crap about the cruise, he said, "Well, that explains it." Turns out Missy was the one who had told Hef's friend the story about Maria and me hooking on the ship. She'd been a makeup artist at Maria's wedding and that was the only time I had ever met her. I was Maid of Honor and Tommy Thayer, (who would later become guitarist for KISS), was Best Man. Hef told me that she had been turned down as a Playmate thirteen times. She'd made it into *Playboy's* newsstand special, *The Book of Lingerie*, though, so in her mind she was a celebrity. I'd bumped into her once at the Playboy Mansion and I said, "Oh, hey, I know you. You're the makeup artist." I wasn't trying to offend her, that's how I knew her, but she took it as an insult. The irony is that she got to go to Brunei because of me. Maria had sent me her photos, and I'd passed them on to the guy in charge. I was responsible for her making a lot of money and now she was tattling to *Playboy* to try and

Carrie with Hugh Hefner
(top, and bottom two photos);
and with Playmates Tiffany
Fallon and Renee Tenison
(photo at right).

destroy my chances of being Playmate of the Year. That's the thanks I got. On top of all this, Missy was now dating Eric Singer, the drummer who'd replaced Eric Carr in KISS. Irony upon irony. It wasn't enough for her to take my place in the KISS family, she wanted to ruin my *Playboy* career out of sheer jealousy. But karma got her: Hef banned Missy from the mansion and from ever appearing again in any *Playboy* publication.

*****

One day not long afterwards, I got a call from Hef that he needed to talk to me. He wanted to come over to my place, which was unusual. I thought perhaps he wanted to take me out somewhere. Or perhaps he expected me to sleep with him to secure the Playmate of the Year title. As quickly as that thought entered my head, I erased it. I didn't really think he'd pull something like that. We'd developed a friendship and that wasn't the Hugh Hefner I knew. We didn't go out that night. We didn't get any further than my driveway. Sitting in the back of his stretch limo he broke the news.

"Darling, I have decided we cannot have you as our Playmate of the Year."

After all the drama with the editors, the lawyers and the P.R. people, I knew why. Brunei. The poison pen writer had won. Defeated, I slumped over, my head in his lap, bawling my eyes out. When I looked up, Hef was teary-eyed, and said, "Now I feel like I'm going to cry."

"Why?" I asked, puzzled.

"Because I'm the one who did this to you."

"Then why do it?"

I wanted to know.

Gently, Hef said, "You won't understand this now. But you will later. I'm doing it to protect you."

Hef was right. Although the decision had largely been made to protect the Playboy brand, I realized I would have been the focus of some nasty publicity. The only time in the history of Playboy that the Playmate of the Year issue was July, not June, was because of me and the Brunei scandal.

During the time he was married to Kimberly, Hef was a recluse. The famous mansion parties ceased as he embraced family life. When he was going through his divorce with Kimberly, he told me how much he appreciated me supporting him through that rough time, so I invited him to my 1997 Christmas party knowing that he would appreciate the gesture. But I didn't think he'd accept. He'd barely been seen in public in a decade, so when he walked in my front door, crickets! Don Henley was sitting on a barstool in my kitchen, David Schwimmer was in my living room telling jokes to giggling Playmates, but all went silent when Hef walked in. It was like seeing a ghost. People couldn't believe their eyes. It was great having him there. He graciously took photos with anyone who asked, including me. We posed for photos in front of my framed centerfold that hung on my powder room wall. Before cell phones had the capability of taking photos, Hef was enamored with those cardboard disposable cameras, so he always had plenty of extras for his entourage.

*****

After his separation from Kimberly, Hef would resurrect the wildly elaborate parties that the mansion was famous for, and I was often at them. I saw a lot of celebrities at those parties. One image that is etched in my memory is Brian Austin Green standing naked in the waterfall. I once witnessed an orgy in the grotto, but I didn't get close enough to recognize anyone involved. My favorite celebrity regular at the mansion parties was Leonardo DiCaprio. He was really down to earth, and we had a lot of mutual friends. After the mansion parties shut down, he'd invite some of us over to his house. One night three or four other Playmates and Paris Hilton (before she was famous) were all there at Leo's, and we all changed out of our clothes and into his white T-shirts and boxers so we could go in his Jacuzzi. We were playing truth or dare. Leo's dare was for me to kiss Paris, so she and I jumped out of the water, I gave her a quick, tiny peck, and that was it. We jumped back in. It was all in good fun.

Another night a group of us ended up at my house after a mansion party, and Leo was confiding in me about his relationship with Giselle, the supermodel who later married Tom Brady. I gave him some good advice, and I gave him a book called *How to Make a Girl Squirt* that had been part of a kinky holiday gift basket from my friend Marc Bell who owned Penthouse Magazine at the time. I suggested that he read it and use the techniques on Giselle. It was one of those half-joking late-night conversations. We had a brother and sister kind of energy, but after that, he and Giselle got really serious. I'd tease him that it was all thanks to me.

It was around this time that Hef had three girlfriends, Brande and twin sisters Mandy and Sandy, and even though they were his "dates," he'd follow me around the parties and say, "Carrie, when you're ready for a serious relationship, you let me know." I let him down easy. Jokingly, I said, "But Hef, I feel inadequate. I don't have a Terry and a Sherry to take with me. You'd be getting a bum deal compared to the one you have now." One night I was high on ecstasy when he yet again suggested a serious relationship. I was so out of my brain, I declared, "I'm ready. I love you, Hef. I'm ready." The next morning, I woke up back at home and thought, "Oh, fuck. What did I say? Now he's gonna call me. What am I going to do?" Sure enough, he called, and I invited him over. I filled a crystal ice bucket and served Jack Daniels and Diet Pepsi. That was all Hef ever drank, besides milk. I prepared a nice rejection speech and was ready for him to be mad at me.

"I have a confession to make," I declared, as he nursed his drink. "The other night when I told you I loved you and I was ready I was high on ecstasy."

"Well, where's the ecstasy now?" he laughed.

It was a big, genuine belly laugh. He thought it was funny. I also laughed, with relief. Then he told me Barbi Benton had just visited the mansion and brought him some reefer. He called marijuana "reefer," like old hippies did. Barbi had been the love of Hef's life for nine years back in the '70s. "You laugh like Barbi; your voice sounds just like Barbi's did... you like to travel just like Barbi did... you love animals like Barbi." I wanted to scream, "I am not Barbi!" But the words wouldn't come out. I was too high. The message my brain was sending to my voice malfunctioned.

I can't handle pot. One hit and I become paralyzed. I began to hallucinate. It seemed like I was shifting from being present in my living room to floating out of this world on a spaceship with alien doctors and nurses poking and prodding me. My head swirled in waves backwards and forwards. I couldn't move. I couldn't feel my body. My arms and legs wouldn't obey when my brain told them to move. I was trippin,' slurring my words: "I'm shorry. I'm shorry." I was aware enough to be paranoid that he thought I was pretending so I didn't have to sleep with him. But he was the perfect gentleman. He helped me get up from the couch and even though he was seventy-two or seventy-three, half-carried me to bed and tucked me in. For a while Hef continued to pursue me romantically, but eventually settled for what became a wonderful twenty-year friendship. Years later Hef's bodyguard, Kent Moyer, told me I was oblivious as to how much Hef was in love with me.

It wasn't unusual for Hef to let the Playmates bring their significant others, parents, or siblings to the Playboy Mansion. Easter was the one event a year to which the Playmates' children were invited. Hef would host a big Easter

Egg Hunt and give prizes out. I took my son Jaxon for the first time at Easter when he was just two months old. But just a few years later he became a regular. When Jaxon was little, I'd often go up to the mansion on Friday or Sunday nights for dinner and a movie while Jaxon stayed home with a babysitter. One night, sitting at the head of his regal mahogany dining table, Hef said to me, "Why don't you bring Jaxon up to see the animals?" It was so sweet. It was almost like he was pleading with me. So, I made the appointment with his secretary and assumed I would show Jaxon around. As a Playmate I was paid to give tours to corporate groups and VIP visitors. But Hef himself walked us around the entire property, proudly showing Jaxon all the monkeys, peacocks, rabbits, and reptiles. The next day, I got a call from Hef's personal secretary Mary telling me that I no longer needed to call ahead. Jaxon and I were on Hef's permanent guest list. We could come and go as we pleased on weekends for dinner and movies.

I think Hef had an especially big heart when it came to me and included us because I was a young single mom who didn't have any family in L.A. Either that, or he really did mean it when he said he loved me.

Jaxon and I spent many memorable Christmases and Thanksgivings at the mansion. Of course, he was not permitted on the wilder nights, like the lingerie/sleep-wear attire required theme parties such as Midsummer Night's Dream or Halloween. But one Halloween when my son was eight years old, and Hef had a big scary house built for an adult party that director and horror enthusiast Rich Correll created. He invited Jaxon to experience it the day before. And again, he walked us through the property, personally showing us all the Halloween decorations. My son was terrified in the scary house and started crying. So, they shut down all the electronic noises and dismissed the live performers and walked my son through while it was quiet to comfort him.

Often, Hef would beckon the photographers over because he wanted a photo with Jaxon. During dinners, Jaxon liked to help the staff bus the tables. It was so cute. When he was six or seven, we were standing by the patio one day and he asked, "Mommy, what is a Playmate, anyway?"

How was I going to explain that?

I said, "Well, it's a model but she has her clothes off."

He said, "But you wear your underwear, right?"

I said, "Yes, of course."

It wasn't a complete lie. They might have been hanging from a toe or around my ankles. Well, they're somewhere in most of my *Playboy* pictorials, right?

There was only one other child in the last two decades of Hef's life that he welcomed into his home like Jaxon, and that was Trease, daughter of Victoria Fuller, Miss January 1996, who was Mary O'Connor's close friend. We were family. Even though we lived only a ten-minute drive away, we called the mansion "our home away from home." My son thought of Hef as a father figure and felt special when he received attention from the legend. We always felt loved while we were surrounded by the magic of the Playboy Mansion. It was a place where we were accepted and adored.

Sometimes when I broke up with jerky boyfriends, I would wonder if I should have given it a chance with Hef. I'll never know if he would have given up the other women in his life, but that was the deal breaker for me. I am a one-on-one kind of woman. I know what went on upstairs in his bedroom when he had multiple girlfriends, and I don't judge anybody, but group sex never appealed to me. Hef never asked me to be a part of that anyway.

Every weekend Hef hosted "Fun-in-the-Sun Day." He and his closest friends would play backgammon poolside, while babes in bikinis were swimming and sunbathing. After spending the early part of a sunny Sunday afternoon attending a friend's baby shower at the Beverly Hills Hotel, I decided to pop by the Mansion, since it was on my way home. I was sitting with the men, who had their very serious game faces on. I was bored with their silence. I was also uncomfortably hot. So, I made an announcement:

"I'm overdressed!"

I unbuttoned my blouse and whipped off my bra, fully aware that Hef's personal photographer was standing right there. It provoked an impromptu topless photoshoot with me on Hef's lap. He loved it! Everyone was laughing so hard, especially Hef.

On August 31, 2009 I received some of the photos and a letter of appreciation. Hef wrote, "Dear Carrie, What a lovely pair! You and I, that is. Thanks for the memories (and mammaries as well). See you soon. Hopefully, topless. Much love, Hef."

Now that I think about it, maybe it wasn't just my honesty that he loved me for. We shared a sense of humor, and a fearless spirit.

I have to say, though, it *was* a little weird, when Hef had the seven girlfriends who each got an allowance of $1,000 a week. When you think about it, it's another irony. I lost the Playmate of the Year title because someone threatened to expose my time in the harem in Brunei. But Hef had a harem of his own. It's interesting that his ex-girlfriend Holly Madison wrote a book trashing him for not acknowledging her depression, because I recall visiting him one afternoon to console him after their break-up. We were sitting alone in his informal dining room while he told me that she was depressed, and he was clearly very concerned about her.

*****

Sometimes the Playmates partied like rock stars and other times we worked alongside them. I was really excited when I got the call to host an all-day 80s rock festival in Albuquerque, New Mexico. The show's promoter hired me and Kalin Olson, Miss August 1997, to kick off the concert, driving us around in an open convertible while we threw into the crowd copies of *Playboy,* the ones in which we were featured. Kalin was a lot younger than I; she was twenty-two, I was twenty-eight. She didn't grow up in the 80s, so she didn't appreciate the music like I did. I think she got bored and went back to the hotel early. But I was in my element.

The show featured L.A. Guns, Warrant, and Quiet Riot. I sat on the side of the stage watching Rudy Sarzo tear it up on bass while I swigged shots of Jack Daniels and Tequila with Tracii Guns and threw more copies of my *Playboy* issue to the screaming fans. After the show, some of the guys and I decided to go to a dive bar. Standing in my way was this little old man who'd been assigned as my chaperone. Poor guy, he tried to tell me I had to go back to the hotel. I didn't hire him, but I fired him. In the middle of the sidewalk, in front of all the guys. At the bar some of the guys jammed, and we drank shots, and toasted Eric's memory.

Afterwards, we went to Warrant's hotel to party some more. I ended up in bassist Jerry Dixon's room. We didn't hook up, but we did brush each other's teeth. I don't know why, we were just drunk and silly. When I decided to leave, I realized I didn't know where I was staying. I was traveling so much it wasn't unusual to forget my room number, but this time I couldn't even remember which hotel I'd been checked into. I had the room key, but it was useless, just a white plastic card. Jerry and I went to the front desk with our minty fresh breath, grabbed the Yellow Pages and called every hotel in Albuquerque, asking for Carrie Stevens until we found where I was staying. I got to my room by 5:00 a.m. but missed my 7:00 a.m. flight.

*****

One day Jeanie from the P.R. department phoned to tell me that Bret Michaels had been in touch to say he'd met me at a club the night before and had lost my phone number.

"I stayed in last night," I told her, suggesting it must have been another Playmate. "Maybe it was Carrie Westcott or Kerri Kendall?"

"No, he definitely said Carrie Stevens."

I told her to forget about it. I was amused and flattered, but not interested. I forgot the whole thing until the day my hair stylist handed me an autographed Poison CD and a signed 8 x 10 glossy from Bret. Apparently, when she told him she did my hair he got all excited. The next time I went to the salon I reciprocated and gave her one of my signed *Playboy* magazines to pass on to him. Then he got my number from her.

I was reluctant to meet with him. I'd moved away from the rock scene and had no intention of revisiting it. But Bret was persuasive and on May 20, 2000 I agreed to see him for drinks at Casa Vega. I'd often been there. One time when I was on a date with Michael Keaton, they gave our table away to Slash.

Bret was charming, fun to be with, and really cute. Many margaritas later, we were laughing and holding hands when some girl stormed up and started angrily screaming at him, my cue to quickly excuse myself and go to the bathroom. When I got back to the table, the angry girl had gone. Bret, having already paid the check, offered to give me a ride home. At my place I invited him inside and had barely closed the door before he started kissing me. We ended up in my bedroom, where he enthusiastically went down on me, until we were interrupted by his ringing phone. He couldn't finish what he started. He had to rush to the hospital. It turned out that the angry girl at Casa Vega was the best friend of his girlfriend, who was in the hospital, in labor. As I was seeing him out, Playmate of the Year Victoria Silvstedt, who'd become my best friend, was knocking on my front door. She was on the cover of the June 1997 issue that I had autographed for him. Bad time to have to leave, Bret.

*****

One afternoon I was hired along with about ten other Playmates to host a premier at the mansion for a film called *Orgasmo*. It was an ordinary assignment except that Metallica, one of my all-time favorite bands, performed. After the show, the guys invited some of us to have drinks at their hotel, the Sunset Marquis in West Hollywood. Lenora, wife of Gary Corbett, KISS's offstage keyboard player, was visiting me from NYC with her friend Roberta. The three of us joined the band at the hotel bar. Marilyn Manson and Twiggy Ramirez were there. I was sitting on a sofa and Lars Ulrich, Metallica's drummer, was sitting on the arm, chatting me up, and smiling like a man does when he's interested in you. Suddenly he got up, walked across the room and started making out with Metallica's lead guitarist, Kirk Hammett. Roberta, Lenora, and I were freaked out. What a buzzkill. As we got up and left, the band's manager chased after us apologizing for their behavior. He said that they just liked to shock people. Well, it worked. I still love their music, regardless.

*****

Playboy was a stepping-stone, a gateway to my dreams and aspirations. But like my father always told me, "Don't get too excited or too disappointed about anything. The thing you think is the most exciting thing that's ever happened to you could turn into the worst thing that ever happened, and the thing you think is the worst could turn out to be the best." Dad was right. One of the most exciting things was when I was chosen for a coveted *Rolling Stone* cover. But I almost forgot all about it. I must have blocked it out of my head until I read Rose McGowan's account of her *Rolling Stone* cover shoot when she appeared ass cheek to ass cheek with Rosario Dawson, both of them wearing nothing but strings of bullets.

The photoshoot, said Rose, was the point where she snapped out of her "Hollywood brainwashing." She wrote, "I realized I was being photographed by a gay male who was imagining me as what he thinks a straight man wants to fuck. I knew I had to do something about what I'd let my life become." Well, I would have been thrilled to appear on the cover of *Rolling Stone* looking as gorgeous as Rose did. I'd have loved to trade places with her.

In 1999 my dear friend and modeling agent Kurt Clements called with the thrilling news I'd been chosen for a *Rolling Stone* cover with Nine Inch Nails, and the photographer would be the renowned Mark Seliger. I was beyond excited. I was a huge Nine Inch Nails fan. And Mark

Seliger was Rolling Stone's photographer of choice. It all started well. When I got to the set in Los Feliz everything was very professional. I was immediately led into the hair and makeup trailer and told to change out of my clothes into a white terry cloth robe. Nothing unusual there, either, as you often strip off to avoid getting lines on your body from wearing tight clothes. Then we were summoned to the set to block the scene.

Basically, the set was a pit. A hole in the ground which used to be the basement of a house before it burned down. Standing in the pit, the band and I were told the concept for the shoot. I was to lie naked in the dirt and play dead while the guys stood around my lifeless, dirty body, looking cool and unfazed. I was horrified. The band looked just as horrified. One of them went over to their publicist, and I'm sure he was refusing to do it. I didn't wait to find out. The only thing worse than being told to get naked and die in the dirt would have been the humiliation of doing it. I snuck off set, rushed to my trailer, got dressed, jumped into my car, and drove away as fast as I could. Fuck *Rolling Stone*. I called my agent in tears. He'd had no idea that was going to be the concept. He said leaving the set was the right thing to do.

The next day the photographer sent me a big flower arrangement with a card of apology and the promise of a good job soon. Of course, it never happened. No doubt Rose McGowan was objectified by wearing nothing but bullets for her *Rolling Stone* cover. But I'd like to think she understands why I would have traded places with her any day.

I was just a small-time actress and a centerfold, so did that make it okay to treat me as if I weren't a human being? Lie down in the dirt, naked, play dead, and be unrecognizable? A nameless, faceless, dirty dead girl? It was a demeaning and disturbing experience.

Early in my *Playboy* career, not long after I was Miss June, I had a different kind of encounter with world-famous photographer Helmut Newton, who was doing a pictorial for the magazine. Pubic bush was out, and landing strips were in. Helmut, however, didn't appreciate my lack of pubic hair and asked the stylist to create a little toupee for my mound. I was appalled, so I quickly pivoted my hips to show less crotch and asked, "How about this?" He liked the pose and dropped the idea of the toupee. Thank God. I didn't want the world to think I had a big bush. Those were out of style. It was all about the landing strip.

*****

The year after I became a Playmate, I got cast in a show on the FX cable network, playing a centerfold. In one scene I had to pose nude for a photoshoot except, as it was for TV, I wasn't really nude. I had a feather boa and pasties and a nude-colored thong to cover the bits the television audience wasn't allowed to see. When we broke for lunch, the director asked me to stay behind. Alone, on set, he instructed me to do the scene again, but without the feather boa and pasties. I was twenty-nine, and nobody's fool. "I'm sure the Screen Actors Guild would be very interested in why a director would dismiss the crew and ask an actress to perform a nude scene especially on television," I told him. "Shall I call them now?"

"Scratch that," he hastily responded. "My apologies. Enjoy your lunch."

This was the first time I stood up to a creep in the motion picture industry. What's interesting is that after I posed for *Playboy,* I felt strong enough to stand up to predators. There was something about becoming a Playmate (which was like being stamped "Grade A Meat") that made me feel like an equal to the men whom I had previously let intimidate me. For the longest time, I didn't even realize how wrong it was when directors, producers, and others in and out of the industry pushed themselves on me. Sometimes it was physical, sometimes verbal, suggestive or demeaning comments. I got angry at myself for not having the backbone to handle it. My self-esteem was so low that I froze, reverting back to childhood when I felt small, invisible and worthless. I actually blamed myself instead of the predators. I should have been infuriated, but instead I sank into a dark, hopeless state.

After I became a Playmate, I felt empowered. I had an iconic brand behind me. I was protected by Hef and his security staff. I know that the corporate offices had my back. For example, there was a cooking competition show on television, starring a celebrity chef who is notorious for being an asshole. When I told *Playboy* that he had sexually harassed me, James Gonis, who was head of the Playmate promotions department, called the show's production company and told them that they would no longer send any

Playmate talent for their projects. That's power. In complete contrast, I never had a problem on Playboy sets. The crew was so used to seeing naked women every day, they yawned when I walked by butt naked. But when I was on a movie or mainstream TV set in a mini skirt, the guys were whistling and cat calling me, and I was expected to ignore it.

*****

I seemed to do everything in reverse. Most girls posed for *Playboy* and then went to Brunei. Most girls posed for *Playboy* and then dated rock stars. Most girls were broke when they did *Playboy*. There weren't many, like me, who owned their own home before becoming Playmate of the Month. All of this threw Hef for a loop when he developed romantic feelings for me. He was used to dangling a *Playboy* pictorial and the opportunity to live in the Playboy Mansion. I'd already done my centerfold. I already had my own house just a few miles down the road. I couldn't be bought. I had what's known as "fuck-you money."

Matt LeBlanc was the first person I ever heard use the term. Soon after I got back from Brunei, I went to see his new house. With some apprehension I confessed where I'd been the previous six months. His response, with a sly smile, was, "Now you've got fuck-you money." I did, and it felt great. But money can't buy the amazing experience of being a Playmate. I have Hef to thank for that. I loved him very much and always will. Being a Playmate afforded me an extraordinary life. I became an expert in the art of using my looks for gain and prosperity, and I enjoyed all of the perks that went along with it, which is why I rarely complain about being objectified.

I take full responsibility for how I used those opportunities. Some I am proud of and others not, but I can never regret posing for *Playboy*. Because of my Playmate status, I have a place in history. Anytime you have visibility, it gives you a platform to use your voice. That's exactly what I am doing by writing this book. I wouldn't be able to do it without all of the experiences I gained from being a part of the *Playboy* legacy.

Chapter 7

Don't Have an Affair with a Married Man

The casting director took one look at me and shook her head. I'd barely got inside her office, and I was dismissed.

"Oh, no!" she exclaimed. "You're way too beautiful for these roles. If I bring you in to audition, the producers will just laugh at me."

I flashed back to 8th grade biology class and Mrs. Marshall's remarks about my looks. I was mortified, not at all flattered to be called beautiful. Again, it was a case of pretty girls should be seen and not heard. All I wanted to do was audition, but I wasn't even given the dignity of opening my mouth. I walked out of her office, head hung low, and cried all the way home. I'd spent the entire weekend learning lines for roles in two different TV series that she was casting. Instead of going out with friends, I'd stayed home rehearsing, only to be abruptly rejected. It didn't make sense. I got the audition because my agent submitted my headshot, so obviously the casting director knew what I looked like. If she didn't want my type for the role, then why waste my time? I was pissed and in tears. It was Monday morning, and my week was off to a lousy start.

Then I got a call from James Gonis at the *Playboy* offices. Would I like to do a promotion, hosting a party for the Broncos in Miami? It was sponsored by EAS Sports, the big sports nutrition company, and would pay $3,000 a day for two days. I had the choice to fly there either commercially or on a private jet.

"The Broncos," I asked, "Isn't that a hockey team?"

I'm sure James was rolling his eyeballs at the other end of the line, but he patiently explained, "No. It's a football team. It's the Super Bowl."

Okay, I thought. Things are looking up. I'm not too beautiful for the Super Bowl. I'm not too beautiful for a private jet either. Why would I choose to fly commercial? I knew nothing about football, obviously. My high school was too small to have a football team, so I didn't grow up with the sport. I'd never even seen a game in my life, at any level. My first experience of a game would be Super Bowl XXXIII, January 31, 1999, between the Denver Broncos, the defending champions, and the Atlanta Falcons.

I was flown by private jet from L.A. to Miami with a brief stopover in Denver to pick up Bill Phillips, owner of EAS, and his entourage. In Miami we were whisked off to a mansion on Star Island, an exclusive, private island in Biscayne Bay that holds just a few dozen multi-multi-million-dollar homes. I'd been given an option to stay in a hotel or at the mansion. Well, which would you choose? This was party central. I may not have known anything about football, but I knew a good time when I saw one coming.

Later that night Bill took all of us to The Dollhouse, a strip joint in Fort Lauderdale. He said we were going to meet up with the "Quarterback Club." I didn't really know what that meant, but it was exactly what it sounded like. A bunch of quarterbacks getting lap dances in a private room. When the night was over, we all piled into the stretch limo to drop off the quarterbacks at their hotel before heading back to the Star Island mansion. I was sandwiched between Bubby Brister and Brian Griese. Bubby was harassing me. Just a typical drunk with too much testosterone. Brian thought it was funny, but I didn't. Having had a few too many myself, my idea of putting him in his place was to threaten, "Hugh Hefner is going to kick your ass." As if! But my ego could rival theirs. The fact that they were star quarterbacks didn't impress me in the least. I was accustomed to hanging out with rock stars and movie stars, a celebrity in my own right. And besides, I was not a sports fan, so athletes meant nothing to me. I had no problem sparring with them.

One guy, sitting on the other side of the limo, came to my rescue. He scolded Brister and Griese like they were school kids, "You, and you...you treat her like a lady." This tall, good looking guy oozed strength and self-confidence. He exited the limo, leaving me wide-eyed and impressed. What a gentleman! I had no idea who he was. I was probably the only person in America who wouldn't have recognized John Elway.

The next night there was a phenomenal party at the mansion and on the huge yacht that dominated the boat dock. Besides me, three other Playmates, Echo Johnson, Nicole Wood and Corinna Harney, and twenty local Miami models had been hired to entertain the team. Before the party got underway, I was walking from the yacht along a path leading back to the mansion. Walking right towards me was my hero from the night before. Our eyes locked. It was love at second sight. With the whole football team watching.

My grandma always told me you know when you find "the one," because it hits you over the head like a ton of bricks. And that's how I felt. Spinning. Intoxicated. Blown away. John and I spent the entire evening glued together. We ignored everyone else as the party swarmed around us. Like maniacs, we screwed everywhere: in the mansion, on the yacht, in the bathrooms, the Jacuzzi. We had sex seven times. It was not deliberate, but I discovered later he was famous as "Number Seven." All I knew was we couldn't get enough of each other. I was a little taken aback, however, when one of the guys offered me half a hit of ecstasy. I hadn't expected that from football players. Not that John was loaded down with drugs or anything. He wasn't. But he was no amateur.

It was a magical night and the most elaborate party I'd ever been to. Besides the yacht, a helicopter provided chopper rides over the Atlantic. The ecstasy turned the stars overhead into an amazing light show. John and I couldn't keep our hands of each other. He put my cheeks in his big strong hands and said, "You have the most beautiful face I have ever seen; I want your hair off of your face." Then he paid one of the girls that worked on the yacht a hundred bucks for her hair clip, an old brownish tortoise shell hair clip faded from the sea and the sun. I pulled my hair back for him, and he told me to keep that hair clip forever. Never throw it away. It had had a special significance to us.

At one point, we spied on Brian Griese and Playmate of the Year Corinna Harney, who were relaxing in the yacht's Jacuzzi. Brian thought he was going to get lucky, but Corinna is a devout Christian. When Brian made his move, we heard Corinna ask him, "Are you a believer? Do you take Jesus as your savior?" Brian looked baffled. John and I laughed so hard it hurt.

This was my second night with the football crowd, and these guys partied like rock stars. The funny thing was, they partied *more than* rock stars. In all my time on tour with KISS I never saw anyone do drugs. Gene Simmons and Paul Stanley didn't even drink. Some of these sports stars you see as role models on the Wheaties cereal boxes are still out partying while you're having your breakfast. I had always thought football players were supposed to keep in perfect physical shape. You know, your body is a temple, and all that. But they were not going to let a little thing like a hangover get in their way, even though the Super Bowl was just a week away. During the party, John announced, "I think I'm in love," and decided I was "Lady Luck." He'd lose the game if I wasn't there.

I was supposed to leave the next day, but no one wanted to run the risk of the Broncos losing because "Lady Luck" had left town. Bill Phillips and his team urged me to stay. As I'd expected to fly back to L.A., I didn't have any clothes to wear for the rest of the week, a problem Bill generously solved by sending me on an Ocean Drive shopping spree with my new friend Heidi, one of the fitness models. Armed with credit cards and no spending limit and a limo driver to carry our bags, it was quite an excursion. Bill even flew in my friend Peggy to keep me company and make sure I was happy. We had mani-pedis by the pool, a limo at our disposal twenty-four hours a day, chopper rides off the deck of the yacht. They called me the "Queen of Miami." Apparently, whatever John Elway wanted, John Elway got.

The night of the party, I'd thrown caution to the wind. There was such a magnetic attraction that I'd gone with the passion of the moment with no thought as to what might or might not happen later. When the party came to an end, around 5:00 a.m., we said goodnight and I went to bed in my room in the mansion. All was quiet. Dressed in my little baby doll teddy, I was nodding off, when I heard footsteps. It was John. He could not leave without fucking me for an eighth time. That was my clue that he was married: he was acting like he'd never been laid before and might never get laid again. But I ignored my intuition and enjoyed one last roll in the hay with him.

The next morning, I awoke to the sound of someone outside, calling up to me, "Carrie, Carrie." I stepped onto the balcony wearing the burgundy teddy I'd been sleeping in and no, it wasn't Elway. It wasn't a Romeo and Juliet scene. There was a messenger, sent by John. He threw an envelope up to me and left. Inside were two tickets for the Super Bowl. I showed them to Bill Phillips.

"You've got to be kidding me," he said, "What an idiot. He put you in the seats right next to his wife." **My jaw dropped.**

Lucky for John, Bill Phillips exchanged seats with me.

I watched John on TV that day, press day, being interviewed by a crowd of journalists, he seemed to get more camera time than anyone else. All of the players were now in a kind of quarantine leading up to the big game. They weren't allowed any distractions. Just a few nights later, though, I was having dinner at a restaurant called The Forge with a group of people including Bill Phillips, his brother Shawn, Heidi, and Jim Nagle, an EAS employee whom I knew because he used to work for *Playboy*. In total, there were ten or twelve of us. Halfway through dinner, one of the guys told me to follow him into a private dining room, and there was John. He'd snuck out just to see me. He was sitting by himself, hands crossed, looking down like a shy schoolboy. It was like he couldn't even look at me. So adorable.

"I couldn't stay away. I just had to see you again," he told me.

We chatted for about twenty minutes before he returned to the team's hotel.

Still, my brain didn't fully register why everyone had been kissing my ass all week until the day of the Super Bowl when I arrived at the 75,000-seat Pro Player Stadium to see tens of thousands of fans wearing shirts bearing the name Elway and his number 7. Then I got it. To them, this man was a god. And this game meant everything. Huge bets had been placed and careers were at stake. Suddenly, being "Lady Luck" felt like a lot of pressure.

Peggy and I watched the game from the seats I'd traded Bill. I couldn't see much of the game, and what I did see I didn't understand, but the halftime show was all too familiar. As pyrotechnics exploded, KISS appeared onstage. I was stunned to see them in full makeup and costumes, which they had given up in 1983. When the surprise wore off and I let myself feel the music, my heart tore apart, and my eyes welled up. This was the first time I'd seen KISS play since Eric died. I didn't even listen to their music anymore. I always changed radio stations when they came on. How could I listen to KISS and not relive all the memories of watching Eric play those songs on tour? Now here I was trapped at the Super Bowl, of all places, forced to watch KISS in concert. Seven years after Eric passed, number seven had come along.

When KISS was offstage and the game restarted, I snapped back to the present, cheering wildly along with thousands of ecstatic Broncos fans when John threw a dynamite eighty-yard touchdown pass. The Broncos won 34–19. At the age of thirty-eight, he became the oldest player to be named Super Bowl MVP. As Lady Luck, I had done my part, but I had never felt so alone in a crowd. Here I was, haunted by my lost love while watching my new love...and realizing that he wasn't mine at all.

It was a magical week, perhaps the most enthralling of my life I had been treated like royalty and showered with attention. The mansion. The yacht. The chopper rides. Jet skis. The 24-hour limo. Poolside massages and manicures. A new wardrobe, new friends. And a passionate encounter with a man I could never forget. But now it was over. I didn't pine over it. After so many years of missing Eric, I was used to wanting what I couldn't have. I chalked it up to a Super Bowl fantasy, something I'd tell my grandchildren while sitting in my rocking chair. I was content knowing I'd had the experience of a lifetime. As I boarded the plane back to L.A., I giggled to myself, seeing so many passengers reading newspapers with John's face splashed on every front page. If only they knew!

A month later, he tracked me down. He was in L.A. to do *The Tonight Show* with Jay Leno. In Miami, I'd mentioned that my friend Peggy Trentini had dated his golf buddy, actor Jack Wagner, and it didn't take much detective work to find me through her. Against my better judgment, I agreed to meet up with him at a sports bar in Santa Monica. Broncos coach Mike Shanahan was with him. It was actually quite hilarious as these two back-to-back Super Bowl winners tried to give me a crash course in football. They did everything they could to explain the rules of the game, all about offense and defense and linebackers and running backs. They might just as well have been trying to explain how to land on the moon. I could understand their passion for their sport but that was about it. Teaching me about football was a losing proposition even for two of the most winning football champions of all time. I didn't get it, and I still don't.

I later took John to a Hollywood nightclub, hoping the friendly doorman I knew would be on duty. Doormen usually waved hot girls in, no problem, unless you were with a guy. Well, as it turned out, I could have been standing there stark naked and no one would have noticed me. All eyes were on John. It was strange for me, the adulation he was getting. I'd achieved rock royalty status and Playmate status on my own. I didn't go to a rock concert without a backstage pass. I was accustomed to having bottle service in clubs with stars like Leonardo DiCaprio. But John's celebrity status was off the charts. I was truly naive. I thought sports fans were sports fans and only hung out in sports bars, and rock fans were rock fans who went to rock concerts. I didn't realize that the fans crossed over and that John would be recognized and celebrated in my Hollywood scene. In almost any scene, in fact.

Dennis Rodman was in the club that night. It was noisy, of course, and I didn't hear something he said to John, but it must have been some smart-assed comment about me. John was pissed.

"You apologize to the lady. And go buy her a drink. Right now."

Dennis, shamefaced, did as he was ordered. When he returned with my drink, John in full alpha-male mode, switched gears, "You're not drinking that. We're out of here."

My heart fluttered. He was my knight in shining armor again, my protector. He always seemed to be in command. Little did I know.

Years later, I ran into Dennis in a club in Miami. The waitress told me he wanted to send me a drink.

"Tell him I've met him before, and I don't want to meet him again," I instructed.

Rodman being Rodman, ignored the rejection and came over anyway. We talked, and he revealed he hadn't said anything derogatory about me to John that night in L.A.

All he said to him was, "That's not your wife you're with."

*****

As John was a spokesman for EAS, he got me invited to work at a promotion in Vegas along with some fitness models.

He told the company, "I'm not going unless Carrie is going." And, as John always got what John wanted, there I was.

Walking through the casino in the Bellagio, the newest, plushest hotel on the strip at the time, I heard one of the other football players shout, "Yo, Lady Luck! Yo, Lady Luck," waving me over to the roulette table. John was there, of course. He loved to gamble. One of the players, I don't even remember which one, handed me a chip. A thousand-dollar chip. I looked across the table and my eyes locked with John's. I gave him a subtle smile and a wink and placed the bet on number seven — his number. They all followed suit. And we watched the wheel spin and the ball tumble from number to number until it finally came to rest...on number seven. The cheering was deafening. You'd think they'd all just won another Super Bowl. It was awesome. Lady Luck had come through again. I collected my winnings and went straight up the escalator to the shoe store.

*****

I couldn't escape a relationship with John. I was Miss Killian's Irish Red Beer and he was the Coors guy. Coincidentally, Killian's was owned by Coors. So, we worked all the beer conventions together. We were thrust together even if we'd wanted to avoid each other, which we didn't. I fell madly, deeply, crazily in love with him. He came to L.A. frequently because he was in talks to partner with local billionaire, Eli Broad, to co-own and launch a football team. We went out to trendy nightclubs. He wasn't concerned about being seen in public, which to me today is totally shocking. It wasn't an exclusive relationship, though, no matter how deeply I cared for him. He was married, after all, something I had to live with and didn't feel good about. At the same time, I was into my third year of casually dating Enrique Iglesias, and it seemed like every other weekend, he or John was in town.

I couldn't sleep in the same bed with Enrique. I'd usually drive home from his hotel around 4:00 a.m. I couldn't spend the whole night with him because I wasn't in love with him, and he wasn't in love with me. We were just having fun, as two young, healthy attractive people should. But then I'd head out to go sleep in my own bed in my own home.

With John it was different. I couldn't tear myself away. I felt his love, and I fell in love in return. I literally trembled with emotion when it was time to leave his hotel room. I'd put my sunglasses on to hide my tears from the valet parkers. Sometimes, I'd pull over on the way home and dry heave. Sometimes, after seeing him, I would stay in bed for three days. I couldn't sleep. I couldn't eat. He had such a powerful hold on me. I even consulted a past life regressionist to help me try to figure it out. Later, I confessed all this to him. He never believed me. He'd say, "How could a girl like you love me? What would a girl like you see in a guy like me?"

For someone who was such a superstar, he was full of insecurities. I saw the sensitive side of John Elway, the side football fans never got to see. There were times when he would bury his head in my lap and cry like a baby, "You can never, never leave me... I will die." Of course, he was liquored up at the time.

I loved him not for his looks — he had unusually deep wrinkles for his age, maybe from never wearing sunscreen when he played golf or football — but for the way he made me feel about myself. I was a sucker for the attention he gave me. He made me feel so special. It was equivalent to a rock star picking you out of the audience, but even more special because I was his Lady Luck. It wasn't a band with the same shtick every night. This was the culmination of his career, and he gave me credit. My beauty gave him confidence. His adoration made me feel powerful. We fed off each other's shallowest needs.

*****

Our relationship came to a head at a Coors convention in Hawaii in 2000. I told John that if he brought his wife and kids, I would bring a date. I was half-joking. I didn't really expect him to show up with his family. The morning of the flight, however, he emailed to let me know his family would be with him. Seriously? He must have known this for a long time. You don't make travel plans for your wife and four children at the last moment.

In the hotel I overheard people excitedly say things like, "Look! Elway's over there by the elevator with his wife and kids. What a cute family." It killed me. I'd never had to deal with this kind of situation before. I'd never seen his family up close and personal, and I couldn't bear the pressures of being in the same room with the man I loved *and* his family. Holding that secret inside of me was sheer agony. I was torn apart. The Coors and Killian's employees knew about the affair, and it made me all the more uncomfortable wondering what they were thinking as they saw fans asking for photographs of John and me together while his family looked on. He couldn't really talk to me. He couldn't call me. We couldn't go out for dinner together. I felt lost and alone. I was in love yet feeling shame. It was all too much.

That night I tried to drink away the nerves and the pain, but it backfired. I had too much beer. I fell over, cutting and bruising myself above my eye. The next morning, struggling with his football injuries, John limped up to my Killian's booth with the sportscaster Dan Patrick. They wanted a photo of the three of us together, and I said no. The way I looked there was no way I wanted to be in a picture with anyone, especially John.

Flying back to L.A. I looked in my compact mirror, examining my swollen eye and the gash under my brow.

It was a reflection of the way I felt. I said to myself, "Carrie, God is showing you on the outside, what you can't see on the inside." I hadn't fully understood why nice girls were not supposed to have affairs with married men. Of course, I knew it was considered wrong. I knew it was against most religious beliefs. I did have respect for other women, but I figured that men who cheat would cheat anyway. I rationalized, if it wasn't me, it would be someone else.

I wasn't suggesting he leave his family. I didn't want to be a homewrecker. I was just having fun. It had never occurred to me that I might fall in love. It took a different kind of fall, a physically hurtful one, to be my wake-up call. I was wounded, deeply wounded. The scar on my face was visible proof that the affair was destroying me. It had to end. I needed to get out. To make sure he couldn't talk me out of it, I made myself unreachable. When I got home, I changed all my phone numbers and blocked his email address. I had to. Like many of the hardest things I have ever done, I did it on autopilot. It was a survival mechanism. It was the right thing to do. And I had to do it while our affair remained a secret, so that we never hurt his wife or children. I forgave myself for my mistake and told myself that my broken heart would mend. I walked away with what little dignity I had left.

AT LEFT: Carrie and Peggy Trentini at the Super Bowl (1999).

BELOW: With Enrique Iglesias (1998).

Chapter 8

Don't Get Knocked Up

An established theatrical agency decided to give me a trial run. My first audition was for a leading role in a TV series *Son of the Beach,* being produced by Howard Stern's company. I got a call back, and then they wanted to bring me in for the screen test. I couldn't make it. I was in the Bahamas shooting a swimwear catalog. Both the agency and I were bitterly disappointed. It's not often an actress gets down to the wire on a series her first time out. The problem with being a professional model was that I was often unavailable for TV and movie auditions. Acting is what I wanted to do, but modeling is what paid the bills.

The agency gave me a second shot. Without knowing my history, they told me about a Mark Wahlberg/Jennifer Aniston film called *Rock Star,* set in the 80s metal scene. The producers were looking to cast people who had actually experienced the era to give the movie some authenticity. It was perfect for me. The prospect of working with major stars on a big budget Warner Brothers' movie was thrilling. I'd always had this feeling that what would catapult my career was a small role in a big movie. This was the role that could change everything, that could transform my life.

Since they were looking for real rocker chicks, I went to the audition wearing my KISS jacket from the *Hot in The*

Shade tour, a black leather motorcycle jacket with an illustration of the Sphinx on the back. As an actor, you naturally want the casting director to be interested in you, to want to get to know you. The worst thing that can happen in an audition is you read a scene and they go, "Okay. Thanks. Next." The jacket worked. It grabbed the attention of the casting director, Sharon Bialy.

"Where did you get that fantastic jacket?" she asked as soon as she saw me.

I was happy to tell her. The jacket was made for the members of KISS: Gene, Paul, Bruce and Eric. Eric had given his jacket to me, saying it looked better on me than it did on him. Inevitably, this revelation invited more questions. I told Sharon enough about life on the road with KISS to prove I'd really lived the 80s metal era. She hung on my every word. I knew she was impressed. I'd established my rock star credentials. All I had to do now was a good reading. Sharon put me on tape for the director, who couldn't be at the audition, and I nailed it.

As she escorted me out, she stopped to show me a bulletin board displaying photos of all the people already cast. First, I saw Stephan Jenkins, the singer for Third Eye Blind.

"Oh, I know Stephan," I told her, "I just starred in his music video for *"Never Let You Go."* It is number two on the VH1 countdown."

I thought this is so awesome. Could this audition possibly have gone any better?

She pointed to another guy's photo and said, "If you get the part, you'll be playing his wife." It was Zakk Wylde, former guitarist for Ozzy Osbourne.

I laughed out loud and told her, "I have a great Zakk story."

Her eyeballs grew wide, and she invited me back into her office to hear it.

This is the story I told her:

In 1989, in the relaxed days of air travel before 9/11, friends could come with you to the departure gate. I was heading from L.A. to New York to see Eric. My friend, Marie, took me to the airport and, while we were having a few drinks at the bar, I met Zakk for the first time. He was on the same flight going to see his longtime girlfriend, Barbara. Zakk was booked in first class, and I was in coach, but there was an empty seat next to me, so he gave up his first-class seat so we could continue the party on the plane. We drank until I passed out. The last thing I remember is Zakk standing in the aisle giving me a shoulder massage. I might have complained my neck hurt; I really don't remember. It was all very innocent. It wasn't as if he was trying to screw me in the mile-high club or anything. All he talked about was Barbara. Anyway, the next thing I knew a flight attendant was waking me up. We were at JFK. Everyone else was off the plane. Once I pulled myself together and walked out to the gate, Eric was waiting for me.

"Hey," he said, "Guess who was on your plane? Zakk Wylde."

"Oh, really?" I shrugged.

I barfed all the way into Manhattan.

Sharon was in stitches, laughing. She let me know she'd cast several movies for this director, and that he trusted her. She had decision-making power. I left that audition beaming, confident it was my lucky break. I could feel Eric's presence around me. Between the jacket he gave me, the flight he arranged, and my connections to the 80s rock scene I had everything going for me. I couldn't have done it without him. Eric was the angel watching over me and making it happen.

When I got the call from Warner Brothers with the offer, my roommate and I jumped around the house, singing *"Never Let You Go,"* popping open bottles of champagne. I signed a contract for thirty days of work for $25,000 plus residuals. I was beyond thrilled. This was the small role in a big film I'd dreamed about.

My first day on set, when I went to craft services for breakfast, I laid eyes on the director, Stephen Herek, for the first time. A short guy with a good build, spikey bleach blonde hair, and piercing blue eyes, he noticed me as he took a bite of his donut and his jaw dropped. His face said, "Oh my God, who is that?" I giggled to myself.

Then I noticed Zakk. I hadn't seen him since our flight a decade earlier.

"Hey, remember me?" I asked.

What were the chances of us being reunited, cast together as husband and wife? Now he was married to Barbara and they had two kids (later a third). And just like on the plane, she was all he talked about. I got to hear how he'd bang Barbara in their walk-in closet in the morning so the kids wouldn't catch them in the act. Zakk is awesome and possibly the most loyal rock star on the planet.

The *Rock Star* movie set had the reputation throughout Hollywood of being one big raging party every day, and it wasn't far from the truth. It was a blast. On any movie set there's a lot of sitting around and waiting, often cooped up alone in your trailer. But there was never a dull moment on this set. We all parked ourselves in lawn chairs outside our trailers like it was a backyard barbecue. Jennifer Aniston made margaritas for everyone and would sweetly ask if we were okay waiting while she made them. Her then-husband, Brad Pitt, often came to visit her. On days when the call time was too early for alcohol, I'd visit Jeff Pilson, bass player for Dokken and Foreigner, in his trailer. As we drank cappuccinos, we had deep discussions about life, and, of course, about Eric.

A Who's Who of guys from the glory days of heavy metal had been recruited for supporting roles in the movie including Blas Elias, a good friend who was the drummer of Slaughter. When Blas first joined Slaughter, Mark Slaughter was dating my friend Marie. Blas gave me Slaughter's demo tape. I gave it to Eric who gave it to Gene Simmons. And that's how Slaughter got the gig opening up for KISS on the *Hot in The Shade* tour.

I played hard, but I worked even harder. I was on the set of *Rock Star* five days a week. On weekends I traveled, mostly to the Midwest, for my ongoing role as the Killian's Irish Red girl. Sometimes I did as many as thirteen appearances a day, catching flights to different cities. I might have breakfast in Minneapolis with a grocery store owner, do a radio interview, and then have lunch with contest winners. After that, I'd jump on a plane to Indianapolis to sign autographs at bars, liquor stores, conventions, nightclubs, anywhere they sold beer. I was the only Killian's girl for three consecutive years. They said I could hold my liquor, and I was a good man handler, until I punched a guy at *Hooters* for asking me how many guys I had to fuck to get my job. He deserved it. But that was the end of my career as the Killian's girl, since he tried to sue them.

While we were filming *Rock Star*, the director, Stephen Herek, wasn't shy about flirting with me. "I just get weak in the knees every time I see you," he'd say. He sent flowers and bottles of Patron Silver to my trailer. He kept asking me out. I was flattered. He was cute. But he was also married. I thought God must be testing me to see if I'd make the same mistake twice.

After the movie wrapped, Steve and I kept in touch. We had lunch once, dinner once. After dinner we went to the Crazy Girls titty bar in Hollywood. With a few drinks under his belt, he kissed me. I quickly pulled away and reminded him he was married. "Well, it's rocky and I'm not sure how much longer it's going to last," he insisted. I let that go in one ear and out the other, figuring it was the booze and lust talking. Steve scored points, however, by getting his high-profile agent to take a meeting with me, even though I knew realistically that it was just a favor to Steve whom he could not afford to displease. After all, he'd directed high-grossing movies like *Mr. Holland's Opus*, *The Three Musketeers*, *101 Dalmatians*, and *The Mighty Ducks*. The agent told me to keep in touch, let them know how my career was going, that kind of Hollywood bullshit. They represented movie stars, not newcomers like me.

I was not a big name, but I was on my way. After *Rock Star,* I was booked on movies back to back. I was finally so busy that I didn't have time to audition, which is every actor's dream. I filmed *Redemption,* with Chris Penn, and *The Backlot Murders,* with Corey Haim. *Redemption,* also featuring Don "The Dragon" Wilson, was an excellent script, and I was excited to have scenes opposite Chris because of his reputation as a great actor. But it never happened. It turned out he was insane, out of his brains on drugs and alcohol, and prone to random violent outbursts. The first day on the set he punched a producer in the face for no reason. Later, he virtually kidnapped a production assistant to bring him to downtown L.A. to buy crack. Every day they rewrote scenes to accommodate Chris's lunacy. They even walked me in a circle around the set to avoid him. Concerned for my safety they had one of the producers read the part of Chris's character with me, instead of Chris. That was fine, except the producer couldn't act. I was so disappointed. Don "The Dragon" was fantastic to work with and tried to keep Chris sober long enough to shoot a scene, but it was a lost cause.

Afterwards, the same production company offered me a role in *The Backlot Murders* which was wonderful since I didn't have to audition. Even better, they let me choose which role I wanted. So, I picked the part of Corey Haim's girlfriend, basically because she was the only girl who didn't have to take her top off. I don't know why I cared at that point in my life. But I did. Despite whatever drugs he was doing, Corey was a really sweet guy. Acting opposite someone who is tweaked out, cold, clammy, and shaking, is not the best experience in the world. But what really creeped me out was that I had to kiss him. Regardless, I got through it like a pro. *The Backlot Murders* involved numerous night shoots. We'd have a call time of 6:00 p.m. and wouldn't get done until six the next morning. Filming is not as glamorous as most people think; it's hard work. Wearing nothing more than a skimpy mini-skirt and a tank top, I froze my ass off and was exhausted all the time. Following *The Backlot Murders,* I lived at the Las Vegas Hilton for a month, shooting a movie with John Taylor from Duran Duran. At least he wasn't on drugs! It also involved brutal night shoots. I was tired of life in the fast lane. I was ready to settle down.

About nine months after the *Rock Star* shoot, Steve called. "I filed for divorce. How about dinner this Friday?" His timing was perfect. Friday happened to be Valentine's Day. Steve wasn't a rock star or a football star. He was kind of conservative and had a real job, if being a movie director counts as a real job. To my surprise, he came on really strong. On the second date, he asked me to be his girlfriend. But I was in no hurry. I waited a month before even making out with him. And it was three months before I slept with him, a record for me. For once in my life, I wanted to do things the right way. The relationship with Steve quickly became intense. He'd call me in the afternoon just to say, "I'm so fucking in love with you." He took me on his arm to the industry pre-screenings of *Rock Star*. I felt completely adored. I truly thought he was the one.

One night, Steve took me to Spago for dinner and booked a room at the Hotel Bel-Air (ironically owned by Prince Jefri). I knew we were going to sleep together. In between caviar blinis and sips of champagne, I found the right moment to tell him upfront, "You need to know something. I am almost 32 years old, and I've never been pregnant. If I get pregnant now, I don't want to have an abortion."

He said, "I wouldn't want you to."

Not long afterwards, Steve was on location in Seattle directing Angelina Jolie in the movie *Life or Something Like It* and arranged for me to fly there to see him. The night before, I went out with a couple of friends to have dinner at Robert de Niro's Italian restaurant, *AGO*. No sooner had we ordered a pitcher of peach martinis when Steve phoned. I went outside with my drink in hand to take the call and spoke with him so long that I missed dinner. My friends came out, ready to go clubbing. I quickly hopped into the driver's seat. On Sunset Boulevard, I got pulled over for tailgating, which was ridiculous because the traffic was back to back. At first, I figured the cops couldn't resist checking out a bunch of hot girls in a big white Lexus SUV. But it was more than that. They made me do all the sobriety tests, including touching my nose, walking in a straight line, and saying the alphabet backwards. Thanks to not having time for more than one martini, I was sharp as a tack. I performed perfectly. But I failed the breathalyzer.

They slapped handcuffs on me and hauled me off to jail. My friend Donna rode with me in the back of the cruiser. I wasn't upset at all. In fact, we were laughing and chatting up the cops. Once inside the community jail cell, I earned the nickname "Miss Congeniality." Genuinely interested in the lives of the hookers, I asked about their upbringing and their love lives. I let them use my calling card to call their pimps and their kids. I always make the best of any experience, and this was no exception. Two hours later, when my roommate bailed me out, she expected to find me crying. Instead, I was all smiles. I explained to her that as an actress it was an opportunity to do character study. She looked at me in disbelief. She was expecting the reaction of a normal, rational person. Me? Jail was fun, I told her. Not that I ever wanted to go back.

The next morning, as planned, I flew up to see Steve. We spent the afternoon exploring the city. He took me to Tiffany's and bought me a pair of one-carat diamond earrings to replace the cubic zirconias that I'd lost in his bed back in L.A. Instinctively, as we chatted over dinner in the revolving restaurant at the top of Seattle's Space Needle, I kept the DUI to myself. And then we went to bed. As we were making love, something out of this world happened. Something spiritual. I felt like I left my body for a few moments, and my soul floated above us. It was something so extremely powerful, so unique, something I'd never experienced before, or since. Two and half months later when I found out I was pregnant I knew with all the certainty in the world that what I'd experienced was a spirit entering my body. I'd been warned years earlier by Maren Nelson, my rebirther, that there was a spirit hovering around me that wanted to come in. This spirit must have found his vehicle through Steve.

I suspected I was pregnant while on the Caribbean island of St. Martin for the opening of a Baywatch resort. My friend, who I will refer to as "Baywatch Babe," had been invited to attend the opening and bring a guest. A vacation in paradise. How could I resist? We made the most of it. During the day, we sunned ourselves on the white sand beaches and at night partied with the show's producer Michael Berk and the cast.

One morning I knocked on "Baywatch Babe's" door and told her straight out, "I think I'm pregnant."

"What do you mean you're pregnant?"

"Well, my nipple just woke me up. My right nipple. It's throbbing. It's giant red and screaming at me."

"You're not pregnant. You're not pregnant," was all she could think to say.

But I was adamant.

The second clue I was pregnant came on the flight back to Miami. The guys sitting next to me were drinking beer. Just the smell made me want to barf. On the layover, I called my roommate to tell her: "I'm pregnant. I'm pregnant. I know it."

Back in L.A., I bought one of those EPT pregnancy kits you use when you pee first thing in the morning. I dipped the stick in my urine, nervously awaiting the verdict. It showed two lines. Positive. At 6:00 a.m. I ran into my roommate's room and woke her up by shoving my urine stick in her face. We ran right out to the store and bought three more test kits, three different brands. All were positive. Fuck. My roommate came with me to a doctor to get official confirmation. I didn't want to tell Steve until I was absolutely sure, and my roommate thought I should wait to tell him in person. But I didn't know when that would be. He was still in Seattle, and I couldn't hold off. It was the biggest thing that had ever happened to me. So, I broke the news over the phone. Much to my relief, he was ecstatic. He said he was over the moon.

"I've always wanted more kids," he said.

He said he wanted to shout it from the rooftops.

There was just one obstacle. His second divorce from his second wife wasn't final, and he didn't want news of my pregnancy somehow screwing up his divorce settlement. Hmm. Did he want me to have an abortion, I asked, praying the answer would be no. He practically screamed "No!" He wanted me to have the baby. *Our* baby.

*****

My pregnancy was really rough. For the first four months I had so much morning sickness there was no way I could fly up to Seattle, so instead Steve came down to see me for Memorial Day weekend. He spent the weekend pampering me. He went to California Pizza Kitchen for the Sedona Tortilla soup I could tolerate, and, to calm my nausea, stocked the nightstand with saltines and ginger ale. All weekend he was loving and attentive, everything you'd want in a proud, expectant dad.

On a glorious sunny day, as he got ready to leave, he knelt before me, kissed my swollen belly, and told our unborn baby, "Be strong for her. Take good care of her." Then he gazed into my eyes, kissed me, and said, "I love you. I'll call you later." And off he went to catch a first-class flight back to work on the film with Angelina Jolie.

He never called me again.

He ignored my voice mails.

I wrote intense, emotional emails, asking, "Are you going to be with me? Are you going to stand by me?" I sent lots of emails, but never got a response. He just stopped communicating. His phone number changed. He'd ditched me. What's now known as "ghosting." And he did it when I was four months pregnant with his child and without any kind of explanation. I thought he was being sweet when he told the baby to be strong for me and to take care of me. I later realized it was a send-off. He was telling the baby to take care of me because he had no intention of doing it himself. I hadn't seen it coming. How could I? Nothing bad had ever happened between us. No fights. No warning signs. Nothing. He simply walked out the front door and never looked back.

My premonition that my little part in *Rock Star* would be the role that transformed my life came true, only not in the way I thought it would. I wasn't prepared for a blow like this. To make it in this business you have to be a bit self-centered and strong. And, God knows, I had a healthy ego and a thick skin. But this betrayal was way beyond anything I could have imagined. I waited and hoped for the phone to ring, staring out my window for hours at a big eucalyptus tree. I watched for the leaves to sway with the wind, my way of knowing that time was indeed moving; otherwise, it seemed to stand still. I was distraught. I cried, a lot. Whenever I thought about Steve, which was all the time considering his baby was growing inside my body, I had to puke. I don't know how much of it was the morning sickness and how much was heartbreak, but I barfed all the time.

At my sixteen-week appointment, an ultrasound revealed the baby's sex. I called to tell Steve. He didn't answer, of course, so I left a message: *We're having a boy!* He didn't call me back. The premier of *Rock Star* was just days away, so I assumed he was busy, but I also figured he was avoiding me because he didn't want me to go. I was home alone sulking over missing my red-carpet moment and pining over why he didn't want to proudly have me on his arm that evening, when the phone rang. Steve finally called me! Not to invite me to the premiere, but to frantically scream at me. Warner Brothers had questioned him after *The New York Post* printed a September 7, 2001 article exposing the situation. It read: "You'd think the gossip from the set of *Rock Star* would be about the film's star, Mark Wahlberg, but it is actually about the film's director, Stephen Herek and actress, Carrie Stevens. A source says, Stephen and Carrie had been dating for like five months and she's pregnant now. He has turned very cold and wants nothing to do with her or her child." To add insult to injury, he accused my sister Jill and I of being the mules who leaked it.

When 9/11 happened and everybody called anybody they cared about, I called him again. He never responded. Now he was in Vancouver directing *Life or Something Like it*. Once again, I foolishly told myself that he was busy. I didn't want to bother him. I knew he was under a lot of pressure and I thought I should let him focus on his work. When I knew the film had wrapped, I wrote an emotional three-page letter and hand delivered it to the mailbox of his Encino home.

He never replied. Under other circumstances I would have downed a few Margaritas, or found a new boyfriend, or at least been able to swallow an aspirin to help deaden the pain. This time I was trapped. My future, once as bright as my smile, came to a screeching halt.

I wondered why it's often said men are "trapped" when a woman gets pregnant because I was the one whose choices had narrowed to almost nothing. Meanwhile, Steve was out having a good time. My friend Adi saw him having dinner with a woman in Santa Monica. My roommate ran into him having drinks at the Hotel Bel-Air. He didn't even ask about me. My girlfriends, however, told me he'd be back one day. They assured me he was just scared. When the baby was born, he'd do the right thing, they insisted. It made sense. I mean, I'd never heard of a middle-aged, white-collar, twice-divorced father doing a disappearing act.

I tried to be patient, even though I wondered how I could have been such a poor judge of character. How did I let this happen? I'd lost my virginity at the age of fourteen and never been pregnant before. I reflected on all the times I tried to get Steve to wear a condom, and he wouldn't. I nagged about it. I all but threw him off me. I told him many times after sex, "You know, you could have worn a condom." Although it probably wouldn't have offered us much protection anyway. Condoms tend to slip right off of small dicks.

I asked myself again and again, how he could permanently alter my life, so carelessly create a new life, and just walk away. Other than my conviction that our son deserved to have a father in his life, I don't know why I wanted him back. This was a man who'd never even asked if I had health insurance. Never offered a penny of financial support. His actions were inhumane. How could this be the same man that sat up with me until four in the morning talking, talking, talking? Then it hit me: I'd done all the talking. *What I should have done was ask questions.* He sure seemed like he was interested in what I had to say, but now he was treating me like someone he'd fucked in a bathroom stall without getting her name.

Knocked up and bored, I went online and looked up David Lee Roth. Googling his name led me to the website slawterhouse.com and a competition for Miss Slawterhouse. I'd been a Playmate of the Month. I'd been the Killian's Red girl. Why not add Miss Slawterhouse to my collection of titles? Sitting at my desk on my fat, pregnant ass that no longer resembled that of a centerfold, I sent in my *Playboy* photos, and won. My prize: all of Van Halen's and David Lee Roth's CDs, a copy of his autobiography *Crazy from the Heat,* and a piece of artwork. He drew two ships, some ocean waves and seagulls.

He autographed it, "To Carrie, You babe! David Lee Roth."

My contact at Slawterhouse, via email, was a guy called T.K. who wrote one day, "Keep it under your hat, but Dave would like you to have his phone number." Hmm. I was convinced that T.K. was, in reality, Dave, sitting at home just as bored as I was, and pretending he had an assistant working for him. I knew from hanging out with Dave that 'Keep it under your hat' was something he'd say. I wrote back. Yes. I'd love to call him, but I happened to be eight months pregnant. It was honest, but probably a little too much information. I wasn't going to be pregnant much longer. I should have kept that detail out, because of course, after *that* revelation I didn't hear a thing. Sometime later, months after Jaxon was born, when I was in better physical shape than ever, I thought it would be fun to reconnect with Dave. I'd written his phone number on a piece of paper and left it in my desk drawer. But I couldn't find it! How the fuck I lost that number, I have no idea.

I'd finally slept with David Lee Roth but was too drunk to remember it. I ruined my chances with him by babbling on about Eric, then I'd got back in touch through becoming Miss Slawterhouse when I was heavily pregnant, only to lose his number. I wondered if he even realized that his new Miss

Slawterhouse was someone he knew personally. Maybe he was just like those guys at Sanctuary who didn't connect me, Miss June, with the girl they'd formerly known as a hostess. How fitting his artwork was. Maybe his drawing represented two ships passing in the night?

*****

As a young girl I'd dreamt of being pregnant, supposedly the most beautiful time of a woman's life. I'd fantasized about having three kids and taking photography classes while I was pregnant. Instead, it was the loneliest time of my life. The man whose child I was carrying, took all that I had going for me away. I couldn't work. I couldn't date. I'd lost my looks. I was a whale, with barnacles. Well, acne. Bad acne. And because my license had been suspended as a result of the DUI, I couldn't even drive myself to my doctors' appointments. Even though I got the DUI before I got pregnant, it took so long to process that I had to attend DUI school up until I was eight months along. Even worse was the mandatory attendance at the Mothers Against Drunk Driving event. Two hundred women glared at me, assuming I'd been drunk during my pregnancy.

Thankfully, I had wonderful people in my life who went to Lamaze and baby care classes with me (even if some of the couples asked if Peggy and I were life partners). There was one amusing incident when I went to Florida for my sister's lesbian wedding. My mother gave a funny speech.

"Where did I go wrong?" she asked. "I have one daughter who's marrying her girlfriend and another daughter who's pregnant and not married."

Another person who was super supportive was Howard Stern. I met him when he was broadcasting live from an event at the Playboy Mansion. A bunch of us Playmates were sitting at a round table with Hef, and Howard did his thing, trying to embarrass girls with wildly provocative questions. I don't remember what he asked me, except it was something obscene and obnoxious so I gave him a sarcastic, smart-ass answer.

"Come on, you're my type," was his flirtatious response.

Later in the game house, a small private house on the grounds of the Playboy Mansion, the male lead singer of the band that performed was blatantly hitting on Howard. Howard turned to me, desperate to be rescued. He needed someone, anyone, to turn to at that moment, and I happened to be standing there. He struck up a conversation

I told him flat out, "I hate your show. I'd never go on."

In a very calm tone, he said, "You don't have to."

We sat down on the floor of the van room, a room in the game house decorated to look like the back of a 70s van, complete with wall-to-wall carpet. He was intelligent and engaging. He told me that he wasn't into the whole Hef having multiple girlfriends thing. What do you know? He wasn't the pig I'd always assumed him to be, not the person he portrayed on the radio, not a sexist asshole at all. I liked him. A lot.

We ended up going out in his limo with a group of people. The two of us danced closely for hours at a club in Hollywood that had glass walls around the dance floor. Afterwards, Howard's limo took us all to the parking garage in Century City where we'd left our cars before catching the shuttle to the

Playboy Mansion. I was about to exit the limo when Howard rightfully insisted that I should not drive and that he would take me home. I don't know what I was thinking at two in the morning asking Howard if he wanted to see my house. Well, of course, he did. We were in my downstairs family room when we started making out and his glasses fell off onto the floor. We went upstairs to my bedroom. In the morning, I served him breakfast in bed. He lay on his back while I, wearing nothing but the diamond belly chain I had on the night before, straddled him like a cowgirl and spoon-fed him an egg-white frittata. His poor driver spent the night in the limo in front of my house.

After he left, I went back to bed only to be awakened by my roommate bursting open my door with a pair of eyeglasses in her hand.

She said, "Oh my God, are these Howard Stern's?"

I said, "How did you know?"

She was a huge fan of his and had recognized them right away.

Howard called me from the plane on his way back to New York City and asked if I could mail them to him. He was in between marriages at the time, and this happened not too long before I dated Steve and got pregnant. When I broke the news to Howard about my pregnancy, I quickly joked, "Don't worry, it's not yours." Howard already knew from our mutual friend A.J. Benza that I was dating some director. We kept in touch and when things went south with Steve, he was amazing. He called me from time to time just being a supportive friend, talking about the realities of my situation. It was Howard Stern, the notoriously chauvinistic shock jock, with whom I'd had a one-night stand, who helped me get through the abandonment. Go figure.

Regardless of how hideous I looked I was still part of the Playboy family. Hef always welcomed me at the mansion for dinner and movie nights even though, as the months went by, I looked less and less like my centerfold. Nevertheless, my pregnancy was a painful and lonely time. I felt that everyone, from the couples at Lamaze classes to my own family, were thinking: "She must have done something really awful for him to abandon her."

What I hated most was when people told me I mustn't feel depressed and angry because the unborn baby can feel everything. Well, first of all, I was not a robot. Feelings cannot simply be banished just because they are unwelcome. Second, wouldn't the hurt and sadness from the guilt trip they were laying on me damage the baby just as much? Did it not occur to them the baby would feel that, too? It was easy for people to make those kinds of comments, but I was the one suffering through it.

About a month before I was due, the harsh realization that I'd soon be experiencing childbirth hit me. This baby had to come out of my body, and I didn't like any of the options for getting him out. I went to interview a doula (a midwife who helps you through your delivery), who showed me videos of gargantuan vaginas with babies emerging, crying, and covered in blood and mucus. She spoke of it as though it were a beautiful thing, but I had an anxiety attack and ran out of the office, hyperventilating. I also watched videos of C-sections where they slice up a woman and take the baby out of the side of her stomach like an alien from outer space.

I was beyond horrified. I couldn't sleep. Not just from anxiety but because my baby had his foot stuck in my rib cage. Instead of lying down, I was forced arched up on all fours like a cat, as I tried to get him to take his foot out of my ribs. I gained sixty-eight pounds and had a hard time walking. I had to wear flip flops in December because I couldn't reach my feet. It was time. I knew it was time.

My doctor, however, insisted I wasn't ready to deliver, that my due date was two weeks later. I argued with him. I knew exactly when I'd conceived. I'd had that intense experience, felt the precise moment my son's spirit entered my body. Besides, the only time I could have gotten pregnant was when I had gone to visit Steve in Seattle. That would put me at forty-two weeks. I told my obstetrician that he had three choices. He could induce labor, or he could give me a C-section, or he could let me go home and drink a bottle of castor oil. He thought I was kidding, but I wasn't. I'd read a homeopathic book about using castor oil to induce labor. My sister Jill came home with me. We followed the instructions, mixing castor oil and orange juice in a shot glass. Within hours my water broke, and I was in labor.

Labor was hellacious. I couldn't help but scream "Fuck!" at the top of my lungs, hour after hour while my mother and my sister tried to give me whatever comfort they could. My friend Adi showed up to film the birth. She was at the nurses' desk, asking where I was, when she heard: "Fuuuuuuuuck!"

"Never mind," she said, "I think I found her."

Crying, I told Adi not to film anything and to leave, because my horrific labor might scare her off from ever having children. I didn't know how anyone could endure such pain. And it wasn't supposed to be painful. I wasn't one of those women who said no to drugs. I was happy to take whatever they would give me. Yes. Give me an epidural. Yes. Stick that tube in my lower back and do anything to get rid of the pain. But something unheard of happened. The anesthesiologist made a mistake and inserted it incorrectly. It was only effective on my right side. I could opt to have him take it out and reinsert it, they said, but there was a risk of permanent paralysis. So, I chose to leave it be. But my labor went on and on, as the effects of the anesthesia wore off. They administered more and more until the left side of my body was paralyzed. On my left side, I felt nothing. On my right side, I felt the excruciating pain of natural childbirth. Eric was paralyzed on his left side after his coma. Is this what it was like for him? I was crying hysterically, so they gave me a heroin-like drug called Stadol, a type of opiate that stops the pain just long enough to make you forget you're about to have another contraction. For those thirty seconds between contractions, my mind drifted off with thoughts of Eric. I had prayed to God to give me some of his pain. Had I asked for this?

Another contraction. "Fuuuuuuuuuuck!"

Because I could only move the left side of my face, I could not properly scream. The nurses, who'd dubbed me "Miss Potty Mouth," were probably glad. They say you forget all the pain of labor when you see the baby, but I didn't. I vividly remember the agonizing horror of shoulders and feet coming out of me. When the doctor saw my placenta, he admitted I was right. I was two weeks overdue, proving that I got pregnant exactly when I said I had. My spiritual experience of feeling my son's spirit enter my body was real.

After nine months, two weeks, and twenty-eight hours, I finally met this divine spirit and instantly knew the meaning of true love. He was a healthy nine-pound two-ounce beautiful bundle of joy, whom I named Jaxon Gene. The first name is traditional, strong, and masculine, with the spelling fit for a rock star, and the middle name is after my father, not Gene Simmons. As soon as my mom and sister left the room, I tried to reach Steve. I left him a voicemail: *I just gave birth to our son.* Then I slept for twelve straight hours. Finally.

The next day Steve unexpectedly showed up at the hospital. He held our son in his arms for a few minutes and looked genuinely touched. I thought I saw a tear in his eye. How could he not be emotional after meeting his newborn baby boy? He left, saying he'd call later that week.

He never called.

Warned to say goodbye to sleep, my new life revolved around burping, breastfeeding and changing diapers. I loved waking up with Jaxon to feed him in the middle of the night. I couldn't wait to see his little eyes look up at me no matter what time it was. Even so, I had the energy to get myself back in shape. I had sixty-eight pounds to lose. Fueled by anger and determined not to let Steve take my hotness away, I embarked on a routine of weight training, spinning classes, hiking, and eating egg whites. Once Alex Van Halen and his wife came into my spinning class. He got on the bike right next to mine. I was so starstruck that I twisted my neck and stared at him during the whole ride. No wonder he never came back to the class. Oh, well. Six months and seventy-four lost pounds later, I was in the best shape of my life.

*****

I'm not sure why Steve was surprised when I slapped him with a paternity suit. After all, it's the modern-day equivalent of someone's father putting a shotgun to your head. That's what it took to get a fucking reaction from him. He finally called, furious because I had sued him. The nice letters I'd written had been ignored. Even after holding his baby in his arms, he wanted nothing to do with us. It took an attack on his wallet to get his attention.

"You could have had an abortion!" he yelled, conveniently forgetting he'd insisted he didn't want me to have one. Maybe he'd just said that at the time out of some kind of Catholic guilt. I don't know. I was done making excuses for him. This wasn't about the two of us anymore, I told him. He had a son, and he was running away from his responsibilities.

The legal battle began.

The first unpleasant step was complying with his lawyer's order that we submit to saliva swabs for DNA to prove Steve was the father. I was offended at the suggestion that it could have been some other guy's baby, but after the way he treated me why should I expect anything else? After his paternity was proven, he fought tooth and nail to avoid paying child support. He was still paying for his other "mistakes," giving his two ex-wives alimony and child support, so I guess he thought he shouldn't have to take care of Jaxon as well. Custody was never an issue. He didn't fight for that, only for his bank account.

His lawyers tried their best to get him a bargain. I received a smarmy letter saying that Steve promised "a smooth parenting relationship" if I settled for half of what I was entitled to. Steve was in the high-income earner bracket and I was entitled to a lot. My lawyer and all my friends told me I'd be stupid to accept the offer, that Steve and his lawyers were manipulating me. But I wanted Jaxon to have a father and couldn't risk making a decision that might deprive him of that. Also, Steve had suddenly become attentive, sending flowers on my birthday and Mother's Day. He took me for dinner at Mexicali, a Studio City restaurant we used to frequent. He told me I looked hot. He was right. The confidence I gained from going through hell and back gave me an undeniable glow. I loved flaunting myself in front of him. You always want the one that rejected you to want you back.

He was cunning, though, and stayed one step ahead of me. He knew exactly what he was doing. He was deceiving me with false hope, making me think that perhaps we could be a family after all. After dinner at Mexicali, we stood over our son's crib, admiring the life we had created. Steve leaned in for a kiss. Our lips met for a moment and I pulled away. I asked him the question that was burning in my brain. Why did he abandon me when I was pregnant? All he said was: "I just couldn't handle it at the time." Not much of an explanation, but I forgave him. The love I felt for my son overpowered the anger I felt for his father.

Of course, I wanted to be back with Steve. What mother of a newborn wouldn't want to make a family work? At his lawyer's suggestion, we agreed that Steve would visit Jaxon for one hour every Sunday. Once he brought his 13-year-old daughter, Samantha, to meet her half-brother. It gave me hope that he was sincere about being a father. But then on one of his visitation days, he stayed for only five minutes. At the suggestion of my attorney, I documented all of Steve's visits. There were six in all. On the last visit, I videotaped Jaxon, eight months old, as he slithered on the floor, trying to crawl for the first time.

Recently, on Jaxon's sixteenth birthday, we watched the video.

"Look. I was smart," Jaxon said.

"What do you mean?" I asked.

He had me back up the video and explained, "I'm crawling towards you and not towards him."

I don't know how any man can hold his baby, see him crawl, bring his daughter to visit, and then walk away with no conscience, but that's exactly what Steve did. The day that Jaxon first crawled is the same day I signed the paper settling for half of what Steve was required to pay in child support. He had tricked me, and he never looked back. I've always wondered what he told his little girl. She must have asked, whatever happened to that baby brother of mine?

I went to three different therapists, seeking answers as to how I could have been attracted to such a heinous man. They didn't have any answers. It plagued me to think about it. I wanted to make sure I understood it, so I'd never make the same mistake again. The only person who gave me any peace of mind was my son's godfather. He said, "Carrie, some people chop other people up and eat them for dinner. You won't figure them out because you don't think like they do." His words released me.

*****

There were times when the absence of a father was heartbreaking. Once, when Jaxon was four years old, I picked him up from Sunday School, and he had a temper tantrum, pushing me away, crying.

"I don't want you! I want my daddy!"

He'd seen all the other little kids' daddies picking them up.

Managing to remain calm, I knelt down, looked him in the eyes, and asked, "If you could talk to your daddy right now, what would you say?"

He pointed to a plane that was flying overhead. "I would say, 'Daddy, is that you up there in the sky? I need you. I love you, Daddy.'"

"Do you want to call him and ask him that?"

He did.

I dialed Steve's number and Jaxon left a message. His so-called dad never called back.

It was one thing to reject me, but how can you ignore the pleading of your four-year-old son telling you he needs you? It made me angrier than I'd ever been. I wished I could take one of my five-inch stilettos, drive it through his eyeball, and twist it hard. Nothing would have given me greater pleasure. It was at that point that I gave up trying to get Steve to be a father. My son was better off without him.

Steve has missed out on the sheer joy of having a son as wonderful as Jaxon. I don't feel sorry for him. I got the better deal. The day I brought Jaxon home from the hospital, my house became a home. I had an overwhelming feeling that everything would be okay. God would take care of us. And he has. My son was meant to be with me, and that is all that matters. I never think of Steve as a part of Jaxon. God and I made him. May he bless us all.

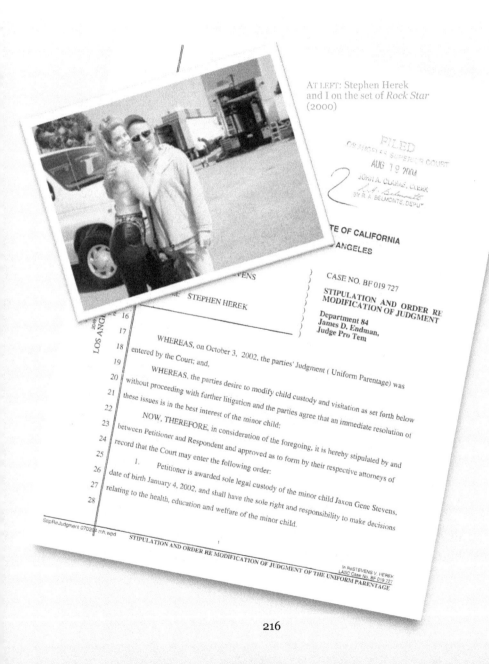

AT LEFT: Stephen Herek and I on the set of *Rock Star* (2000)

NADIA PANDOLFO PHOTO

NADIA PANDOLFO PHOTO

Carrie and son Jaxon *(all images);*
dressed for Halloween 2002 *(photo at right).*

Chapter 9

Don't Fall in Love with a Legend

The email was from an address I didn't recognize: jelway@... My heart skipped a beat. Could it be? Three years and three months had passed with no contact. I assumed he'd forgotten me. I opened it and read, "A lot of things have changed in my life. I'd really like to talk to you." Well, a lot of things had changed in my life as well. I wasn't a jet-setting celebrity anymore. I was a single mom. I was embarrassed to tell Mr. Family Man what Steve had done to me.

I called John Elway anyway.

"How are you"? he asked.

"Good...good," I nervously replied. "Well, I have a one-and-a-half-year-old son now."

He'd heard that I had a baby. He said he'd love to meet my son. Not only did he not judge me, he'd also been keeping tabs on me. I was flattered to hear he'd never stopped thinking about me. It made sense, as I'd never stopped thinking about him either. I always had a theory that if you feel that strongly about someone, they must feel it too. Some mornings when I woke up in Steve's bed, I caught myself thinking of John, even though I was supposed to be in love and hoping to have a family with Steve. Obviously, I thought, John and I must have a very special connection, one that just might stand the test of time.

We spent hours on the phone. He told me he'd been separated for six months, that his wife, Janet, had left him. I knew he would never leave his family. That's why I was shocked to get his email. I never expected the chance to have a real relationship with him. Nor did I weigh the consequences. My knight in shining armor had arrived. He was perfect! A few days later I was on a flight to join him at a celebrity golf tournament in Philadelphia. Even though I wasn't accustomed to being at sporting events, there were some familiar friendly faces there. Jack Wagner for one, who'd dated my friend Peggy Trentini. At the awards dinner, Michael Jordan was seated at our table. He kept looking at us and repeating, "You two are in love." We agreed.

When we got back to our room, Elway gushed over me. "I love everything about you. I love your teeth, I love your eyes, I love the way you dress. You make my heart go pitter-patter." Then he reached for my French-manicured hands, gently held my ring finger, and said, "Someday, I am going to put a ring on this finger."

When I returned to L.A., three dozen red roses were waiting for me and a balloon for Jaxon, along with a note from Elway thanking me for making the trip. The same huge arrangement was delivered to me every two weeks, like clockwork, for the next year.

I remembered something he'd once said. In bed together in his room at the Peninsula Hotel in Beverly Hills, he whispered, "Someday somebody's going to come along and sweep you off your feet." It made me sad when he said it because I wished it could be him. Now my wish was coming true. I was a new woman. On cloud nine. I finally stopped agonizing over Steve abandoning Jaxon and me. I understood the big picture now. I was meant to be with the one I truly loved. God had a better plan for me, and his name was John Elway.

A couple of weeks later, Elway flew me to Tampa where he had to make an appearance at an NFL event. Since my sister and my mother lived in Florida, I brought Jaxon along so that he could spend time getting to know my family. This was only our second time seeing each other now that he was single, but he wasn't wasting any time. As we enjoyed a late lunch on the patio of our hotel room, he said, "I want to marry you and adopt Jaxon." I was the happiest girl in the world. We had some hurdles to cross, of course, but I was confident that our love was meant to be. It would be another six months before his divorce was final. Then I'd be introduced to his four teenage kids, we would merge families, and Jaxon and I would move to Denver. Elway even drew for me the layout of his house to show where Jaxon's nursery would be, and where the nanny would live.

Jaxon's nanny, Amy was trained in kidnapping prevention and defensive driving. We got along very well. It was a pleasure having her live with us. The only thing that kept me from being able to travel was my work, so Elway saw to it that I stopped working. He was insecure about me staying in hotels alone, anyway, so whenever *Playboy* booked an appearance for me, he'd ask what it paid and double it if I turned the job down.

He only had to do it twice before I burned my bridges with "Bunny Mother" Pat Lacey. She was a Playboy bunny in the 1960s and was now in charge of hiring us for promotions. Even though I got her a signed football from Elway to try and make up for it, she knew she could no longer depend on me and she stopped hiring me. I don't blame her, and I regret it every day.

I also lost a lot of momentum in my acting career. Although my agents were impressed that I was dating John Elway, they weren't happy I was traveling with him so much that I was rarely in town for auditions. My priority wasn't my career anymore though; my family was. Elway was going to be my husband and the adoptive father of Jaxon, so I put him first. I did whatever Elway wanted. That's the way it always was with Elway. Whatever Elway wanted Elway got.

John Elway's mother told me more than once that the family's life revolved around sitting on a bench watching him play. She was a charming little spitfire. I basked in her positive energy. But one day she said to me, "Every Sunday John's sisters and I had to watch the game. It was always about John." I looked at Elway as she said it. He didn't like it and rolled his eyes. The fact is Elway was born and bred to be a champion. To me, his upbringing sounded like more of that of a racehorse than a human being. His father was a football coach. They moved the entire family from Washington state to California's San Fernando Valley so that his only son could play for Granada Hills High School, the best high school football team in the country at the time. I understood what his mother was saying. It must have been tedious for the family to have to support him the way they did, although she was obviously pleased with his success. It was Elway's reaction that I did not fully understand, as I still knew nothing about the game. I didn't know the reputation that quarterbacks have.

Elway and I were inseparable for a while. The first year, he was amazing. All I talked about to my friends for a whole year, was how cute Jaxon was and how in love I was with John Elway, the football hero, the successful businessman, the generous man who, liking me to dress conservatively, bought me cream-colored Armani pants suits, Dolce & Gabbana dresses, Gucci shoes, and Louis Vuitton luggage. He gave me 2.5 carat diamond earrings for Christmas, a Chopard diamond necklace for Valentine's Day, and a trip to Tahiti for my birthday. We couldn't keep our hands off of each other. His private jet had nine passenger seats, but I never sat in any of them. I was always on Elway's lap. Even when we went to restaurants and the host asked how many in our party, we'd say three if we were a group of four, and five if we were a group of six. And we'd giggle. I never sat in my chair. I was always on John's lap. We were head-over-heels in love with each other, and our chemistry was off the charts.

The sex just got better and better and better. We were always doing it on his plane. We joined the mile-high club on a commercial flight to Tahiti. How did we fit in the bathroom? Well, where there's a will, there's a way. Elway got what he wanted. We jokingly called my couch "The Fucking Couch," like, *"Want to go watch TV on the fucking couch?"* Because, well, you get it. After watching TV there, he looked at me... sweat dripping down his face and said, "No one has better sex than we do." Just one of the many ways John's competitive personality showed through.

John was born to win. But now he was retired. Heroics were gone from his life. I didn't need to know anything about the game to recognize the challenges of no longer being a champion on the field. Football was his everything. The truth of this came out when he was drinking. He was a lot of fun up until three or four vodka-cranberries. At which point he'd pick fights with me, making nonsensical comments like, "Maybe if you knew who I was, you'd love me."

I protested, "I love you for you. I don't need to know how many passes you made or how many times you were sacked, I love you for who you are as a person."

But he doubted I could possibly love him without appreciating his prowess on the football field. It's the only thing he had ever been valued for. Just as I was told a narrative about myself as a little girl, so was he, as a little boy. The message he got was: "You are a winner. No one else matters."

The first time I got a glimpse into just how dark and demented Elway's mind could get was the night we were driving back from a romantic weekend in Santa Barbara. We stopped at *Koi* restaurant because my friend Elena Terrones had told us she would be there with a fun group of people. Even though I was exhausted from a day of wine tasting, we stopped in because I wanted John to meet my friends. I was unusually quiet, though, since I was so tired. Elena teased me: "I bet you'd be excited if Mariah Carey were here." She was thinking of the time that Mariah and I met on a dance floor in Aspen on New Year's Eve. We danced together with glow sticks while the crowd watched. My friends love that story.

After we got home, John left my house and wandered around the neighborhood in the middle of the night. He needed to blow off steam. It turned out that Elena's innocent joke had inflamed him. He'd imagined a lesbian encounter between me and Mariah Carey! All we'd done was share a dance floor. No bodily fluids, or even words for that matter, were exchanged. Even though his bizarre interpretation was a red flag, I forgave his accusations.

After John's divorce was final, he brought me into his world. It was a lot of pressure to be introduced to his kids, his friends, and the press as the first new woman in his life since his divorce. Denver loved Janet Elway. I was grateful word never got out about our affair three years before or I'm sure I would not have been so well received, especially by his kids. We spent less time in California and more in Denver, in the same house he had shared with Janet. There were two huge his and hers master bath suites at the end of a corridor. Janet's room was now mine. I didn't feel guilty about it, since I wasn't responsible for the break up of their marriage, but it gave me the creeps, nevertheless. I desperately wanted John to sell that house so we could start our new lives together in a home free of marital memories.

Vestiges of their life together were everywhere. For example, I always kept the door to my dressing area open, since the toilet had a separate door. I had never noticed anything unusual until one day when Jaxon was playing, and I heard a rattling noise. Curious, I went to see what he was playing with. I discovered, to my confusion, that he was playing with one of six deadbolts fastened to the door. I walked across the hall to John's dressing area and examined his door. No locks at all. So, I asked him why Janet had six deadbolts on hers. He said it was so she could lock herself in whenever she wanted. I thought nothing of it. I guessed she had her reasons.

Another remnant of their marriage was the bookcase next to what was now my side of the bed. Why had she taken all of her belongings except the books in the case, all self-help books? Maybe she didn't need them anymore now that she'd got away from John. Was it possible she wasn't reading them for herself? Was she trying to figure out a way to help John?

Unfortunately, I asked these questions much later.

Love sure is blind.

I far preferred John's vacation home, an eight-bedroom house in Coeur d'Alene, Idaho, to his Denver home. We planned to get married there on the lake. John had speed boats and jet skis, and all kinds of toys. Sometimes we'd bring the kids for family time; sometimes we'd fill his plane with friends and make a party of it. Sometimes it would be just the two of us, for a romantic weekend. I preferred the family time because there was less chance of drama. When his friends were with us, there was more alcohol. After just a few stiff drinks, it was a complete transformation. Like something out of *The Exorcist,* he'd spit obscene insults. No one wanted to be the last one awake with him at the end of the night.

John and I were mismatched in many ways. I don't like sports. I don't get it. I like music. He doesn't get it. I'd blast the same Journey, Rolling Stones, Van Halen or Tom Petty album all day long while we were out on his boat, and later when I'd talk about the music, it would be like he'd never heard it before. Looking back, we really just had one thing in common: we were good in bed. Like the Eagles song lyrics:

> *Life in the fast lane*
> *Surely makes you lose your mind*

But some nights John wouldn't come to bed at all. I didn't understand it. I took it as rejection. It would be two or three o'clock, and I'd find him outside, staring at the lake, drinking and smoking cigarettes, lost in gloomy thought. I'd ask him what was wrong, and he'd blow up at me. I'd cry myself to sleep wondering how he could be so hurtful.

Alcohol made him aggressive and made me hyper-sensitive, a terrible combination, but if I didn't drink with him, he'd say I was no fun. It came between us and changed our personalities. We had an awful dark cloud around us. I knew that these indulgences were a dead-end road that our relationship could not survive. But I was terrified of losing him. I did whatever he wanted.

More than John's marital status had changed in the three years that we had not been in contact. Not only had he retired from football, but his twin sister had died of lung cancer, and his father, who was also his best friend, had died of a heart attack. He had four teenage kids. He was a phenomenal father to them, but now they were a broken family. John hadn't processed any of the pain. His inner torture was all dumped on me. Maybe I deserved it for having an affair with him, but I got sold a bag of damaged goods.

I suggested we go to therapy. I must have looked surprised when he agreed, because he said, "Carrie, do you think I want to be an asshole my whole life?"

At least he admitted it. I'll give him that. But the truth was, he was simply unwilling or unable to change. We hired a couple's therapist in L.A. and another one in Denver. But the "we" soon turned into me going to therapy alone. As soon as he had experienced the pain of facing his buried emotions, he told me he'd take physical pain over emotional pain any day. He had decided that he didn't want to work on himself. He said flat out that he'd rather date a doormat than someone who made him face his problems. He knew I wanted to help him heal. I loved him too much to watch him self-destruct. As it turned out, I didn't have to. He broke up with me. Then we got back together. Over and over, and over again. So many times, I lost count.

For a man who'd achieved so much glory in his life, he was strangely insecure. John was jealous of everyone, including women, my dead boyfriend, and my son. Whenever we got to a hotel, immediately after checking in we had to go to the bar for a drink. Normal people go to their rooms and get settled, but not John. He needed a cocktail, pronto. Once we arrived at the lobby bar of Atlantis Resort in the Bahamas. We were there for Michael Jordan's golf tournament. Like clockwork, after three drinks down the hatch, the cruel, irrational comments began. "Carrie, I could never be the love of your life because if Eric had stayed alive you would have married him." I was taken aback. Why was he bringing Eric up? Just to hurt me? This was nuts. Then John slurred, "And I can never be the love of your life because you have Jaxon."

"But you have four kids. You were married to their mother for twenty years. All those Christmases and birthdays. Eric and I never had the chance."

Trying to reason with an intoxicated asshole is a losing battle. On the other hand, he was right. I would have married Eric, and Jaxon would always come first. He couldn't understand why Steve had abandoned me and Jaxon, and he'd constantly ask me to repeat the story about the way it happened. It was almost as if he expected me to say something different, which really pissed me off because reliving it over and over again was torture. But like most decent fathers, John could not fathom what Steve did. At the end of the day, he had my back. He wrote an email to Steve standing up for me. What do you think Steve did? Something no man has ever done. He ignored Elway. Just like he ignored my entire pregnancy. Just like he ignored his son. Steve ignored Elway.

Soon Elway ignored me. He wouldn't speak to me the night of the big gala in the Bahamas. I took refuge in talking with Wayne and Janet Gretzky who were seated with us, a lovely couple. I was hurt and embarrassed. I hoped they didn't notice that John was ignoring me. Maybe they did. Maybe that's why they were nice to me. What had set him off that night? I thought he was mad at me because that afternoon I'd said hello to Paris Hilton, whom I knew from Playboy Mansion parties, when we bumped into her at the pool bar. I adored Paris, but John was repelled because her infamous sex tape had just come out. But the silent treatment turned out to be for nothing more than that John was pissed off because he couldn't get the telephone in our hotel room to work. He was like a toddler having a tantrum. He ruined our trip over a phone. He was impossible to deal with, but I stayed with him because I wanted the fantasy to be real. I wanted him to marry me and adopt Jaxon. I wanted us to live happily ever after.

We went to the Lake Tahoe golf tournament in 2004, the same tournament where Stormy Daniels allegedly hooked up with Donald Trump the following year. Trump was there and, while Jay Leno performed, we sat at the same dinner table. Throughout the show, Trump leaned his entire body across the table, leered at me and repeatedly said to John, "Your girlfriend is so beautiful, your girlfriend is gorgeous." I was amused. But John got mad. Not at Trump, at me! Whenever anyone gave me compliments, instead of being proud, he came unglued. He was used to it being all about him; he couldn't share the spotlight.

John grew more and more antagonistic. On the last night of a vacation to Italy he stayed out drinking all night with a friend. He showed up so late the next morning, I thought we were going to miss our flight. He was drunk, bloody, and battered. He looked like he'd been in a bar fight. On our way to Milan-Malpensa Airport, he went for the jugular. "Carrie, you don't know how to be loved because no one's ever loved you."

"Really?" I snapped. "Because the only reason anyone even talks to you is because you used to know how to throw an inflated pigskin."

Immediately, the enormity of what I'd said hit me. I ran to the ladies' room where he couldn't follow me. I kept out of his way until the flight was called. I got on the plane, put my ear plugs in, face mask on, and pretended to sleep. Eventually, he tapped me on the shoulder and apologized. We landed in Denver in time for the naming ceremony of *John Elway Drive* outside Mile High Stadium.

*****

One night a group of us were having dinner in the bar at his Denver restaurant, *Elway's*. Another girl, Shawna, who'd just arrived with one of John's male friends, wanted to use the bathroom, and so did I. So, we got up and went together, working our way through the crowd. To make sure we wouldn't get separated Shawna and I held hands, or wrists, I forget. Just what girls normally do. We peed, washed our hands, put on our lip gloss, and we were done. As we walked back to the table John stormed past us, angrily raised his middle finger at me, and mouthed, "Fuck off." I had no idea what could be wrong with him. He was drunk, of course. What was wrong this time? A little while later the valet manager, Scott Eirish, came over and asked if I needed a ride home.

"No, thanks," I said, "I'm with John."

"Well, I know. That's why I'm concerned. He just left."

Scott rescued me and took me back to John's house. When we got there, John's teenage daughter and my three-year-old son, whom she was babysitting, were both terrified, in her bedroom, balling their eyes out. John and one of his flunkies had packed all my stuff up and thrown it out into the snow in the front yard. I went into the bedroom where the kids were and locked the door behind me. John was going wild. Crazy drunk. Beating on the door, screaming at me to get the hell away from his daughter, who didn't want me to leave. When I told her I was so sorry, but I had to go, she cried, "Can't you do what my mom used to do and just get a hotel for the night?"

With my son in my arms, I got the hell out of there. Scott drove us to a friend's apartment and made sure we were safe. But the storm got worse. We were snowed in for three days. John kept calling me, but my heart couldn't take more drama, so I let the calls go to voicemail. I was devastated. I couldn't understand what had triggered his insane behavior. Later, back in L.A., after I'd had time to decompress, I listened to the dozens of abusive foul-mouthed messages he left for me that horrible night. One in particular explained his bizarre behavior.

"I sure hope Shawna tasted good," he slurred.

Oh. My. God.

Apparently, he'd got it into his twisted imagination that we'd gone down on each other in the bathroom. Where that came from, I had no clue. I certainly didn't have a history of hooking up with women in public restrooms.

After that episode, I told myself I was finished with him. The jealousy and the ludicrous accusations might have been forgivable, but this time he'd kicked my toddler out in a snowstorm. He'd crossed a line. I had to be done with him. John didn't remember doing any of the awful things he did that night. Not even when I played all his messages to him. He was disgusted with himself. He was sorry. He got sober for three months. I took him back. Again.

Things were better for a while. But tension mounted as I felt torn between John and Jaxon. After the first year, John stopped welcoming my son and our nanny on trips. He wanted my undivided attention. Amy was complaining because she expected the job to include more travel. And when I was away with John, I missed my baby. I felt guilty being an only parent and letting a nanny raise him. I tried to talk to John about it, but he just said, "When my kids come, then yours can." But he didn't hold to that. There were trips when his kids were included, but Jaxon excluded, with the excuse that he was too little. I grew to resent him. He wasn't exactly sensitive to my needs. This wasn't what I signed up for. Where was the John Elway who took my son to SeaWorld and carried him around on his shoulders? Where were the roses and the balloons?

In 2004, when John was inducted into the Pro Football Hall of Fame in his first year of eligibility, it was a big deal.

Not only was it the pinnacle of his career, but it was a huge event, like having a wedding with a big reception and everyone you ever knew invited. As we flew on his plane to Ohio for the ceremony, all his kids were with us. But not Jaxon. We were still climbing to the cruising altitude, when John began reading that morning's *Denver Post*. He had the paper gripped in both hands. I could see he was seething, a vein bulging on his forehead. I knew it was my fault, and I felt terrible about it. I hadn't intended to tarnish his big day, but I'd screwed up.

You see, he'd given me the honor of being part of a huge feature story on his induction, but when the reporter asked about John's heavy drinking, which was pretty well known at the time, I wasn't savvy enough to deflect the question. I answered honestly and was quoted as saying it was a problem in our relationship, and I wished he'd quit. This was one occasion when he would have been justified lashing out at me, but he handled it calmly. He didn't make a big deal about it. His sister did. She wanted to kill me.

I was proud to be on his arm in Canton, Ohio while he was applauded by thousands of fans. I was pleasantly surprised when he had me walking the football field with him, waving to his fans and posing for photos with his family. I felt that he honored and respected me. Bill Phillips from EAS was there, the man responsible for the two of us getting together in the first place at the Miami Super Bowl. He said, "Well, you got what you wanted Carrie." He was right. We'd come a long way from the Dollhouse in Ft. Lauderdale.

*****

John Elway was friendly with Jon Bon Jovi. They were both co-owners of Arena football teams and had appeared on TV together. I met Jon Bon Jovi a few times at the games and on set. As chance would have it, they were both going to be at a Toyota dealership convention in Chicago, as Elway owned dealerships and Bon Jovi was hired to perform. It sounded like fun, but I couldn't go. I had already been traveling with Elway for a week, and I needed to get home to my son.

Back in L.A., I knew not to answer my phone after 10:00 p.m. because of Elway's drunk dialing. In the morning, when I checked my voicemail, he had left me a slurring message: "You've been around, and it's over. Whore." I was livid and didn't speak to him for a week. But we had a big trip planned to Washington, D.C. for a U.S.O. event, to the University of Virginia to visit his daughter, to a Basset store in Florida to launch his furniture line, and to South Beach for a few days of relaxation. I didn't cancel, but I was still fuming when I got on a United Airlines flight to Denver. We then flew on his private jet to Washington. I was there but I wasn't there. I looked out the window, refusing to speak. Finally, I broke my silence.

"I want to know why you called me and said, 'You've been around and it's over.' And why you called me a whore."

"Well, how many times have you been with Jon Bon Jovi?"

I almost choked. "The only times I've ever met him have been with you. Why?"

"Because he asked about you."

"What did he say?"

"He said, 'Is your girlfriend here with you?'"

This is what it was all about? Good Lord.

I said, "He was just making conversation. It meant nothing. He doesn't even know my name."

From Jon Bon Jovi's innocent, polite inquiry, Elway's fevered imagination had concocted an entirely different scenario. That's what I had to contend with.

But Elway didn't have to worry about Jon Bon Jovi. He should have been more concerned about Peyton Manning. I'd met Peyton when Elway took me to a *Sports Illustrated* party at the Super Bowl in Houston, and we sat at the same table. When he saw me the following year with my girlfriends in Hawaii during Pro Bowl, he knew I was John's girlfriend. A friend of Peyton's invited us to a party and got my phone number to text the address. But no text came. Instead, I got a call from Peyton.

"Hi, beautiful. I'd love for us to get together."

"Aren't you here with your wife," I asked him. "Where is she?"

"She's out on the balcony. She can't hear me," he replied.

I managed to evade him in Hawaii but when I got back to L.A., he called again and asked me to get together with him in Denver. He was still playing for Indianapolis but had business in Denver.

"Are you out of your mind?" I asked him. "Do you want a double murder story in the papers? John would kill us."

I could imagine the headlines: *Hall of Fame Quarterbacks in Murder Love Triangle!*

I was stunned that Manning was hitting on me. I figured he would have had more respect not only for his wife but for Elway. These quarterbacks have way more testosterone than they know what to do with. I was tempted to tell John about Peyton, but I didn't want to hurt his fragile ego, so I kept my mouth shut. Years later, when I read that John was managing the Broncos and had hired Peyton, I laughed. Had I opened my mouth I could have changed the entire course of football history!

"You are not the easiest person to be in love with," John would say to me. Maybe he had a point, but he did have all my attention. I never even thought about other guys when I was with him. Brad Pitt or Tom Cruise could have hit on me and no way would I have been interested. I was madly addicted to John.

*****

After yet another breakup, I read one of those dumb relationship books. This one's gimmick was a sixty day rule. Basically, the rule was don't contact the man. If he really loves you, he'll come back within sixty days. On day fifty nine of the sixty day test period, I got an audition for a John Stamos TV show. I was so depressed, I could barely get out of bed, but my close friend and talent manager Christina (who was once married to KISS guitar player Bruce Kulick), pushed me to do it.

"You have to go. Just pick yourself up and go," she insisted.

At the audition my survival skills took over. It was another of those "hot girl" roles. My specialty. I needed a distraction to get over Elway, so I made a point of accidentally bumping into Stamos. I introduced myself as a single mom who would love to get involved with his pet charity, saving abandoned babies with Project Cuddle. I'd recently read a magazine article about his involvement with the organization in People Magazine, so I was armed with knowledge. Impressed, he gave me his email and we began a flirtation. Plus, I had a legitimate reason to get in touch. Without any help from him, I'd landed the role. Stamos is renowned for being good looking, but he also has a fantastic sense of humor. He made me laugh and cheered me up. He was really slow about asking me out, however, until we were both invited to see Vince Neil perform at the birthday party of a mutual friend, *Full House* producer Jeff Franklin.

Unlike Elway, Stamos and I had music in common. He's a talented musician who sometimes plays with the Beach Boys. We'd hang out at this house with his friends while they jammed classic rock tunes. John played drums, guitar and piano. We went to Disneyland with groups of people. He loves Disney. He also invited me to Las Vegas for Super Bowl weekend. The sixty day rule had already been broken. It was now about day ninety, and I'd heard nothing from Elway. So off we went to Vegas in a private plane along with Stamos's mother, sister, and a couple of his cousins. We started drinking on the plane at eleven that morning, which is always a mistake.

When the plane landed in Vegas, it taxied and parked right next to a Citation with the tailwind numbers 777MX. Holy shit. Elway's plane. I wasn't expecting him to be there. Elway's pilot, Sid, was a good friend who'd married one of my best friends, Nicki, so I texted him and invited him to hang out with us. Another bad idea. As much as I love hanging out with Sid, I associated him with Elway. I didn't need to think about Elway more; I needed to think about him less. The group of us spent the day drinking, gambling, and having fun. We dined at *Nobu* and cruised the strip in a convertible driven by an Elvis impersonator.

That night I did the worst thing I've ever done to anyone. It's a story I'm ashamed of. It had been a long day, when we got back to our suite at the *Hard Rock Hotel,* Stamos crashed. Alcohol makes some people sleepy, but not me. I took off my clothes and my makeup and got ready for bed, but the sugar in the booze had me wide awake and ready to party. I got this whacked idea to call Elway. There was no logic to it. I hadn't called him in months. It was just a dumb, drunk move.

He answered, and we arranged to meet for a drink. I was putting my clothes back on, still talking on the phone, when I realized Stamos had woken up and overheard the conversation. He grabbed the phone and screamed at Elway. Neither guy knew who each other was, at this point. Stamos was rightfully pissed off and told me to get the fuck out. He called a friend to take me to Harrah's where he had other rooms booked. Instead, I made my way to the Venetian where Elway was staying. What was I thinking? I go on a trip with a gorgeous TV star, a really nice guy, and I pull a stunt like that? But I wasn't over Elway. I swear he had an evil spell on me. I went to his room and we made love all night. John Elway couldn't stand it when I called it having sex. I had to say, "making love."

The next morning, Elway and I were talking. I would have assumed Sid told him I was with John Stamos. When I mentioned how guilty I felt that I had ditched Stamos the night before, Elway flinched.

"You're seeing John Stamos?"

I will never forget the look on his face. There couldn't have been a bigger burn. I knew he'd never get past it. For the first time Elway actually had a legitimate reason to be insanely jealous about: one of the sexiest guys in the world. Among Elway's nonsensical drunken claims was that I had once said to him, "I can have any guy I want." It's not something I would ever say, but simply to start a fight, he'd insist that I'd said it. Now that I was with Stamos, it was an argument I'd lose.

In the middle of all this, Stamos called me. "You're not in your room at Harrah's. You're with your ex-boyfriend, aren't you?"

"Yes, but he has a two-bedroom suite."

"Did you have sex with him?

"No. No. I swear I didn't."

Stamos isn't stupid. He didn't believe me. Well, who would?

"Well, since you decided to go there, I'll let him figure out how to get you home."

John Stamos was a nice guy to even consider how I would get home. He's the one that should have told me to fuck off. Instead it was Elway who didn't care how I got home. He just left me there in his hotel room with barely a goodbye. Two famous men, two private jets, and I ended up having to buy my own plane ticket back to L.A. on Southwest. I guess I deserved it.

How could I have done something so stupid? I hated myself. Humiliated, I wrote Stamos a sincere letter of apology and he called me. What made me feel even worse was how understanding he was. It took my sacrificing a really nice guy, probably the best catch in Hollywood, for me to gain some self worth. Maybe just to make me feel better, Stamos told me he'd done worse things in his drunker days, and that mutual friends had told him my behavior was out of character. It was too bad it went down the way it did, Stamos said, because he thought we had a really sweet thing. He was right. But the damage was done.

Elway and I stayed in contact. He came to L.A. to get hair plugs and I took him to the doctor. This was the second surgery; the procedure had to be spaced six months apart. It takes about eight hours while the patient is awake, and they sew one hair at a time in your scalp to get a natural result. We had lots of time to talk. But the end of our relationship was in sight.

"I wish I'd met you later. I wished I'd met you after I'd sorted through all of this stuff," he told me.

On one level, I was satisfied to hear him say he knew how fucked up he was, but at the same time, it was the first time he had ever broken up with me in a rational manner, so I knew it was for real this time. He was sober and sincere. He said he was sorry, that he was just trying to cope, and I got caught in the crossfire. He'd been working with a Christian-based psychologist, who specialized in helping retired sports figures, and he'd realized that he'd not even begun to deal with his divorce. Two and a half years into our relationship, and he just figures this out? A giant tear rolled down my cheek.

"Do you think this is our bad karma for having an affair?" I asked.

His eyes welled up, too.

As much as Elway was a tormented man, fighting his own demons, I had a few of my own. Losing Eric to cancer and being abandoned while I was pregnant did a number on my head that I have never gotten over. Elway was just a big bandaid for the wounds inflicted on me by Steve. I'd justified that ordeal, telling myself I'd had to endure it because Elway and I were meant to be together. If I now accepted that he and I weren't meant to be, there went the comforting rationalization that everything that happened with Steve was for a reason. The fear of accepting my own reality kept me putting up with Elway's abuse.

After our final breakup, I felt like someone had tied my wrists to the hubcaps of a car and dragged me along, skinning me alive before leaving me to die on the side of the road. I told myself I'd rather stay single than ever have to break up again. With every loss, I relived the previous one. My emotional memories lingered in every inch of my mind, body, and soul.

I learned the hard way not to help men with their hair plugs; it turns out I was just fixing him up for the next girl. John Elway cheated on me with a former Raiderette cheerleader whom he eventually married. I saw the photos on Facebook. They even used my wedding plan. Now my master bath suite is hers. I hope she never needs the deadbolts.

ABOVE PHOTO:
With John Stamos and Elena
Terrones in Kona, Hawaii.

Chapter 10

Don't Blow Off Billionaires

My son Jaxon was raised hanging out at the Playboy Mansion, flying on private jets, sleeping on tour buses, and going to concerts with all access passes. Not exactly a conventional upbringing. After my breakup with Elway, Michael Keaton and I started dating again. One day Jaxon went to preschool wearing a cute little cream-colored sweater with a brown teddy bear that Michael had bought him at the Gap. When the teachers admired it, he told them, "Batman gave it to me." They called me into the office because they thought he was making up stories. I got a kick out of telling them it was true.

When Jaxon started preschool, I was the only single parent at the school. To help him cope, I used to read to him those illustrated books with an animal kingdom theme that explained different kinds of families. By the time he was in elementary school, a lot of parents were divorced, so he got to see it first-hand. Some kids were being raised by grandparents, and his best friend was being raised by an aunt and uncle, because the mother and father were in prison. Not shocking since we lived in Los Angeles. Two other Playmate moms, Angel Boris and Daphne Duplaix, had kids at the same elementary school, so being the offspring of a centerfold was nothing unusual. Strange as it might sound, being able to say that he grew up at the Playboy Mansion somewhat made up for my son's father abandoning him. Jaxon thought of Hef as a surrogate dad, and it was a privilege to call the Playboy Mansion our home away from home. It always cheered me up when we went there on weekends, even now, when getting myself to go anywhere was a battle. It wasn't fair of me to date Michael because I was emotionally unavailable, and it didn't last. He told me I wasn't sexy like I used to be. He was right. I just wasn't into it. But we remained friends.

The final break up with Elway had left me devastated, as though I'd barely survived a war. My entire vision of the future had been obliterated. I spent weeks alone in my dark bedroom. Sometimes I'd sit on the floor, my back against the door in case my son tried to open it, sobbing on the phone with Nicki. I would never let my little boy see me like that. I always put on a happy smile for him. But I knew I couldn't fake it forever. I had to pick myself up and be strong. Survival mode kicked in. Where was that spirited girl with a sparkle in her eyes and the spring in her step? I was determined to find her.

I recalled one of the fights I had with Elway the year before. We were in Idaho, out on his boat with a group of his friends. I took the liberty of looking at his phone and saw he'd made a call to a number I knew, a girl he'd gone out with before me. In his contacts, it was listed under a man's name, but I have a photographic memory, so he didn't fool me. I was so pissed I jumped off his boat into the icy cold lake, screaming at him, "I'm going back to Monte Carlo and Ibiza!" I furiously swam to shore and quickly packed my things. Walking out of the bedroom I spied the remote control on the nightstand. John couldn't fall asleep without the TV on, so I grabbed the remote and hurled it into the lake. I knew that mentioning Monaco and Ibiza would hit John where it hurt. But now that was all behind me. The more I thought about it, it was exactly what I needed to do. Revisit those opportunities. Reconnect with some of the friends I'd made over the years, friends in high places.

I'd met a grocery store tycoon named Ron when I was working at Sanctuary. He took me on lots of exciting trips on his private jet, a 737 with a red velvet interior. Puff Daddy (Sean Combs) was on the plane with us once when we flew home from Miami. He'd just begun to date J. Lo, and it was supposed to be a secret. Another time, the Reverend Jesse Jackson was on the plane. My friend Layla Roberts, Miss October 1997, was afraid to fly and buried her head in the reverend's lap. He was not offended or uncomfortable. Never a dull moment.

Ron would call me up and say, "Grab your friends and let's go." At just a moment's notice we'd be on our way to Paris or Ibiza or Monaco for the Grand Prix. That's where I encountered Richard Branson. One crazy night at the Monte Carlo nightclub *Jimmy'z,* he drank champagne out of

"Baywatch Babe's" stiletto and came back to the yacht to carry on partying. Richard and "Baywatch Babe" were in the cabin next door, so Layla and I stood in the bathtub giggling as we held drinking glasses between our ears and the wall trying to hear what was going on. Suddenly our door flew open and "Baywatch Babe" appeared, wearing nothing but a sweatshirt. She needed to barf. We didn't stand in her way. Afterwards, I cleaned the puke off her face and gave her some mouthwash. Then we ordered her, "Get back in there. He owns an island!"

Considering "Baywatch Babe's" condition, I don't think Branson got lucky, but the next morning, as I enjoyed my breakfast on the deck, it was funny to witness Branson do his walk of shame. Ron's friend Marcus called out to him, "So how's it going with the hot air balloon?" — a reference to his attempt to fly around the world. Branson just laughed and got off the yacht as fast as he could.

That was also the first time I'd met Prince Albert. I returned to the 2005 Monaco Grand Prix and Cannes Film Festival and met the prince again at a yacht party attended by Bono, Jay Z, and numerous other celebrities and socialites. Mutual friends introduced me to the charming prince, and I reminded him we'd met before. We shared a few laughs, and I walked away to mingle. A little while later, security guards subtly requested my phone number for the prince. Unfortunately, I'd rented a French cell phone and accidentally wrote down the wrong digits.

The royal opportunities didn't stop there. It was the prince's twenty-one-year-old nephew, Princess Grace's grandson, that I woke up in bed with. He just happened to be partying on the yacht I was staying on and needed somewhere to sleep, so he crawled under the covers with me. We just cuddled. Not that I was celibate the entire trip. I did hook up with a dashingly handsome French race car driver. He bent me over the track in the middle of the night when the streets were empty. A Formula One experience like no other, an experience money can't buy. What a way to see the city lights bouncing on the horizon! I conquered Monaco and returned to the states, over John Elway, and ready to be me again.

However, my bubble quickly burst. As soon as I got home, Stephen Herek served me with papers to modify child support. There's this horrible law in California that enables a man to renege on payments if he files a motion to modify the amount. Then he can just pay whatever he wants until it's settled in court. The asshole started paying me a measly hundred dollars a month and dragged out the legal process for as long as he could. I was in a bad position. In the time I'd spent with Elway, I burned through my savings. He didn't want me to work, so I had no income. And he didn't pay my bills. When we split up, I was broke. A hundred dollars a month certainly wasn't going to cut it. I had to take out a second mortgage to pay a lawyer and put food on the table.

Somehow Steve won a reduction of child support to less than a fifth of what we had originally agreed on. You'd think he would have been more than happy with that. He wasn't. Greed or plain callousness got the better of him. He simply ignored the court order and continued to pay just $100 a month. He'd seen my financial records and knew I didn't have the money to fight him. What do you expect from a man who abandons his own child?

At the same time, my son's godmother was also taking advantage of me. She stayed with me for free for eighteen months and never chipped in towards even one bill. She watched me lose everything and never offered to pay for a thing. As the legal battle dragged on over the course of a year, I lost my rich boyfriend and my best friend, and accumulated a ton of debt.

I was emotionally ravaged. So, when another billionaire named Ron, a New York cosmetics mogul, invited me to join him on his yacht moored at the Caribbean island of St. Barth's, I jumped at the chance. Years before, he'd called *Playboy* to get in touch with me, and we'd met for coffee a few times. Now I was open to spending time with him. Naturally, I assumed he expected it to be a romantic trip. After all, he'd pursued me for a decade. I was surprised, therefore, when he brought along his thirteen-year-old daughter and three of her friends. They were sweet; I didn't mind at all.

I hadn't expected a G-rated trip, but I got an even bigger surprise when nine rabbis with their wives and kids joined us on the boat. It was a major Jewish holiday, so we all wore yarmulkes, held hands in a circle, and prayed. I'm not Jewish and wasn't familiar with their religious practices, so it was a fascinating experience. I certainly wasn't prepared for the rules, however. The Jews didn't believe in using transportation on Saturdays, so I took the small boat into town by myself, and enjoyed the jet skis with Ron's personal doctor, the only other non-Jew on the trip. On Saturday evening, I went to the yacht's kitchen to get a snack only to be told no eating was allowed after 6:00 p.m.

The morning we left the island, as I was having breakfast with Ron, he took a call. He told someone that he missed her. It sure sounded like he already had a girlfriend. He wasn't trying to hide it; he just hadn't told me about it. I should have figured as much, considering he did nothing more affectionate the entire weekend than hold my hand once. I'm still not sure why he invited me. Maybe he was like Prince Jefri. Maybe he wanted a decoration for his boat. Anyway, it was an amusing experience unlike any other, and a great distraction from my problems. Not every relationship needs to be romantic. I was grateful for the good time, even though it didn't turn out to be a love connection.

Lucky for me, billionaires named Ron were coming out of the woodwork. My friend Sarah suggested she set me up with her husband's billionaire friend, also called Ron. So, the four of us went out. This Ron, who'd made his fortune in construction, had a magnetic personality and muscular biceps, and we hit it off immediately. On our second date, I confided in him about the legal battle with Steve. Ron had been divorced a couple of times, but deeply loved all his children. He couldn't fathom how Steve had not only turned his back on his own child, but also wasn't willing to provide financial support. Ron intended to do something about it.

"I want you to find the best lawyer in L.A. Tell him money is no object. And you fuck that guy!"

My heart swelled. This was the man for me. He was badass. So that's what I did. I found the best lawyer in L.A., Ron Litz (another Ron). Ron paid for Ron, who proved in court that Steve had lied. He showed that every month Steve spent more money for pet food than he did in child support. He told the judge, "This man cares less than zero, if possible, about his own child."

The judge announced he wanted to see Steve in his courtroom. Steve's lawyer had to stand up and admit, "I'm sorry your honor, my client is busy directing a movie in Canada." Huh. Previously, he'd used the pathetic excuse that Steve couldn't pay child support because he couldn't get work. "You're only as good as your last picture," he claimed. The judge had been manipulated and lied to, and he wasn't happy about it. He awarded me an Ostler-Smith order, which means that once a year I have the right to look at Steve's tax returns and put him in the correct bracket for what he's supposed to pay according to his income. That is what happens when an absent parent tries to lie and cheat their way out of paying child support.

Ron had saved the day. Steve is still probably scratching his head trying to figure out how I came up with the $60,000 in legal fees, which the judge then ordered him to pay. Win-win for me. Steve may have learned his lesson about trying to screw over the legal system, but he certainly hasn't learned any lessons about how to be a decent human being. He still has never reached out to see his son. Not a call, never a card. Nothing.

After our fourth date, Ron called and told me he hadn't been able to sleep the night before. Why, I asked. He wanted to know if I had car payments. Well, I did. He insisted I fax the paperwork to his assistant, and my car was paid off that day. His generosity knew no bounds. Ron's idea of a date was to take me to Neiman Marcus for the afternoon and blow fifty grand on me. Once we flew on his main jet, his 737, from L.A. to France, just to yacht shop and have lunch for a few hours. He said his Gulfstream was mine and the 737 was his. Ron was head over heels for me, and he adored my son. We talked marriage. We discussed having our wedding ceremony at the legendary Hotel du Cap-Eden-Roc Cap d'Antibes, which sits between Nice and Cannes and has stunning panoramic views of the Mediterranean coastline. He had his personal jeweler come to the house, and we picked out a nine-carat stone for my ring.

*****

Not all billionaires are named Ron. There's one named Don. I was basically naked when I had my first encounter with Donald Trump. It was September 2000 during New

York Fashion Week, when designer Betsey Johnson had the concept of using a group of Playmates to showcase her designs. I was doing a quick-change backstage, wearing nothing but a pair of nude-colored panties when I felt someone staring at me. I turned around and there was Trump, a big lecherous grin on his face, winking at me, an exaggerated wink-wink, with his hairy eyebrows jiggling up and down. Standing right next to him, stone-faced, was the woman he was dating, Melania. It was kind of creepy.

Later, Donald and Melania gave me and two other Playmates, Victoria Silvstedt and Layla Roberts, a lift to the after-party. Victoria had been roommates with Melania during their days modeling in Paris, which was why they extended the invitation. All the way there he did the same thing. Wink-wink-wink. Melania stared out the window, not uttering a word. All very strange. At the end of the evening, he gave us a lift home. Melania was dropped off first at her apartment, Donald got out at Trump Tower, and the limo took us back to our hotel. To be fair, he didn't try to go home with any of us.

The Playmate whom he did infamously have an affair with, Karen McDougal, was a friend of mine. She wasn't a part of that fashion show, but six years later she met him at a Playboy Mansion party for *The Apprentice*. Soon after, in June 2006, they began an affair that she claims lasted ten months. She first told me about it when we went out for lunch one day. She said she was having an affair with one of the most powerful people in the world, but she wouldn't say who. Later that night, I sent her an email saying, "Now you have me curious." And I put together a list of candidates. It was part funny, part serious. I included Bill Gates, Bill Clinton, P. Diddy, Rupert Murdoch, Oprah — and Trump! She wrote back, "You're too funny. I will ask him if I can tell you. I just don't want him to get upset (especially since I told a friend and she can't be trusted now). I do want to tell you!!! Oh, he is on the list."

Later, she told me who it was and spilled stories of her escapades with Donald Trump. She told me details so obscene that if I repeated them in this book, my memoir would turn into trash. So, I won't.

After the affair became explosive worldwide news, Karen told Anderson Cooper on CNN that she had first decided to disclose her story about the affair because "an ex-friend or an old friend of mine started on social media talking about my relationship, and she was part of that, she knows everything." Well, she had told me a lot about the relationship, but it didn't all match what she told Anderson.

She told him that the first night that she and Trump had sex in a private bungalow at the Beverly Hills Hotel, he tried to hand her cash. She never told me that. She also claimed on CNN that there were real feelings between the two of them, that she hoped the relationship could lead to marriage, and that Trump "always told me that he loved me." She never told me any of that either. She never said anything nice about him.

All she did was complain that he promised her Christmas and birthday gifts, Cartier jewelry and watches, and then never delivered.

Karen's relationship with Trump overlapped her relationship with Bruce Willis. She was crazy in love with Bruce. I never heard her speak about Trump the way she did about Bruce. She and Bruce had a steamy sex life. I know, for sure, because Karen once brought me over to Bruce's house, and the three of us partied and... ahem, let's just say I personally witnessed the steaminess. Karen dated Bruce for six months, but then one day she told me that he suddenly he ghosted her, refusing to take her calls. I had a theory as to why. Photos of Bruce and Karen vacationing in Italy had hit the tabloids not long before. I suggested that Trump could have seen them and called Bruce to boast about his affair with her. My theory must have hit home, because her face fell, and her eyes welled up with tears.

Karen's relationship with Trump would probably never have been of any consequence if Trump had not run for the presidency. Of course, she used my silly tweets on May 7, 2016, four days after Trump won the Republican nomination, as her excuse for selling her story for $150,000 to AMI, publisher of the *National Enquirer*. As I explained in my preface, I had never imagined those tweets would help create such a firestorm. But Karen found them useful to justify exploiting her affair. She claimed that if the story was going to become international news, she wanted to be the one to tell it, to ensure that the account was accurate and not lurid grist for the tabloid mill. But that was Karen's style. In fact, it wasn't the first time she had sold a story to the tabloids.

One day, Karen called me for advice. A foreign publication was offering a hefty sum if she would do a topless photoshoot and spill the details about her relationship with Willis. Apparently, my opinion didn't matter. In 2008, the Spanish tabloid called *Interviu* published new topless photos and a "tell all" interview about her relationship with Bruce Willis. It came out soon after Bruce started dating model Emma Hemming, whom he later married. I was surprised when the White House or AMI, or Fox News didn't use that information to destroy her credibility.

It had been a decade since I'd heard from Karen McDougal, but somehow I became the centerpiece of her story. Karen's claim that I was the first to expose her affair with Trump came when she filed a lawsuit against AMI on March 20, 2018. By using my name and my nearly two-year-old deleted tweets in court documents, which are public records, she dragged me into her drama. The press was already in a feeding frenzy over porn star Stormy Daniels' association with Trump. The barrage of media calls started all over again. I could have said a lot, but I refused to speak to any of the reporters. I didn't want to risk the information being manipulated for a political agenda or to inadvertently hurt other alleged victims. And I certainly didn't want to spread more rumors.

*****

Ron and I never went through with the wedding, and I never got the ring. Once the newness of the relationship wore off, we stopped being perfect people. We got grumpy with each other. I didn't appreciate the good things about him and focused on the flaws. I became annoyed at the way he spoke down to waiters and his staff. One day when he was mean to his daughter's friend, I packed my bags and left his house. He came after me and apologized. He didn't understand why it upset me, but I'm really sensitive. I was a fourteen-year-old once and felt the girl's humiliation. Unfortunately, I started being bitchy and, eventually, he just called it off. We tried once to get back together, but the magic wasn't there anymore. He was a great guy, and I'll always appreciate the kind things he did to help me and my son.

I used to assume I would meet the perfect stepfather for Jaxon, but as an only parent, it's hard to cultivate a relationship. My divorced friends who shared custody every other week had the time for dating, but I didn't. Another pressure on me was the deep pain my son felt living without a father. When he was eight years old, Jaxon went to *The School of Rock* where my mother had bought him guitar lessons, but instead, he wanted to learn the drums. Ironically, the first show in which he was cast was a KISS tribute show. The kids all wore KISS makeup and I did Jaxon's just like Eric's "The Fox." He even used Eric's gloves and sticks that

I'd saved. It was adorable. But his desire for a dad led him to go around telling everyone Eric Carr from KISS was his father. The teachers could do the math and knew it was impossible and called me into the office because of it. When I explained that his father had abandoned him, and he wished Eric was his dad instead, they understood.

Although I kick myself now for blowing it with Ron, it wasn't a difficult breakup. A friend and I went out and celebrated my freedom. I got us front row center seats to a Van Halen show because David Lee Roth was reunited with the band. It was a big deal. I had been waiting twenty years for this moment. Dave sang to me the entire show, and I know every word to every song, so I sang along with him. It was like I was the only person in the whole arena. What was funny was the confused look on his face. Rather than focusing on the audience, it seemed like he was more intent on trying to figure out where he knew me from throughout his performance. They showed my friend and me on the Jumbotron during the whole show, so on our way out we were famous. Everyone was like, "Hey, it's the Jumbotron chicks!" Of course, I was a little disappointed that Dave didn't invite me backstage, but the music had made me so happy. The seats were expensive, but feeling sixteen again? Priceless.

*****

My grandmother on my mother's side, Grandma Jo, always told me it was just as easy to fall in love with a rich man as a poor man. I wish. My lucky streak finding billionaires named Ron ended. My carriage turned into a pumpkin. Instead of a rich Ron, I fell in love with a poor Roni, a flamenco guitarist, of all things. When I first saw Roni perform, I had one of those "where have you been my whole life?" moments. He was gorgeous. Long wavy brown hair and a smile that lit up the world, the epitome of anyone's Latin lover fantasy. Only he was from Nebraska and didn't speak a word of Spanish. It was just part of his act when he toured with his ethnically diverse band and back-up dancers.

Roni and I dated for a year and a half. He was great with Jaxon. As my friend Lisa had moved in with us and was willing to babysit, I had the freedom to go out. I didn't see any signs of insecurity for the whole first year. Then one night, we were talking about our favorite films, and he asked me who my favorite actor was. Leonardo DiCaprio, I instantly answered, but not necessarily because of his movie roles, but because of the special person that he is. I told him the story about the night I'd been standing in line for the bathroom at exclusive nightclub Hyde, when Leo came up, said he hadn't seen me in a long time, and asked how I was.

"Well," I replied, pulling out a photo of Jaxon, "I had your baby."

He laughed. Leo and I had never been intimate, so obviously I was kidding. The joke had only occurred to me because when Jaxon was born everyone had said he looked just like Leonardo DiCaprio. Leo asked me who the father really was, and I told him about Jaxon's father.

"Wow. Some people are such assholes," he said.

Some months later I was at another club and he waved me over to his table.

"I just want to tell you something," he said, "The best people are raised by single moms."

"Was yours a single mom?"

"Yeah."

"Well, you tell your mom she has a fan."

It just meant so much to me that he went out of his way to be supportive and make me feel better during the worst and most challenging time in my life. When somebody abandons you the way I was abandoned, I imagine people ask what's wrong with her? Like I must be a psycho or have done something horrific to drive a man to abandon his pregnant girlfriend. Leo's comments meant more to me than he could ever know.

I related the whole story to Roni who didn't share my appreciation. He became insanely jealous. In the coming weeks, if Leo appeared on TV, or a girl walked by wearing a Titanic shirt, or we overheard a couple at the next dinner table mention "Leonardo DiCaprio," I'd get the silent treatment for the rest of the night. On a trip to the Cayman Islands, as the flight descended, I was flipping through a magazine and there was Leo in an ad for Tag Heuer watches. Roni saw it and huffed and puffed and crossed his arms. Three days of cold silence followed. I sat on the beach in the stunning Cayman Islands, crying because Roni refused to speak to me.

"What is your problem?" I kept asking.

I finally got my answer. Roni told me that Leo was representative of all the famous men I had gone out with. Why he had chosen Leo, whom I had never gone out with, to represent the ones I had gone out with made no sense to me. I jokingly suggested we fight about someone I had actually dated. Anyway, he had known about most of my past relationships. We had been together for a year and half, and it had never caused a problem. Why now? My theory is that Roni's career had begun to fail, which made him more and more insecure and jealous, and he felt inadequate when compared to some of the rich and successful men I'd dated.

More than angry, the whole thing just made me sad. Faced with the fact that our relationship had deteriorated to the point of no return, I shared my devastation with my sister in the form of hysterical tears. Jill told me, "This is not about Roni. It's about Eric and John and every other loss you've experienced." She was right. With each loss I relive the previous ones. Why did I still hold my exes in my heart? Why did they continue to have power over me?

The answer was simple. When I gave them my heart, I truly meant it. I couldn't fault myself for that. So, I examined my choices in men instead. I looked at it as my father would when conducting a scientific study. I considered all my exes and tried to name the common denominators. On the surface, there didn't seem to be a pattern or a specific type. They were various ages and their physical attributes differed drastically. But when I really dug deep, I saw what they all had in common. They were *exciting*. I was attracted to excitement. Even though Roni wasn't rich, he was a beautiful dreamer. I fell in love with the fantasy that we were going to build an empire together. As his dream crumbled, he wanted to take me down with it.

As much as it hurts to be at rock bottom, I am glad that he pushed me to that point of realizing that none of those men or their lifestyles were the answer anymore. I had to find a way out from under the wrath of Roni and discover a way to satisfy my quest for excitement on my own.

Over the following months, he berated me. With a psychotic look in his eyes, he obsessively demanded to know what other celebrities I'd dated. This tore me apart. He wanted to know my past only so that he could use it against me. He had turned into John Elway. I wasn't happy with someone who didn't accept me for who I was, and who was clearly digging for a reason to leave me. I am a public figure. It's hard to hide my past but I tried. I paid a company called Web Sheriff a lot of money to erase my past off the internet, particularly web sites like *WhosDatedWho.com*. But everyone has their limits and there came a point when I was done hiding and done apologizing. I gave him what he asked for.

At least I was considerate about it. Before I dropped the bomb, I asked him:

"Are you sure you want to know? It might kill you."

He was defiant. "Yes! Tell me, now!"

I could have chosen David Lee Roth. We had run smack into him when Roni took my son and me to a Van Halen concert. We entered the venue through the artists entrance at the same time Dave was arriving. It was the one time I didn't want him to recognize me, so, of course, he did. I'd quickly turned my head away and walked on. It would have been a huge slap in the face to Roni to find out I had a thing with Diamond Dave, especially after he'd drained his savings account for our incredible seats.

Instead of drawing the torture out, I squashed Roni like a bug.

"Tell me," he demanded.

"Howard Stern."

Roni was the biggest Howard fan in the world. Even though he was a musician, he never played music in his car, only Howard on Sirius radio.

He'd asked for it, and he got it.

That was how I got rid of Roni.

Chapter 11

Don't Believe in Fairytales

While writing this book, one question nagged at me: *How do you end the story of a life that is still in very much in progress?* In the spring of 2018, that question was on my mind as I boarded a plane to Indianapolis for my first KISS Expo. For years I had been invited to these things, but I had always declined. Held all over the world — Atlanta, Tokyo, Helsinki— KISS Expos offer fans and band members a chance to mingle for a weekend of fun and tribute. I had a lot of reasons to be apprehensive about attending, but mainly it was because I knew that meeting so many of Eric's fans would dredge up a lot of painful memories.

As I boarded the plane, I was still not sure why I had let Bruce Kulick change my mind this year. Was it because he had assured me that KISS fans were wonderful people? Was it that it was the twentieth anniversary of the Expo? Or was it that the writing of this book had made me less afraid to confront my past?

As chance would have it, the past was sitting right next to me on the plane, in the form of my old friend Bobby Rock. Bobby and I had become friends twenty-five years earlier, after his pregnant girlfriend, Sherri Foreman, was murdered.

While our bond comes from tragic loss, a club no one wants to join, it doesn't make it any less cherished. Talking with Bobby is better than therapy.

As Bobby puts it, "Deep is what we do."

Now, completely different paths had led us to the same spot. His main connection to the Expo was that he was formerly in a band with ex-KISS guitarist Vinnie Vincent. Bobby had written about his experience with The Vinnie Vincent Invasion, and was launching his book, *The Boy is Gonna Rock,* at the KISS Expo. He had also been in a band with Mark Slaughter, whose band opened for KISS, and is the current drummer for Lita Ford, both of whom were also appearing at the Expo. As I knew Bobby to be a talented writer who has been published multiple times, I told him all about my memoir and my worries about the ending. Was I supposed to come up with some dramatic world-shattering truth, some awe-inspiring revelation. We kicked around some ideas, more than a few related to the Expo.

Half-jokingly, Bobby said, "Maybe something will happen this weekend at the Expo that will bring your past full circle."

I explained how daunting the event was for me. Meeting KISS fans could be painful sometimes, especially when I met a super fan who knew more about Eric than I did. For example, I'd worked hard to forget painful reminders like what kind of cologne Eric wore, but certain fans love to approach me with, "Remember how Eric wore Halston for Women?" Others reminded me of what Eric liked to eat for breakfast. I knew that there would be fans like this at the

Expo, but for the first time I was pretty sure that I was strong enough to get through it.

When I entered the venue the next morning, I understood why the event was already being hailed as "The Mother of All Expos." It was a mob scene. A fan named Mark, who had brought me tons of stuff to autograph, was crying so hard he could barely speak. He said meeting me was bringing him closure in regard to Eric's death. The next thing I knew, I was crying too. It would not be the only time that weekend. A lot of fans said that meeting me meant so much to them because I was the closest they would ever get to meeting Eric. Others told me that I was as personable and sweet as Eric was, which I considered the ultimate compliment because Eric was known for being the friendliest, most down-to-earth guy in rock.

When fans at the Expo asked me to sign KISS memorabilia, I was taken aback at first – I was no stranger to signing autographs, always on a photo of myself. It's a glory that I have earned. Now I was being asked to sign next to those of band members, where Eric's should have gone. I never imagined I would be representing Eric this way, but it was my duty and honor to do so. I had an overwhelming feeling that Eric was looking down on me from heaven with gratitude.

Overall, the first day of the Expo was not nearly as difficult as I had imagined it would be. Meeting the fans brought me great comfort. Over the years, I had often felt self-conscious and awkward talking about Eric to my friends and family. I worried they would think something was wrong with me that I hadn't let go of Eric yet. What I found out was that his fans hadn't let go either.

The second day of the Expo, I found myself crying more and more often. Hardly surprising, given that I had now been talking about Eric for two days straight. Also, I was exposed to my first Eric Carr impersonators. They posed for photos with me, wearing his Fox makeup and his costume with the platform boots and the fur collar. I kissed one on the cheek for a photo op and everyone said "Aww!" as if we were an estranged couple getting back together. Pretty odd when you consider it was like Priscilla kissing an Elvis impersonator. It all seemed so surreal. Is this what my life had come to? It felt like a parody, only it was my reality.

As the Expo wound down, I was enjoying a chat with Judy, a fan who was there with her grown son. As we bonded over the single mom thing, our conversation was cut short by a tall, skinny kid with shoulder-length black hair, eyeliner, and chalk-white skin. He was wearing a rabbit-head logo Playboy T-shirt in my honor, and carrying a bouquet of balloons, one of which had a "21" on it. He said his name was Krys and that he was an aspiring rock journalist. A huge KISS fan, he knew everything about Eric and me, and would it be okay if he interviewed me for his twenty-first birthday commemoration, which he was videotaping for YouTube. He suddenly broke away and started thrashing his head, playing air guitar. At first everyone looked over in alarm, but then they started smiling and laughing, realizing it was just a hyper kid celebrating life. People everywhere, including me, whipped out our cameras and recorded him. In our interview, videotaped by his adorable girlfriend, I told him how Eric had sent me roses on my twenty-first birthday with a card that read, "You are only 21 once, make the day as special as you are." He impressed me as the happiest, most energetic dude at the convention. When it was time to say good-bye, I saw a red rose on the table. I didn't know how it got there or where it came from, but I gave it to Krys.

When the Expo ended, a group of us planned on meeting up for dinner before going to the concert where Bob and Bruce Kulick, Ace Frehley, Lita Ford, Bobby Rock, Eric Singer, and the guys from Gene Simmons solo band were set to jam for the second night in a row. I had gone the night before and it was an awesome show, but now I was simply too exhausted. I went up to my hotel room, ordered some room service, and promptly began to sob.

The feelings that I had been pushing down for decades had risen and taken complete control of me. This was more than simply remembering something. It was my body reacting to trauma as if it had happened yesterday — a raw trembling, gasping for breath, giant tears rolling down my face in a flash flood. From my training as an actress, I knew that our bodies have a physical memory that we tap into when we need emotion for a scene. Now, for the first time, it was happening without my consent or control.

While trying to get over Eric's death, I had discovered that my life's purpose was to love and to learn. That is all I was meant to do. Well, I learned more about myself by facing my fears and attending that KISS Expo than I had known about myself before. I had a gift to give. I took the love that Eric left me with, and I shared it with his fans. Love doesn't always have to be romantic, and it only grows if you aren't afraid of sharing it. This is why I don't regret attending the Expo. If you don't experience life, you don't get the lessons. As painful as it was to relive my buried emotions, representing Eric in death had made me feel more bonded to him than an actual marriage would have. And spreading the excess love in my heart, kept the spirit of Eric alive.

The next morning, I got on the plane and there was Bobby again, who saved me a seat right next to him.

"So," he asked, "Did you get your ending?"

My answer was, "I am sure that I got part of it. But not all of it."

"What makes you sure?"

"I just have a feeling when this part of my life is complete, I'll know it, and that's how I'll end my book."

We had a four-hour conversation about the emotional impact the Expo had on me, and how I might potentially end my book. Each scenario circled back to the KISS Expo.

Half-jokingly, I said, "Maybe the book ends with me sitting next to you on a plane after the KISS Expo."

Months passed, the writing of my book progressed, but no matter how I wracked my brain, the ending still eluded me. Then, just days before I needed to begin writing this final chapter, something happened out of the blue that felt like a miracle. Could this be the ending I had been waiting for?

It involved my first celebrity crush.

First, let me backtrack. For many years I have been supporting The Brent Shapiro Foundation by attending their annual fundraiser. The event is hosted by famed attorney Robert Shapiro, who helped defend O.J. Simpson, and who launched the foundation after his son Brent died of a drug overdose. Its mission is to help keep kids sober, uniquely rewarding them for each clean drug test. Because I have witnessed firsthand the ravages of alcohol and drug abuse, and I have great empathy for his family's loss, I always support the cause.

Performing at this year's event was none other than David Lee Roth. I was excited to learn this, but not surprised. He had performed at the event the previous year. In fact, during that performance, he had spotted me in the crowd, pointed directly at me, and said, "I know you." It was thrilling, but I wasn't sure if he really knew who I was or had just vaguely recognized me as some random girl he had slept with many moons ago.

Last year I never got my answer.

Maybe this year I would.

As I have said, my plan was to marry Dave when I was twenty and he was thirty-four. Okay, so I had my dates wrong, but it could still happen, right? Maybe there was a happily-ever-after waiting for me. Maybe we would finally fall in love, and I would have my last chapter.

I was full of excitement when I dressed for this year's event. I went for broke, choosing a stunning Herve Leger blue bandage dress trimmed with black sequins. Cleavage for days. I planted myself right up front. When he took the stage, Dave devoured me with his grin, announcing to the audience, "I need a tall, cool glass of water." He kept a firm glance on me as I danced my ass off and sang along with him.

When the lights came up, the crowd dispersed, and reality set in. I felt like an absolute idiot for having ever thought that tonight was going to be our date with destiny. I would have to end my memoir some other way.

As I gathered my things, a female security guard walked up out of nowhere and said, "Dave would like to see you backstage." I was so shocked that my purse turned sideways, and my phone clattered to the floor. In a sort of trance, I left my phone right there and followed the guard. My faithful friend and talent manager, Christina Scott (the former Mrs. Bruce Kulick), always the sensible one, scooped it up for me. As the guard led me through a labyrinth of security checks, my heart was pounding. My God, it was actually happening just like a dream. My life was charmed, after all. This was my last chapter!

When I entered the backstage, Dave was sitting there, looking right at me, already flashing that dazzling, toothy smile.

"Hello, Carrie."

I looked at him quizzically.

"You remember me?"

He laughed like that was the silliest thing he'd ever heard.

"How could I not, Carrie? I mean, look at you. You light up a room."

I explained to him that maybe I was a little insecure. He took my hands in his and said, "I get insecure, too."

God, he was charming. We sat down and reminisced about our nights at Bordello and Bar One, roughly a quarter century earlier.

"You're just as beautiful now as you were back then."

My heart was about to burst.

"But we never sweetened the deal," he sighed.

"We did!" I insisted.

All these years, I had been kicking myself for drinking straight whiskey the night I finally had sex with Dave. Now here he is, sitting right across from me, drinking Jack Daniels neat, and I find out that he remembers even less than I do. It was pretty deflating that he remembered my smile and my name, but not enjoying my naked, willing body. But then again, did he? Did we? Maybe. Maybe not. I had assumed so all these years, since we woke up together naked on his living room floor. I probably should have played it cool, but I was like a giddy, infatuated adolescent. Everything that came out of my mouth sounded stupid and not at all like what I had intended, but I simply could not stop.

As I babbled, Dave sat across from me, quietly sipping his drink. He couldn't have gotten a word in edgewise even if he had wanted to. I blurted out every single detail of our every encounter. I thanked him for having never offered me cocaine but asked him why he didn't. He replied, "Drugs are what people do when they are bored."

Instead of thanking him for the compliment or engaging in any intelligent conversation about drug use (which would have been more than appropriate considering we were at a charity supporting drug prevention) I jumped ahead in time and blabbed about winning his Miss Slawterhouse contest when I was pregnant. I listed for him every single time I had seen him in concert since, and how each time I had wondered if he recognized me in the crowd. As I was still writing the book, all of these details were fresh on my mind and came flying out of my mouth at warp speed. I even told Dave about the time I took my then eight-year-old son to see Van Halen, and he asked, "Mommy, why is David Lee Roth singing to you? Were you his girlfriend?"

"Of course not," I told Dave I'd replied.

"But he knows you," insisted Jaxon. "He just sang, *I'll wait for you, Carrie!*"

Digging the hole deeper, I revealed to Dave that I was writing a memoir. He asked if he was going to be in it, and I replied, "Oh yeah, you're the first sentence." I proceeded to recite it for him: *I have to wonder what I could have achieved in life if only I had been as ambitious academically as I was in aspiring to fuck David Lee Roth.*

Yes, I actually said this out loud to him.

He was probably thinking, "This chick is still smokin' hot. If only she'd shut the hell up!"

Back in the day, I'd hid my obsession and tried to act

normal in front of him. I had let him tell stories while I quietly adored him. Now, twenty-something years later, I was the one blathering, and he just stared blankly. I had actually rendered the witty David Lee Roth speechless! Was he awed and humbled by my passionate devotion or did he fear I might be deranged and dangerous?

Since neither of us remembered the night we went home together, I wanted to suggest a do-over, but nice girls don't do that, so instead I asked if we could take a photo. He agreed, but then I realized that I had dropped my phone on the floor. Christina had retrieved it for me but had not returned it yet, and so the moment passed.

As we were leaving the venue, I asked if he was going to call me this time.

"You can't catch lightning in a bottle twice," he said.

That didn't sound promising. I told him, "Well, call me if you ever want to have a drink. Or just come over."

Oh. My. God. Where had that come from? I hadn't had a man come over to my house in six years. Not since my son was old enough to understand what it meant.

After a long, excruciating silence, he responded with a non sequitur: "Stay young and skinny, Carrie."

In the next few days, I didn't exactly wait around for the phone to ring, but every time I opened the refrigerator door or looked in the mirror, I would hear his words.

Thanks, Dave.

The following week, I was sitting at my desk, scrolling through social media, and I saw a tweet from Greg Renoff,

Van Halen historian and author of *Van Halen Rising*. He was commenting on a video of Dave performing "*Jump*" that I had hastily posted the night of the event. He wrote: "That look and smile he gives Carrie and the other dancing ladies in the front row at the 8-second mark. Classic. Diamond Dave."

I had no idea what Greg was talking about, so I opened the video and clicked on the eight-second mark. I was momentarily distracted by this dancing girl in the video, flipping her hair and bouncing her rather large, milky-white boobs. Then I realized it was me! No wonder Dave was laughing when I asked how he knew I was there. You couldn't miss me. It wasn't my smile that had lit up the room. It was my boobs! They were like floodlights.

Suddenly, I realized that Jaxon was standing right behind me, looking over my shoulder. Embarrassed, I closed the window, but too late.

"When was that taken?" he asked.

I told him everything, how I had danced all night at the benefit and how Dave had summoned me backstage. How I had talked too much and made a total fool of myself. Now that the excitement had worn off, I felt like a complete idiot.

"He's never going to call me," I said. "I can't believe I'm still stupid enough to believe in fairy tales."

"I think you're missing the message, Mom."

"What message?"

"The one from the universe," Jaxon said. "Your story isn't over. It's still exciting. You're still having adventures."

My son impressed me so much with this insight. The

fact was David Lee Roth represented all that was vital and passionate in me. Just as his mile-high kicks represented the freedom to fly, Dave and his music carried the message that anything is possible. That night he had tapped into the soul of the girl who had worshiped him as a teen, the one who believed in true love, in making her dreams come true. This was long before anyone broke my heart, or my cherry, for that matter. Dave summoning me backstage was confirmation that I was not finished. I still had it. Exciting things still happened to me. I still had so much to look forward to. Was this the ending of my memoir then? Was I going to end on a high note? It might have been, but for a catastrophe.

*****

On Wednesday afternoon, November 8, 2018, I got a text from my neighbor Bridgette Pratt: "Don't come home tonight." It seemed strange. We'd chatted in my driveway just a few hours before as I'd loaded my Yorkshire Terrier and my suitcase into the car. She knew I was going away for a few days to house-sit for a friend in the Pacific Palisades, so why was she telling me not to come home?

Another text arrived. A photo taken from Bridgette's deck. It showed a wall of flame just a few miles away in Bell Canyon and Simi Valley. She said that, driven by hard winds, it was headed our way.

Bridgette and I, along with our friend Elena Grace Soto, began frantic three-way texting, preparing for the worst. (Thank God my son was out of town on a school trip!)

Bridgette suggested that if we were evacuated that night, we should all take shelter together with her sister-in-law in Malibu. It seemed like a great idea until hours later when the winds shifted, the fire turned south west, and Bridgette's sister-in-law's house was burned to the ground.

The following morning Elena, who lives in nearby Agoura Hills, was the first of us to get an evacuation order. With the inferno headed her way, she packed up her three cats, two dogs, two teenagers, and fled.

Bridgette's next texts warned that the fire was spreading with the shifting winds, and no one knew where it would strike next. Since I was housesitting only twenty-five minutes away, she suggested I speed home and rescue whatever valuables I could before it was too late. I read her texts while sitting outside, sipping a smoothie on a glorious fall day. The only way you would ever know that disaster loomed was if you looked due west, out toward Malibu, where huge smoky clouds billowed and gathered on the horizon.

My usual routes home were accessible only by the Pacific Coast Highway, which runs for 650 miles along the coast. I soon discovered to my shock that Pacific Coast Highway heading northwest was jammed solid, and police were directing everyone to head southeast to the Santa Monica freeway. I pulled over and checked for alternate routes home. The 101 Freeway was closed at my exit. This meant returning home was impossible. For the first time it hit me that I could lose everything. I turned on radio news and learned that the Palisades might be next. I was house-sitting directly in the path of the fire. Suddenly, my possessions didn't matter anymore, only my life did.

I called my friend, Peggy, who lives fifty miles away in Newport Beach, and asked if I could stay with her. When she agreed, I turned my car south and floored it. I barely remember the drive. I was in shock, on autopilot, unable to comprehend the magnitude of what was happening.

The next day, the entire city of Calabasas was ordered to evacuate. I was glued to the news, watching as the cities that surrounded my home were being reduced to ashes. If mine was next, what would I miss most? I thought of the ring that my grandfather had given my grandmother on her eighteenth birthday, my photo albums, my KISS tour jacket, my KISS *Lick it Up* gold album, the postcards Eric used to send me when he was on the road. I thought about my son's beloved baseball collection. I owned a fireproof safe, but I couldn't remember what was inside of it. I knew it held the home videos of my son's early years and important legal documents, but what else? Suddenly I remembered things of no sentimental but plenty of monetary value: Chanel Bags, Yves Saint Laurent shoes, my Chopard necklace. Losing them would not break my heart, but it would hurt, nonetheless.

Strangely, what grieved me most that day was not the thought of losing any of the things I've mentioned, but of losing a white coffee mug with a rainbow on it. I had received it a lifetime ago, from Eric, with flowers inside. I had a complicated relationship with that mug. I hated it because it was still here, and Eric wasn't. I loved it because it had been delivered with a card that read: "All of your goals and dreams will come true." I hadn't realized how much the stained, chipped, ugly old thing meant to me until I was on the verge of losing it. I needed it to nag me every morning. I needed it to remind me that brighter days were ahead. On mornings when I woke up without goals or dreams, it reminded me of who I used to be before the cruel world hurt me.

A week later, I returned to my house to discover that it had been untouched by the disaster I was free to resume my old life, but I simply could not do it. I had been altered in ways I still did not understand.

*****

Everything became clearer a week later, when it was time to face another November 24th, the anniversary of Eric's death. What had always been a painful day for me had become far more painful with the birth of social media. Whereas a KISS Expo represents the very best of KISS fans, social media often brings out the worst. As hard as this might be to believe, if I am not the first person to pay tribute to Eric Carr on Facebook, Twitter, and Instagram, I receive messages from KISS fans all over the world, berating me for my callousness. They call me terrible names and accuse me of being unworthy of his love. Even if I were capable of finding closure and moving on, these fans made it impossible.

I'd been altered by the fires in a way that connected me to my new self – a grown woman who is sick of pretending that she is perfect, of trying so hard to please everyone.

Facing mortality makes you want to tell the truth no matter what, even if it is unattractive or risks making you unlikable.

Everything you experience in life contributes to your character and the choices you make going forward. My falling in love with Eric was no accident or twist of fate. It was all part of the life I had envisioned for myself throughout high school. Since I had already been taught early and well that my beauty was my sole worth, I was completely comfortable being a sex object. My goal was to marry a rock star and then become a movie star. I was barely a legal adult, still in my teens, while it happened just as I had imagined it. Life was so easy! Eric and I would get married and be an invincible team. What more could I ask for? Obviously, God or the Universe had something else in mind for me.

Eric saw me as more than a sex object. Before he died, Eric helped me chart a course to achieve my goals. If he had not, I don't know what would have become of me after he was gone forever. I had no depth or complexity when I met him. I had no reason to question my purpose in life or develop a spiritual sense. I didn't really use my mind until Eric's death shattered me. His loss taught me about suffering, pain, compassion and the cruel finality of death. I developed an existential sense.

After Eric died, it was my goal to keep his memory alive in any way I could, and yet suddenly, in the wake of the Woodsley wildfire, in which I had almost lost everything, I simply did not want to be Eric's living memorial anymore. You can't imagine the pressure of receiving Facebook friend requests from fans who use Eric's image as their profile photo. Some of them even call themselves "Carrie Stevens' Boyfriend" and leave me public messages, like "I love you" and "I miss you." One of them writes me lists of his attributes, trying to convince me that he is Eric reincarnated. It's obsessive behavior that nothing prepared me for.

The result of all this unwanted attention is that it had forced me into a surreal bubble of isolation. Who could I talk to about my strange existence? Who would relate to me or even care? What had made it even lonelier was that these same people asked me how I was doing, only on the anniversary, as if when midnight struck Eric would come back to life. Once the hour had passed, they assumed that my pain disappeared, as if I only thought of Eric once a year.

I'm sure most of you have lost people you love, but can you imagine if you were expected to post about them on the anniversary of their deaths and on their birthdays, and if you skipped a year you would be publicly scorned? It was a massive responsibility I never asked for. And so, this year, I could no longer pretend I was okay about it. If almost losing everything teaches us anything, it's how to live in the moment, fully authentic. Instead of just reposting the tributes of others, I decided to state my truth on Facebook, the whole truth on the subject, just as I have expressed it to you in these pages.

I held nothing back. I didn't try to play nice. I didn't worry about who might be offended. What a weight off my shoulders it was! And the best part was that rather than offend Eric's truest fans, they totally understood and released me from carrying the torch. They thanked me for all I had done on behalf of Eric. It was incredibly healing to feel so heard, as well as seen, and respected.

I feel Eric's pride shining upon me. Neither could have foreseen a situation where one of us would have to represent the other in the world. But when you are truly one with another, you are compelled to do so. The irony is that once I was released from the responsibility of keeping Eric's memory alive, it became a privilege to do so. I knew I would do so in the future without resentment. I knew that if I attended further KISS Expos, I would do so with joy and love.

Just hours after posting my feelings on social media, news of a tragedy reached me. I received a text from my friend Mike Suppa, which included a link to an article about a fatal car crash in Indianapolis. The text said, "Have you seen this video? You are in it." Without watching the video, I skimmed the article and my heart about fell out of my chest. It was Krys, the kid celebrating his twenty-first birthday at the KISS Expo. A driver evading the police had sped off and plowed into the driver's side of Krys's car, killing him instantly. Devastating news. His whole life was ahead of him and now he was gone forever. I thought of his adorable girlfriend. I followed a link to the outpouring of love for Krys on his Facebook page, where his name is listed as Krystine Sixteen, after the KISS song "Christine Sixteen." I posted my condolences, and the very next morning on Instagram, Krys's girlfriend, Jessie Henry, sent me a message. She asked how

I got through losing Eric.

"Krys was my soulmate," she wrote. "He was my everything."

I shared with Jessie a lot of advice and insights over the next few days. Here is a small sampling:

I remember you both very well, Jessie. I was devastated when I heard about Krys. I was wondering if you were in the car with him. I am so glad that you're okay, but I know your heart won't be okay for a long time. I wish I could tell you some magic words that would make all of your pain go away. You're going to go through waves of emotions. You'll feel better for a little while, and then it will come back, but the distances between your down days and your up days will get less and less over time. But you never get over someone you lose when you're in love.

Krys and Eric will live inside of us forever. It took a long time for me to see things the way I do, but I am who I am because I lost Eric. I developed parts of my mind and my soul that would have been blank without the inner growth I experienced searching for reasons why Eric died. I couldn't understand how I could still be breathing the air while he wasn't. I'm glad you reached out to me, because when someone dies, you get a surge of sympathy at first, but then no one knows what to say to you anymore. It gets lonely. My heart goes out to you. One thing I have realized is that grief is never over. It's a part of you now. You'll learn to live with it, and you'll find the gifts in it. Krys was so energetic and positive. I didn't know him, but it's obvious he would want you to go on and live a full and happy life. He will be watching over you as you have adventures. You might not believe it now, but you will smile again.

People come into your life for a reason. Maybe I was meant to do that KISS Expo so I could help you. You know how Bobby Rock and I became close friends? His pregnant girlfriend was stabbed to death at an ATM, and I reached out to him because I had lost Eric eighteen months earlier. I told him if he ever needed to talk to someone who had been through it, I would be there for him. All these years later, he and I still lean on each other when we need support. We both agree that some years you don't get very affected by an anniversary or a birthday, and some years you don't know why, but it hits you hard. I'm so sorry you're part of this club now. Just know you're not alone. There are people like me and Bobby who understand what you're going through.

Hold on to everything. I find Eric's drumsticks in the weirdest places. His old cards and letters still help me get through my days. I slept with his toothbrush next to me until just recently, and now I put it in my fireproof safe. By the way, I've had many other boyfriends since, and I've fallen in love again, but the love that I shared with Eric is different. It's been an issue because boyfriends get jealous of Eric, but eventually I'll find one who doesn't get intimidated by my past. I still have letters I wrote to Eric when he was in a coma. I have poems I wrote about him. All these years later *they really helped me remember the frame of mind I was in at the time because I am writing my memoir now. I thought that Eric was only going to be one chapter of it, but he keeps coming back because he's always on my mind. Krys will haunt you for the rest of your life if you let him. This is how true love transcends time.*

In the wake of Krys's death, Jessie Henry needed an angel, in the form of a stranger reaching out to comfort her. Nothing brings me greater joy than to know that I helped get that girl out of bed even if just for one day. She has a long way to go, but I intend to be there for her, for as long as she needs me. Angels don't always have wings, but you can be one if you try.

*****

Out of nowhere, something magical happened that made me feel as though the universe was rewarding me for all of my recent struggles: I got a call from The Van Halen Store. Entirely unrelated to my backstage reunion with Dave, they had seen a series of viral Instagram photos of me in a wet Van Halen T-shirt. They asked if I would like to be the feature model for their official licensed Van Halen merchandise. Next to my becoming a Playboy Playmate, it was the most exciting moment of my modeling career. If it wasn't true love with Dave, it was a hell of a good second prize.

Was this the ending to my book then? *Surely it had to be.* We begin with a girl and her Van Halen poster, and now that same little girl is *in* the poster.

Full Circle.

Music soars.

Credits roll.

Actually, *no!* No. No. No. It was reaching the status of being the Van Halen model (the ultimate teenage dream for me) that made me realize that getting attention doesn't change anything. I am the same girl. I'm just a fan. I'd reached the pinnacle of my fantasy only to feel no different from the way I did the day before. The phone didn't ring. David Lee Roth didn't call. The ego boost of seeing myself in their ads was just about as exciting as going to one of their concerts. It lasted roughly two hours. There was a deeper lesson to be learned. This wasn't about my looks. It was my concept and my actions that created this opportunity. I didn't have it handed to me or negotiated by an agency. I did this all on my own. I learned that I am powerful. My son was right, exciting things still happen to me. Because I am smart. I am not just a pretty face and a pair of tits. I make shit happen. Mrs. Marshall was wrong.

Ever since my mother had told me when I was a little girl that she loved me but didn't like me, I had been trying to prove her wrong, trying to prove that I was likable. That's why I had craved the spotlight and chased fame. But now, at mid-life, having achieved so many of my goals, having stared catastrophe in the face, I was done trying to find validation outside myself. *Now I wanted people to take me or leave me.*

Here's the ugly, sad truth: it's lonely posting hot photos of yourself on Instagram and watching the comments go by as you lie in bed wearing your sweats, feeling unattractive and isolated, like a fraud. I rarely feel like that hot girl in the photo. No matter how many pictures I post, I'm still the same girl. Only it's not 1997 anymore. People want me to look like Miss June 1997 for the rest of my life. Frankly, it's a lot of pressure.

I have asked myself many times in the writing of this book why exactly I was doing it. I knew it wasn't vanity, as I was revealing things about myself for which I knew I would be harshly judged. I wrote this book to find my voice. It's only now, as I reach my ending at long last, that I understand that when you are brave enough to use your voice, you learn that people actually like you better when you are raw, true, and unashamed. More importantly, I like myself better when I am raw, true and unashamed.

As it turns out, my writing led me to revelations that have changed me in fundamental ways, and there is no turning back. My story couldn't end here. What would be the value in publishing the analyzation of my existence before I was sure of my conclusions?

I couldn't just talk the talk. I had to walk the walk.

JAMES **CREIGHTON** PHOTO

ANDRÉ FELIX PHOTO

ALBERTO FIGARONE PHOTO

Chapter 12

Don't Think it's Over

I was struggling with the fact that I was about to turn the *Big 5-0*. I didn't want a birthday party. I didn't want to bring attention to the occasion. But I didn't want to sit around and wallow in it either. So, I took my son to Chicago for the weekend. We took a night-flight helicopter tour over the Windy City. It was my birthday gift to myself, because what could make me happier than to make him happy? I felt that I had already done it all. Seeing Jaxon excited about the chopper ride was enough for me. Happiness for myself seemed to be a thing of the past, anyway.

As we soared above the city lights, I heard the pilot point out Lakeshore Drive. I looked down at the stunning coastal view of Lake Michigan and I suddenly flashed back to a crisp sunny day when I was drawing Eric's name in the sand with a stick. I snapped a photo of him crouched down, smiling in front of his name. Memories of Eric flooded my mind during that short helicopter ride. The first time I'd ever been to Chicago was when Eric flew me there to be with him during the *Hot in the Shade* tour in 1990. I was in tears by the time the helicopter landed. I hated myself for crying when we were supposed to be having fun. Instead of being in the moment, reveling in the spectacular skyline, I was once again sucked back into the past. I further confirmed in my mind that my personal happiness was over. My time was up. I wondered if that was the reason that my father, and many other parents are so generous with their kids. Maybe they felt like me... maybe they wanted to give everything to their kids because they didn't have any hope for themselves. I wasn't normally such a negative person, but these were my thoughts as I was in mid-life crisis mode.

Why I wanted to torture myself I have no idea, but I wanted to take my son out for my birthday dinner at *Gino's East* because that is where Eric took me. He couldn't wait to take me there, and I wanted to pass the delightful tradition of stuffed deep-dish pizza on to my son. Over dinner we discussed the recent parent-teacher conferences. He asked me how they went.

"They were so inspiring!"

Jaxon laughed. "That's the first time I've ever heard you say that about any parent-teacher conference."

I explained to him that the meetings didn't have much to do with his grades, actually. His English teacher told me about his experiences on the remote islands of Panama and his desire to own a second home there one day. I spoke to his science teacher about her plans to take her students on a class trip to Costa Rica. I had a conversation with his history teacher about Cinque Terre. I'd always dreamed of going to the Italian Riviera. I chatted with his German teacher about my impressions of Hamburg and Berlin, the only two cities I'd been to in Germany. I have a passion for traveling so all of it was very interesting to me. But it was his English teacher who had made the most profound impact on me. I told him I was writing a book. He asked what kind of book. When I told him it was a memoir, I naturally had to give him a quick summary of my life. He could not have seemed more reserved and conservative, sitting there behind an old oak desk, and yet, to my surprise, he suddenly opened up to me, confessing that he worked as a DJ in night clubs and played in a band in the 80s. He revealed to me that he'd often wondered what his life would have been like had he had taken the path I did. How would his life had turned out had he moved to the big city to make it in the entertainment industry? He explained to me that he had gotten married instead, had kids and, wanting to give them a stable life, had given up his dreams and become a teacher. We explored the road less traveled. This compelled Jaxon to ask, "By the way, how is your book coming along?"

I had just finished Chapter Ten, *"Don't Blow off Billion-aires."* Jaxon and I shared some laughs over the *'Ron, Ron, Ron, Don'* revelations. I am fortunate to have a wise, old soul for a son. I couldn't find a man who would accept me for who I am, so I birthed one. That's how it seemed. Knowing that Jaxon would understand me and not judge me, I explained to him that after examining my choices in men, I concluded that there is only one thing that all of my exes had in common. They were exciting. I was attracted to excitement. I told him how the chapter climaxes in the revelation that I must find a way to satisfy my quest for excitement on my own.

"That's an easy fix. Travel. Go have an adventure," Jaxon said.

"How does that have anything to do with what I just said to you?"

"Simple! You just told me that you have a passion for travel. You said that you need to create excitement for yourself. Look at your life, Mom. Had you not taken risks you wouldn't have anything to write about. You'd be sitting behind a desk, wondering what could have been. Had you settled... had you played by the rules, you wouldn't have any material. With high risk comes high reward. That's my philosophy."

He was my son, indeed. The apple doesn't fall far from the tree. My thrill-seeking life was finally not condemned, it was justified... by the person I loved most in the world.

I decided to go on a trip to the Dominican Republic to celebrate my birthday with one of my closest friends, Carrie Peterson. My dear friend Pedro lives there and offered to host us. The three of us relaxed at an ocean front resort for four days, and I blew out the 50 candles on my cake. On the day I was to depart I woke up to an email that would change the course of my future. Since my son had accepted a summer job working for my friend Bill Keith's solar company in Indiana, I had rented out our four-bedroom house and got a one bedroom in Santa Monica. It made sense. I didn't need the space, so I would profit handsomely by renting for a few months. I made the mistake of going around Airbnb, because the owner wanted to avoid fees by doing the deal herself. Now I understand why there are rules against that. The bitch canceled on me. The email simply said she changed her mind. And there was nothing I could do about it. Now I was basically homeless. My tenants had already taken occupancy of my house, so I had nowhere to stay. Naturally, I was stressing out.

Carrie Peterson is a pilot for American Airlines. "She said, why don't you do what Jaxon said? Think of this as an adventure. I will give you a buddy pass for your birthday. What is on your bucket list? Where have you never been that you're dying to go?"

As I had been a borderline rebel my whole life, I was torn between doing something sensible and diving into the abyss. I weighed the facts. Now, for the first time in almost eighteen years I didn't have anything holding me back. I was single. I didn't have a kid at home. I had arranged a dog sitter. I was earning income from my renters. I had good credit and some savings. I could use this time to write. Carrie Peterson kept encouraging me to be spontaneous, and Pedro agreed that I should not go back to L.A. My friends knew how lonely I was there, being an empty nester, and what a dark place I had been in for a long time. There was no reason not to take her up on the buddy pass and use this time to unfunk myself. I could reconnect with my soul, just be with myself, and get reacquainted with the person I am. I had never traveled solo. Maybe doing something I'd never done before was the solution to my need for excitement.

I recalled a quotation I had read in an article about Italy: "Feel more. Do less." That sang to me. *Feel more. Do less.* I told Carrie Peterson that I'd always wanted to see Cinque Terre. So, she arranged a buddy pass. I had a layover in Philadelphia that was delayed. I could have made connection by the skin of my teeth had the luggage belt not broken. But alas, my luggage was delayed, and so I missed the flight. In tears, I stumbled along to the airport hotel shuttle vans. I got a room at the Clarion. I woke up sick as a dog. Too sick to fly. One night turned into two. I was on the phone with my sister, Jill, who kindly kept checking on me. I was crying, it was pretty depressing to be stuck in an airport hotel with a head cold instead of going on an adventure. Jill suggested I get on a plane to Tampa since it was only two and a half hours from Philadelphia. She sweetly suggested, "Why don't you let your big sister take care of you?" So, I flew to Tampa and stayed with her and her wife, Elizabeth, for a week. After I recuperated from the nasty head cold, I practiced yoga and got a massage. I had my hair colored and my nails manicured. I was determined not to go back to L.A. with my tail between my legs. I was going to Italy.

I was nervous as I boarded the flight to Milan-Malpensa. I wasn't afraid to fly. The idea of female solo travel didn't scare me. I had no qualms about going on an adventure. But I was still carrying a lot of anxiety over turning fifty. I knew that statistically about two thirds of my life was over. How did I want to spend the rest of it? While writing this memoir, I'd already reflected on the choices I'd made up until this point. I prayed for an epiphany.

After a smooth landing in Milan, I went through customs, collected my luggage (emotional baggage included) and dragged it to the train station where I boarded the train to Monterosso. The Cinque Terre is a string of centuries-old seaside villages on the rugged coastline within the region of Liguria, in the northwest of Italy. Monterosso is the largest of the five villages and the only one that has a direct train from the airport, which is why I chose to spend my first two nights there. I unpacked and then set out to wander the old cobble-stone streets. I heard Black Sabbath coming out of a bar, so I went inside and enjoyed a glass of white wine grown from grapes harvested in the hills behind my hotel. I dined on freshly baked focaccia appetizers that I never ordered. In addition to seafood, white wine and pecorino cheese, focaccia bread is what the region is known for. When I looked at my bill, I noticed I wasn't charged for my food. The bartender explained to me that it's customary to give complimentary focaccia to customers. Then he gave me a complimentary glass of wine and offered to take me out to dinner at the best restaurant in Monterosso and show me the town. I would have enjoyed seeing Monterosso through the eyes of a local but at that point, the wine had made me worse for wear. My jet lag kicked in and I was ready for bed. I didn't want to risk being hung over the next day, because I was excited about hiking the picturesque trails that connect the five villages. This was what I came to the Cinque Terre for, not to get drunk with some Italian guy.

The trails were challenging and crowded, but worth it for the gorgeous views of the Mediterranean that before now I'd admired only in photos. It was incredibly satisfying to know that I'd made my dreams of being there in person come true. The two-hour hike ended in Vernazza, arguably the most picturesque of the five villages. I had worked up an appetite, so I found a ristorante, ordered some pizza and vino and soaked up the satisfaction. I was truly in bliss and wanted nothing more than to breathe in the ocean air and thank God for my life. *La Vita e bella*. Life is beautiful. And so was my waiter, Simone. His English was not so good, but the look in his eyes told me everything I needed to know. He was interested. I made plans to meet Simone later that night after he got off work. He wanted to show me a secret place. It occurred to me that I shouldn't go off with a stranger in the night in a foreign land, to a secret location, but he was twenty-nine, and I was charmed. Besides, I was supposed to be having an adventure, right? Simone took me by the hand and led me across the road, under a natural rock overpass where we climbed past police tape and ignored a sign that read "do not enter." He led me into a dark cave. We turned a corner, and there the moonlight was pointed straight at us in such a way that the whites of the crashing waves were lit up like shooting stars. As I gazed at the splendor, Simone's lips gently kissed my neck. I was having a romance! I created excitement for myself. This was it! Suddenly rain came pouring down and it got chilly. So, we made our way back to the apartment I'd rented. It was freezing in there. The old wall heater was not working well, and I was really cold. Simone kept asking me why I was sad. I kept telling him, "I am not sad. I am cold." But something got lost in the translation. Simone took his hand and tenderly touched my face. In his broken English he said, "Why? Why are you sad? You are too beautiful to be sad." Something about that hit a nerve. I was being judged for my looks again. I was expected to be seen and not heard. I wasn't human. I couldn't be cold or sad because I was pretty? Perhaps I overreacted, but I told poor Simone to get out of my apartment. The very next morning I got on a train to Florence.

As soon as I settled into my apartment and connected to the Wi-Fi, I did what I do in every new city I visit. I googled "rock music." I can't stand to be anywhere that plays bad music. That is how I discovered the Virgin Rock Bar, which became my local hangout. It was there that I met an Egyptian college student named Riccardo who became my friend and tour guide. I found it incredibly difficult to navigate my way around the medieval car-less streets. Riccardo barely spoke English, but he pointed, and I followed. He was also very talented when it came to taking photos of me in front of all the tourist attractions. When I wasn't exploring art museums or hanging out at the Virgin Rock Bar, listening to heavy metal music and eating the delicious free happy hour pasta buffet, I was roaming into old churches and praying for an epiphany. How, I asked God, should I live the rest of my life? What would make me happy? I prayed for wisdom and guidance.

It didn't go off in my head like a lightbulb. I wasn't born again, but I was alone in Italy, where no one knew my last name, no one knew I was a Playmate, no one knew I was an actress or Eric Carr's girlfriend or even someone's mother, for that matter. It was liberating. I didn't realize it at the time, but it was all part of a revelation that I would understand later. I was ready to see some familiar faces, and I still had some time to kill.

I rented an oceanfront place in Galway, Ireland, which has a reputation for being the friendliest city in the world. I had been to Galway the summer before with my son and fallen in love with the artsy culture. There was live music everywhere, mostly "trad," otherwise known as traditional

Irish folk music and classic rock. I'd kept in touch with a few of the locals through social media. It was a good place to plant myself in between being a stranger and a friend. And they speak English in Ireland, so it was easier. I still needed to connect with myself. I didn't know how, but the Emerald Isle might hold the answers.

I arrived in Dublin at 7:30 a.m. after a terrible experience involving canceled flights and disgruntled airline employees. I rented a car and drove two hours west to the other end of Ireland and checked into my apartment in Salthill, a seaside suburb of Galway oozing with charm. I was tired and puffy, so I decided to do a facial mask. The instructions said to apply it and then recline for fifteen minutes. I laid down, reached for my cell phone and played a meditation on an app. My aim was to focus on my breathing, but I was distracted by the sound of children playing outside. The apartment had an ocean view, but there was a playground separating myself and the sea. I started to cry. Why was I crying? I got up and stepped out onto my balcony. It seemed like a century ago that I was pushing Jaxon on a swing set. I mourned his youth. I mourned mine, as well. I felt the sunshine on my face and a salty breeze dry up my tears. Watching parents push their children on the swings was a metaphor for having raised my son right. Jaxon was headed in the right direction. I was proud of myself as a single mother (and only parent) for raising an ambitious young man. I realized that I was crying because I had lost my identity. Just like my son was becoming his own person, I had to evolve, as well. Jaxon was right. I needed an adventure, but my adventure needed to have a purpose. I had a feeling there would be some whiskey involved.

I took the scenic route into town. It was a twenty-five-minute walk along the beach and the Salthill Promenade to the bustling city center. I poked my head into a few busy shops and made my way past crowds gathered to watch street performers. I plopped down in front of the Kings Head restaurant on High Street, and, sipping a pint of Guinness I watched the buskers play. I immediately recognized Johnny, wielding his guitar and crooning on the corner. His ginger hair was so long that his braid was down to his butt. I had met him last summer when I was in Galway, so he came over to give me a hug. I invited him to sit down. Johnny pointed at my pint of Guinness and said, "Ye oughta be having somethin' stronger than that!" I laughed and started complaining about my hay fever. He said, "Ye oughta have a whiskey and jump in the sea." I cringed at the idea of icy-cold ocean water. That didn't appeal to me, but the fish and chips did. I looked at the whiskey menu and noticed one called Writers' Tears. I couldn't resist ordering a double, considering that I was struggling to finish my memoir.

The next day, I went to *The Skeff* on Eyre Square to see my friend Garreth who works there. He's a jolly, tall lad with rosy cheeks and piercing, blue eyes. Garreth pointed out the rather large gin menu. I asked him about the peculiar popularity of gin consumption in Ireland. Gin was now the big trend in Ireland. The first time I got drunk as a teenager, it was gin, so I can't even smell it without recounting the hurls and gags of my youth. Garreth told me there had been a whiskey drought recently.

"Whiskey drought? What? You mean like... like the great potato famine? There was a whiskey famine?"

Garreth explained to me that... gasp! It's all about money. It takes at least twelve years to distill a good whiskey. It's a lot more profitable to quickly crank out some gin. In my mind, I was likening it to Kraft singles compared to Wisconsin cheddar, but I kept my mouth shut. The Irish love to talk about whiskey. I got loads of entertainment out of asking what kind I should drink and how I should take it. Garreth was beaming, as he introduced me to Jameson and ginger ale over crushed ice with a lime. He explained to me that it is how you drink whiskey in the warm weather months. People don't typically think of it as a summertime drink. They think of it as warm and toasty, something you sip in front of a fireplace or drink out of a flask to keep you warm on a winter night. Garreth also advised me that the way to cure a cold is with a hot whiskey. As I sipped my refreshing Jameson & ginger cocktail, I pointed out the nasty burn on my neck I'd gotten from my curling iron. "Ye know what ye ought to do? Have another whiskey and jump in the sea." Okay. I got the point. There is nothing whiskey won't cure! He ordered me another Jameson. It made sense to accept. However, I wasn't so sure about the other piece of advice. "If I jump into the sea," I rationalized, "it would only lead me right back to the bottle to warm up, so why get my hair wet?"

Ireland was definitely my happy place. I spent the whole summer living in the moment. I went to the racetracks and gambled on horses. I explored old castles and toured whiskey distilleries. I chased faeries in sacred fields. Tommy Thayer heard I was overseas and asked if I wanted to catch any of KISS's European *End of the Road* tour shows, so I got on a plane to Glasgow, Scotland to see them. Even though I was quite content to stay in Galway, I kept getting opportunities that I couldn't pass up. When I was tempted to play it safe, I reminded myself that I was supposed to be having an adventure.

A guy named Adam, whom I only knew from chatting with on Twitter, invited me to join him and a group of his friends to see the Foo Fighters in concert. I hopped on a bus to Belfast for the weekend. I had a fabulous time! Before then I'd never even been on a public bus before. Adam and his friends had a car. My plan was to go to Clonmel next, which was in the same direction back to Cork, so they dropped me at my hotel. My desire to go to Clonmel was inspired by Playmate sister Darlene Bernaola, who insisted I needed to visit St. Patrick's Well. She had gone the summer before and had a profound spiritual shift. I had read the historical site described as "one of the 'thin places,' where the presence of God is keenly and easily discernible and the veil between heaven and earth seems remarkably thin." People come from all over the world to be blessed by the holy water in hopes of being healed. There I met a man called David, with eyes so crystal blue they were like a mirror in which I could see my reflection. I am not sure of his formal position there. I'll call him the groundskeeper. He told me to take off my shoes, and together we put our feet in the water and held hands. The water was so freezing, icy cold that I almost couldn't take it. Every time I was about to take my feet out, David gripped my hand a little tighter and smiled at me kindly. Finally, I was past the point of pain where I couldn't feel my feet anymore. We sat together for a long while and prayed. Before I left, David filled my plastic bottle with the holy water and assured me that things were going to be better for me from now on.

I got on a train to Galway and went back to lazy days and whiskey nights. It was so nice to be someplace where no one was arguing about politics that I barely checked my social media anymore. I felt so safe. I wasn't in self-absorbed L.A., where people always had their eyes on the door in case someone more famous or beautiful walked in. Men and women both seemed genuinely interested in getting to know me, with zero ulterior motives. I was learning and growing. I was alive again! I had my own interests (yes, whiskey counts as an interest). Irish people don't care who you know or what you look like or who you used to date. They live in the moment. Even if they were impressed with me, they wouldn't have told me so, because the Irish don't want you to get a big head. It was the perfect place for me to rediscover myself. All the Writers' Tears whiskey I drank didn't fix my writer's block, though. I got absolutely no work done. After nine weeks of pubs, dancing, and debauchery, the winds and the rain finally got to me. Even though I didn't get an earth-shattering epiphany, I'd finally learned to focus outside of myself. It was time to go back to L.A. In the taxi to the airport I told the driver that I didn't really want to leave. I would miss the people. I told him how much nicer they were there and how rude Angelenos could be. He said, "Here's an idea for ye. Why don't ye pretend yer Irish for a week and see what happens?"

I never did jump into the sea, but I dove into the depths of my soul. Turns out I didn't have to pretend. When I got back home, the people in L.A. seemed so much nicer than I had remembered them. My friends were excited to have me home. Strangers were friendly and kind. It wasn't much different than being in Ireland, actually. I realized that it was not other people that were the problem. In fact, it was my perceptions and my projections that were the problem. My journey was about learning to be Carrie Stevens again. I had peeled off fifty years of damage. In taking the time and bravery to be alone with myself, and surround myself with people who had no preconceived notions about me, I was able to shed all of the negativity and false narratives I had come to believe about myself.

Now I understand that Eric's death and all the other heartbreaks, setbacks, and challenges I've endured were meant to teach me to love myself. I learned empathy and independence. I became self-sufficient and resourceful. I respected myself for my accomplishments, mostly raising a son who not only loves me, but also likes me. Yes, it's a simple lesson, pretty much a cliché, right? Without self-love, you have nothing.

And yet some people have to go through multiple heartbreaks and divorces to learn it. (My parents had eight marriages between them.) Other people never learn it at all, no matter how deeply they suffer. Which path you take to get there is irrelevant. Without self-love, you have nothing.

I got back to sunny California and sipped my morning coffee out of my beloved old mug with the rainbow on it. I began believing Eric's words again. All of my dreams and goals would come true. I got back into acting class and started auditioning again. I was dating and began to think that love was not impossible, after all. My positive attitude and my fresh new start would suddenly come to a screeching halt.

Concerts? Canceled.

Dating? Done.

Sex? Not unless it's with myself.

Today is Tuesday, April 28, 2020. My son and I have been quarantined in our home for six weeks, along with two thirds of the world's population. International travel is banned. Schools and all businesses deemed non-essential are closed. No restaurants or pubs are open. Not in Galway, not in L.A....or most anywhere in the world. The grocery store shelves are ravaged. People wearing face masks are fighting over toilet paper. Beaches and hiking trails are blocked off with police tape. Guns and ammunition are sold out. A pandemic, Coronavirus (COVID-19) has swept the globe, claiming over two hundred thousand lives and commanding the end of life as we know it.

Very little is known about the virus, but the media has dubbed it "the invisible enemy." Los Angeles County officials have told us that we should assume everyone is infected. The law says that we must wear face coverings unless we can guarantee six feet from one another, a practice called "social distancing." Only a limited number of people are allowed in stores at a time, while orange cones and one-way lanes are used to enforce the order. Facial expressions are hidden, but you can see the fear and anxiety in the eyes of the people. There is little reason to leave the house except to get food or mail. Before reentering the house, people remove their shoes, clothes and wipe their unemployment checks with Lysol. This is the new normal.

When I started writing this book, I was wondering what to do with the rest of my life. The freedom of choice, which most of us took for granted, is gone, for now. I am hunkered down in my house, facing a different kind of challenge. But I can see the seeds of something familiar. Somewhere in the shadows of this pandemic, there is an opportunity. I will find it! I've endured rejection, earthquakes, wildfires, and grief. I am a survivor. I will do what I was instinctively born to do.

It is at long last, that I reach my final revelation.

I did all of my "Don'ts" because my heart demanded it.

The moral of my story?

I am damn glad I did. DAMN GLAD I DID IT ALL!

*"In my wildest dreams, I could not have
imagined a sweeter life."*

— HUGH HEFNER

Our Baby

Name *Carrie Patricia*

TOP LEFT: Carrie with father and sister Jill.
BOTTOM LEFT: Carrie and Jill with their grandfather.
(All photos from the 1970s)

ABOVE LEFT: Carrie wth Eric Carr and sister Jill

AT RIGHT: Carrie and Eric with "Tiffany the Cat."

AT LEFT: With Eric and,Todd Trent.

BELOW LEFT: with Blas Elias, drummer for Slaughter, and Eric.

BELOW RIGHT: with friend Sandra Lawson, Victoria Mariencheck and Eric Carr in Memphis, TN.

TOP LEFT: Carrie with John Elway
and Hugh Hefner.

TOP RIGHT: With Pauly Shore at his
birthday party (2019).

AT LEFT With Nick Rhodes and
Victoria Silvstedt at Hotel du Cap,
Cannes Film Festival (2005).

AT RIGHT: Carrie with her
father (left) and Hugh Hefner.

BOTTOM LEFT: Carrie with Priscilla Presley
and Playmate Lorraine Michaels-Grant
at the Brent Shapiro Foundation charity
event (2017).

BOTTOM RIGHT: With Gene Simmons
on Easter at the Playboy Mansion (2011).

TOP LEFT: Backstage with Gene Simmons (2010).

AT RIGHT: Carrie with Rod Stewart and fellow Playmates.

AT LEFT: Carrie and son Jaxon at Van Halen concert.

BELOW LEFT: Carrie and Jaxon in the Bahamas (2015).

BELOW RIGHT: With Marq Torien from "The Bullet Boys."

ABOVE LEFT: with Bruce Kulick at the Kiss Expo in Indiana (2018).

ABOVE RIGHT: At Kiss Expo with Bruce Kulick and Todd Billets (Eric Carr tribute artist, as "The Fox").

AT RIGHT: With Jessie Henry and her late boyfriend Krys "Christine Sixteen" at the Kiss Expo.

BELOW LEFT: Carrie and close friend Bobby Rock.

AT RIGHT: Carrie and Todd Billets stand for photos at 2018 Kiss Expo.

TOP LEFT: Jaxon with Hugh Hefner.

TOP RIGHT: With Playmate Audra Lynn at the annual Playboy Family Reunion (2018).

AT RIGHT: With Paris Hilton, Playmate Layla Roberts, and her brother Mondo (1999).

AT LEFT: With Zakk Wylde on the set of *Rock Star* (2000).

BOTTOM LEFT: Playmates Layla Roberts and Victoria Silvstedt (1998).

BOTTOM RIGHT: With Christina Scott on our way to see David Lee Roth perform at the Brent Shapiro Foundation charity event (2018).

TOP LEFT: With baby Jaxon and Gene Simmons (2002).

TOP RIGHT: With Brett Michaels and Lee Ann Tweeden (2014).

AT RIGHT: Carrie and Jaxon.

ABOVE MIDDLE: With Duran Duran's Simon LeBon (2018).

DIRECTLY ABOVE: Playmates with Metallica (1997).

AT RIGHT: With Bobbie Brown (2019).

TOP LEFT: Before the MidSummer Night's Dream Party at the Playboy Mansion with Donna Anderson, Antonia Dorian and Celeste McQueen (2008).

TOP RIGHT: Carrie and Eric Carr.

AT RIGHT: Anita Pressman and I after receiving our Single Moms Planet Awards (2015).

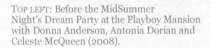

AT LEFT: Carrie with Wendy Griffin and Hugh Hefner.

BELOW LEFT: Carrie and Playmate Barbara Moore and signing autographs in Salt Lake City, Utah with agent Kurt Clements (1997).

BELOW RIGHT: With Elena Grace Soto (2019).

TOP LEFT: Carrie with Goddaughter Julienne Greene after watching her star in the play *Sister Act* (2019).

TOP RIGHT: Carrie and Eric.

AT RIGHT: Carrie at a 1997 audition.

BELOW LEFT: With Carrie Peterson getting photo bombed at Kylemore Abbey in Ireland (2019).

BELOW RIGHT: Photoshoot with baby Jaxon (2002).

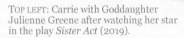

NADIA PANDOLFO PHOTO

TOP LEFT: With Julienne, Gina, Kent Moyer, Wendy and Playmate Shauna Sand at the WPG event, Beverly Hills Hotel (2018).

TOP RIGHT: With Duran Duran's John Taylor.

AT LEFT: Early photo with Eric.

AT RIGHT: Carrie and Kieran O'Malley "The Galway Player" (2019).

BELOW LEFT: Carrie with Eric and his parents, Connie and Al Caravello.

BELOW RIGHT: Carrie and Emma in Galway, Ireland (2019).

About the Author

Carrie Stevens first came into view when she was chosen as *Playboy* Magazine's Miss June 1997. Her centerfold propelled her into a whirlwind life of worldwide appearances on TV and at special events. It also helped jump-start her career as an actor in movies and hit TV shows.

Born in Buffalo, New York, but relocating to the middle of the middle of nowhere and growing up in a small town called Harwick, Massachusetts, Carrie studied Journalism at Memphis State University and modeled locally before packing her bags for Hollywood. She has played opposite Charlie Sheen and Jennifer Aniston, as well as Oscar winner Hilary Swank. She also appeared in the movie *Rock Star* with Mark Wahlberg. Carrie has starred in independent films opposite celebrities such as Jennifer Love Hewitt, John Taylor (of Duran Duran) and Don "The Dragon" Wilson.

Numerous guest and recurring roles on television include *Two and a Half Men, Beverly Hills 90210, Days of Our Lives* and *Black Scorpion*. She has hosted three one-hour shows for E! Entertainment Television including *Wild On* and *FYI*. In Third Eye Blind's music video *"Never Let You Go,"* she starred as the girl climbing the human chain.

Her television commercials include Lexus, Miller Ice, Starwood Resorts, Cyberswim, Toyota, Little Caesar's Pizza. Killian's Irish Red Beer, American Laser Centers, Obagi Skin Care, Botox, Graco Strollers, and Ferro Cosmetics.

In addition to *Playboy* she has been featured in the pages of major magazines such as *Cosmopolitan, Glamour* and *Allure*. Carrie currently resides in Los Angeles with her son Jaxon and is the founder of **StayYoungandSkinny.com.**

PHOTO BY ANDRÉ FELIX

CPSIA information can be obtained
at www.ICGtesting.com
Printed in the USA
BVHW010820290422
635140BV00014B/19/J